Classroom Management

Voices of Experience

Patti Slagle

and

Kay Twaryonas

This edition published by
Dog Ear Publishing
4010 W. 86th Street, Ste H
Indianapolis, IN 46268

www.dogearpublishing.net

ISBN: 978-145750-396-2
This book is printed on acid-free paper.

Printed in the United States of America

Patti dedicates this book to Mildred Daugherty (1920-2008). English Supervisor for the Louisville City Schools when Patti was a beginning teacher, Mildred took Patti under her wing and mentored her throughout her career. Mildred introduced Patti to NCTE which has provided considerable professional and personal enrichment. It was also Mildred, a founder of the Louisville Writing Project, who guided Patti to participate in what was the most significant professional development experience of her career. Patti credits Mildred with playing a substantial role in the kind of teacher into which she grew and cherishes the memory of her friendship.

Kay dedicates this book to
Dr. Marjorie M. Kaiser (1933-2010)
Dear friend, beloved educator, and founder of the Louisville Writing Project

And to Susan,
Of course.

Table of Contents

Meet the Authors

INTRODUCING KAY

I really don't remember any details of my first year of teaching. Sure, I remember my school, Thomas Jefferson High School; my room number, 117 and the school's telephone number, 969-3271. I started my career in April with only two school months left; I had been hired to fill out the year for a pregnant teacher who had made plans to leave school before the school year ended.

I remember the sophomore TV English class of 270 plus students; I had to use a microphone so I could project my inexperienced and shaky voice in the huge room where the television sets were the real purveyors of knowledge. I had no room of my own, but I called an office in the TV teaching complex my home base. I met conventional classes of juniors ready for the year to end. Although I'd never had a dramatics class in undergraduate school, I tried to manage a drama class in a science room with faucets and sinks and other useless equipment, at least for teaching English.

My first year – I remember paying a student price for lunch for six months until the irate cafeteria lady perched by the cash register growled, "Aren't you a Teacher?" I eventually discovered the joys of making lunch at home and brown bagging. I tried to be understanding those first few months- I looked new, I acted new, I was new.

Who am I now? What kind of teacher have I become? What kind of advice can I give after many years on the job?

I'm a veteran teacher with a few of the scars we all have and a great deal of experience. I've taught in only two schools in my career. I've taught remedial sophomores to college-bound seniors. Early on, I taught English to a pilot class of seventeen Korean students and continued to teach English as a Second Language for three years with no training and no degree in other languages. This pilot became the beginning of what is now the ESL program in our school district. I've sponsored just about everything there is to sponsor in high school from cheerleaders to the literary magazine. I've been to more high school graduations and senior plays than I care to admit. I've taught with textbooks and without them. I've had good years and challenging ones. I've sometimes struggled and I've sailed smoothly when the winds of education were just right. I've survived court ordered busing, and I've taught the children of the students I taught.

Through the years, I've accumulated a wealth of strategies for dealing with just about every challenge that has come my way. Those strategies and the advice that goes along with them make up the largest part of the expertise that Patti and I want to share with you in this book – our heritage of successful classroom teaching. People have asked both of us: "How come you STAYED IN THE CLASSROOM?" I smile and reply, "Because the classroom is where the action is." I never doubt that the students in those classrooms are the heart and soul of our educational community. The classroom is where we really make the power plays. Trust us.

K.E.T.

INTRODUCING PATTI

The most important thing to know about me is that I have spent nearly three decades as a classroom language arts teacher - by choice. Everything that I've contributed to this book is based on experiences and observations during those years. During that span I taught them all: ninth, tenth, eleventh, and twelfth grades; "gifted and talented" students, middle-of-the-road classes, and academically challenged students; elective as well as magnet programs; even some speech and drama. Spending my years in three different schools, I had to establish myself in new environments more than once. I learned from every one of those experiences. About a third of the way into my career in education, I began to feel as though I had a grasp on this thing called teaching; but even then, I knew there was more to learn.

When we started this book, students outwardly seemed quite different from the first students I taught. However, twenty-first century students are actually quite similar to the students of that earlier era. In many ways, kids are kids and teens are teens regardless of the decade. What *has* changed are the external factors that affect today's teens. Throughout the years I have strived to remain alert to elements that influence students and have adjusted my methods accordingly. No matter how much we think we know as teachers, there is always more to learn and those who best teach us are our students themselves.

As a beginning teacher I knew little, if anything, about classroom management. I don't recall much instruction about management in college education classes. My first year in the field I was given a teaching assignment, a text, and a schedule that required me to float from room to room. I suppose it was assumed that I knew what I was doing; but I knew I was operating basically on instinct. It helped that my father was a teacher, so I'd grown up with "teacher tales" around the dinner table; but planning lessons, executing them, and managing five classes took a lot more than I had picked up from those anecdotes. After my first month, I took a sick day to stay home and plan. I felt overwhelmed.

I was lucky to have landed in a fine high school English department that actively collaborated in developing elective units. The chair guided our department in this group effort and mentored me before we ever talked about "mentors." He also invited me to my first National Council of Teachers of English (NCTE) local affiliate meeting, which began professional activity that lasts to this day. That collaboration, mentoring, and professional exposure laid the groundwork for the kind of language arts teacher and professional educator into which I developed.

A few years into my teaching adventure, the English supervisor invited me to attend an NCTE convention. What an exciting experience that was! I was hooked. I have attended many NCTE conventions since then. I can honestly say that NCTE taught me as much, if not more, than any of my teacher education courses . . . with the added value that I made many teacher friends, plus it was great fun.

My supervisor also steered me to another significant influence on my professional life: participation in a National Writing Project affiliate institute. Until then, I'd made a respectable stab at teaching writing, but I knew something was missing. In college I had instruction that helped me grow as a writer myself, but nothing about how to *teach* writing. Consequently, writing instruction in my classroom was based on my own reflections of how I went about writing. The writing project affirmed that I had come to some valid conclusions, assured me that writing could be systematically taught, and imparted a wealth of strategies to help my students develop as writers. What enlightenment!

As I approached the latter portion of my teaching career, our school decided to pilot an intensive effort to help heretofore academically unsuccessful students. Our failure rate was too high, and we were searching for methods to rectify that. The administration came up with a school-within-a-school concept in which a team of teachers would focus all of their energies on helping these students experience success. I volunteered to lead that effort. After so many years in teaching, I suppose I was looking for a new challenge. As is often the case when working with striving students, many of them had a history of discipline problems, no idea of productive learning behavior, and minimal self-confidence especially in terms of classroom performance. This endeavor required me to call on every management strategy I had ever encountered and to create some new ones. In addition to shaping positive learning attitudes and behaviors, I helped my students produce state-mandated writing portfolios and prepare for the state assessment test. I wanted a challenge, and I got it! The situation required me to finely hone and refine my classroom management skills. I learned more management-wise from this experience than with any of my previous teaching assignments. Consequently, I can confidently endorse the concepts and strategies I recommend in this book because they have passed that arduous test.

During the second half or so of my teaching career, all of what I had previously learned began to congeal making it possible for me to polish and refine my methodology. My first word of advice would be: never stop learning. Continually seek growth opportunities as well as learn from every experience. Hopefully this book can be a valuable tool in helping you do so.

P.A.S.

I ~ Introduction

WHERE WE'RE COMING FROM
Or, since we're English teachers, "From Where We're Coming"

Teaching is hard work; good teaching is even harder work. Although teaching is one of the most difficult jobs in the world, it can be one of the most personally fulfilling. Successful classroom teaching is a mixture of intense effort, experimentation, risk taking, and patience. No matter how expert teachers may be in a subject area, they can't teach students effectively without sound classroom management strategies.

For a number of years, we have interacted with colleagues in workshop, presentation, in-service and mentoring situations. We've used those opportunities to query both experienced and inexperienced colleagues, pre-service education students, and intern teachers regarding their needs and concerns. **Repeatedly, the biggest frustration expressed by both novice and veteran teachers is classroom management.** Creative and innovative teachers often struggle because they need proven strategies to build management effectiveness in their classrooms. We hope this book will help meet that need.

We have worked with student teachers, formally and informally mentored new teachers, and frequently lent an ear to frustrated colleagues. Teachers, observing our classroom efforts, have asked us to share our successful techniques. While working with beginning teachers, we have realized that methods which contribute to our successful classroom management are valuable to others. That realization prompted us to contemplate our own teaching recollections – both successes and failures. That reflection led to the accumulated knowledge we present. We hope our book will benefit new teachers, veteran teachers, teachers returning after a hiatus, and teacher trainers by presenting some of our methods as well as our stories.

Our successes have come from learning, testing, discarding, listening, reading, conferencing, workshopping – all attempts to find strategies and ideas that *really* work. Yes, we have had our failures, but we made sure to learn from every one. After over sixty years of combined teaching experience, we hope to leave our management insights and strategies as a legacy to future teachers.

We're not "experts" by virtue of title or certification. If we're "experts" at all, it's due to experience. We're not advocating any one particular theory; instead, we're sharing what we've learned and come to believe from our personal teaching experiences. This book reflects our mutual philosophy; but even between the two of us, there are philosophical variations. We don't presume to think that anyone will embrace everything we advocate, but we do endorse the benefits of remaining open to change. We don't have *all* of the answers, and we're not the *only* answer. Think of us as one more resource to add to your reserve of "teacher magic."

WHO WILL FIND THIS BOOK USEFUL?

Experience has demonstrated that numerous ideas and strategies we have used successfully over many years of classroom teaching may be useful to teachers at various stages of their careers. Possible readers might include:

- Pre-service personnel (students, interns, and student teachers)
- New teachers
- Teachers returning from hiatus
- Lateral entries
- Veteran teachers looking for new ideas or reinforcement

Those preparing to enter the teaching profession may not comprehend the impact of classroom management on their ability to instruct. Furthermore, they may not yet possess the skills and strategies to implement classroom management effectively. This book can provide background as well as concrete methods to help these newcomers begin their journey.

Novice educators are often overwhelmed when faced with the reality of the many tasks teachers must juggle. Our book can provide assistance in creating and implementing management techniques to help beginners meet the challenges they will face in the first few years of their teaching careers.

Teachers returning from hiatus may find that classrooms are quite different from the ones they remember. This book can provide them with practical ideas to make the transition from what they remember to what they encounter upon their return.

Entrance into the profession by those in midlife who have already gained experience in another field is a fairly recent educational trend. Often those new teachers receive "on the job" training as part of their entry program. Many times these lateral entries arrive with expectations that do not match the reality of contemporary classrooms. This book could provide ready assistance in meeting the many demands they will face, not the least of which is management.

__Patti's__ principal asked her to help a new teacher with her homeroom duties during the first week of school. This new teacher had decided to enter the education profession after a successful career in banking. To someone without a prior frame of reference, homeroom duties on that first day can easily seem overwhelming, to say the least. This new teacher was bewildered by the mass of paperwork that first day's homeroom entailed, about how to get and hold the students' attention, and about how to accomplish the expected tasks in the allotted amount of time. Patti took over for her and let her observe. After homeroom, Patti made suggestions about ways to organize for the upcoming homeroom sessions and promised to be there all week. When the second day of school arrived, the new teacher had already given up and never returned.

We have discovered in working with veteran teachers that they continually seek fresh strategies due to the ever-changing nature of schools and our society. Conversations with fellow professionals in which we have shared strategies have contributed to our store of techniques. Likewise, our book is a way for veterans to engage in professional exploration.

While we both have spent our careers as high school language arts teachers, we have found that the majority of management concerns and strategies are not limited to our content area or to high school. Major management principles transcend grade levels, although some strategies may be more appropriate for older or younger students. **Middle school** and **high school** teachers will find relevance to their own experience throughout this book. **Elementary** teachers will find that although some of the strategies are not appropriate for younger children, most of the management concepts are clearly relevant for their classrooms.

Although each **subject area** has its own particular management needs, universal management concepts and approaches can be useful for teachers of all contents. Even in the sections specifically addressing reading and writing management, teachers of all subjects can find suggestions that could be applicable in their classrooms. As reading and writing have increasingly become instructional needs across the curriculum, teachers not trained as language arts teachers may find some very functional ideas for use with their own students.

Teaching is a constantly changing, dynamic endeavor that calls for individuals who welcome change and do not fear it. Educators over the years have amassed an incredible stockpile of ideas and approaches. Some ideas have worked beautifully; others have failed; some have been resurrected, refurbished, and put back in business. Education continues to evolve to fit a changing world and a changing clientele. Teachers who adapt will benefit their students by readying them to meet this century's challenges as they leave schools and colleges to enter and work in the real world.

HOW TO USE THIS BOOK

We certainly do not have the intention that any teacher will try to implement everything we have suggested in this book. In fact, we anticipate that some may not agree with all we have written. That's O.K. This book is based on our experiences in our combined sixty plus years in the classroom. Our teaching situations may have been considerably different from those of others. Our philosophy may deviate from yours. Our styles may vary from what you're comfortable with. This book can still be useful for you. Consider our philosophy; then formulate your own. Try a few of the things we've suggested, modifying them to suit your situation and style. Use our experiences to your advantage.

We conceived this book as a "jumping off point," not a prescription. Every suggestion will not work in every situation. Some of our suggestions may not be a comfortable "fit" for you and/or your circumstances. We have shared what worked for us in our teaching environments and what we learned along the way. We suggest that you consider our philosophy and recommendations in light of your own needs, style, preferences, and students then adapt them accordingly. We hope our suggestions will stimulate additional ideas for your classroom.

We do have one cautionary note. You can't struggle with all management issues at once. Effective management is a process; and like any process, it develops over time. We suggest that you choose your management focus for the upcoming grading period, semester or school year and concentrate on *it*. Once you have refined and mastered strategies for that focus, layer on another area for attention. We designed this book to be user-friendly. The arrangement should enable you to readily find support for your specific needs and our answers to questions that you might have.

Our bottom line is that we have tested our suggestions and found them to work for us in our classrooms. Our research is our experience. As teachers, we want to share with other teachers. Our greatest fulfillment would be for this book to save you time, help you be a more effective teacher, enable your students to be more successful, and make your life a little easier. We know from experience how challenging a teacher's life can be.

Good luck! Enjoy! And hang in there!

ADVICE TO NEW TEACHERS

Being a new teacher is tough. New teachers begin with no experience on which to draw, no backlog of materials, no repertoire of strategies. In addition, they often are assigned academically challenged classes because those are frequently perceived as less desirable, so they fall to those with the least seniority. Although we disagree with that perception and practice, we do agree these classes may be some of the most challenging for teachers. However, they can also be some of the most rewarding and fulfilling.

If we were running things, we would give new secondary teachers no more than four classes and two preparations, a planning period *and* a mentoring period, classrooms of their own, no extracurricular sponsorships or coaching assignments, and lots of support. In reality many new teachers may face at least five classes, three preparations, a planning period, an extra-duty assignment, an extracurricular responsibility and minimal opportunity for systematic, productive and practical assistance and support.

We have heard repeatedly from pre-service students, intern teachers, and new teachers that management is their greatest challenge . . . and their biggest frustration. That sentiment is understandable. Comprehending group dynamics is not necessarily instinctive; group management does not occur automatically; and adolescence is a curious developmental stage.

We hope this book will unlock some mysteries for new teachers, but we want to caution you. Even *if* you agree with everything we've written, do not feel that you can implement every management technique the first year. The first few years of teaching you will face numerous challenges in addition to classroom management: lesson planning, materials development, paper work load, and evaluation. You may find yourself planning lessons for multiple teaching preparations. You may be expected to prepare students for satisfactory performance on a state assessment. You may be held accountable for directing student development of mandated writing portfolios with very specific requirements. You may be responsible for coaching students for various kinds of performance assessments. It may be necessary to teach novels that you've never read. Your subject matter may entail setting up and implementing lab experiences including management of the accompanying tools and equipment. You may have to learn how to negotiate a program that includes not only a text, but also a teacher's edition, electronic components, and numerous resource materials. In some cases, you may find that your challenge is how to deal with *too much* material. Don't despair.

Do not feel inadequate if you don't know and can't do everything you know you need to do. **Teaching is a process that takes time to evolve.**

Prioritize the tasks put before you. Then pick and choose the classroom focus and your most compelling management needs for each grading period. Set reasonable targets. For instance, "This semester I will teach my students to begin class by copying the learning log prompt from the board and writing their responses." or "This semester I will teach my students to consistently use a specific format to head all papers." Choose goals that will make your life as a teacher less stressful. Consider the timesaving examples above. By teaching students to begin class with a short writing activity, you have a few minutes to catch your breath, deal with attendance chores and collect your thoughts. When you teach students to consistently head papers, you are helping them to be organized and responsible as well as saving yourself time sorting through papers to determine what they are, who did them, when they were done, and whether they are required or make-up work.

Consider choosing a *handful* of our suggestions to try each grading period. Continue those that work for you and discard ones that don't. Then layer on a few more strategies. Soon your own classroom management plan will begin to take shape. **Form alliances with effective teacher managers** - from your department or others - and benefit from their experience. Ask if you can observe their classes. Observing a master at work during your planning period may be an investment that pays career-long dividends. Talk to teachers in your department. Resist the temptation to skip lunch because you have too much work to do; go where teachers go. Listen to their conversations and ask questions. Actively ignore anyone who is consistently negative. Finally, as you're continually bombarded with new information and experiences, develop the practice of keeping notes or a brief journal of observations and suggestions as well as what works for you.

Don't resist using commercial materials. For many years we both felt that using commercial materials was somehow "cheating." **Patti** nearly drove herself out of the profession by trying to develop everything she needed from scratch:

> *One August, dreading the opening of school, I analyzed my feelings. Even though the prospect was exciting, dread surfaced because I felt that once classes began, school controlled my life and time. I made conscious decisions to help combat my feelings of anxiety. One of those decisions was to use commercial material. I discovered that although much commercial material did not match my teaching style or goals, some good material did. I found that it required less time to adapt material from a commercial source*

> *than to develop resources from scratch. Over the years I became familiar with the quality publishers and stuck with them.*

Think ahead; have some materials in hand when you start planning. Don't throw any teaching materials away. Develop an efficient filing system and begin accumulating materials upon which you can continually draw. Ask colleagues to share materials. Most veterans, remembering their early years, are glad to share with newcomers. Remember to return the favor to even newer members of your department. Be resourceful.

Another of **Patti**'s early choices was that "survival" needs would factor into her classroom framework, student activities, and approach to planning:

> *I justified this move by assuring myself that if I didn't discover some survival strategies, I might leave the profession. Making expedient decisions could keep me in the classroom, thereby benefiting students. Eventually I sufficiently addressed my goal and shifted focus from managing day-to-day needs to instructional pedagogy. Once I developed a backlog of materials and a repertoire of strategies, I could concentrate on employing best practices for instruction. In retrospect, even during those early years of focusing on survival management, my instruction surpassed teachers who had given up in frustration and overload and resorted to one mindless worksheet after another.*

Frequently remind yourself of these concepts:

- Teaching is a process. Everything won't fall into place overnight.
- Mastery won't occur automatically; planning and conscientiously working at management is a likely road to success.

We suggest using these strategies to implement management concepts:

- Make sure that you learn from every experience - good and bad.
- Don't rely on your memory. Note successes and missteps for your future reference.
- Plan rather than wait to see what will happen.
- Learn from those around you who have been where you are.
- Be open to change and new ideas.

INTRODUCING MANAGEMENT

Effective classroom management creates the environment and sustains the time for effective instruction and learning to occur. Sounds simple, but implementation may be one of a teacher's biggest challenges. We don't recall actively planning our classroom management as inexperienced teachers; but we do recall wanting to have it in our classrooms. In those days students came to class on time, sat down in their assigned seats and waited for the teacher to teach. Those days are gone, and that's not necessarily bad. However, in today's society, teachers must create and maintain a safe environment for students, accommodate multiple learning styles, enrich accelerated students, meet the needs of challenged students, prepare all students for assessments, and preserve their own well-being and good nature while doing so. We have learned that effective classroom management can and does promote all of these goals and activities.

Some may think that the purpose of management is to create an orderly classroom. Others may feel that it makes the teacher's life easier. While both are advantages of effective management, its most valuable outcome benefits students and their learning. Haphazard management interferes with effective learning and instruction. Less effective management diminishes learning opportunities, consumes potential learning time, and allows some students to fall through the cracks. **Effective management provides optimum learning opportunities for the maximum number of students and gives all students a foundation for becoming independent and lifelong learners.**

Teachers must have students' attention before they can teach them and before those students can learn. Students will not learn until they are focused on instruction. **Effective management focuses students on instruction and learning;** it conveys verbally and nonverbally that *your* classroom is a learning place.

Yes, **effective management contributes to teacher well being** . . . and this is a good thing. Numerous reports verify that beginning teachers often leave the profession before completing very many years in the classroom.

"Nationally, it is estimated that approximately 30% of beginning teachers leave the profession during the first two years in the classroom." (Darling-Hammond, L. (2001). The challenge of staffing our schools. *Educational Leadership*, 58(8), 12-17.

"According to a new study from the National Education Association, a teachers' union, half of new U.S. teachers are likely to quit within the first five years because of poor working conditions and low salaries." By Lisa Lambert, Reuters, Tuesday, May 9, 2006 (Washington Post)

"Some 20 percent of all new hires leave the classroom within three years. In urban districts, the numbers are worse. Close to 50 percent of newcomers leave the profession during their first five years of teaching." *The High Cost of Teacher Turnover,* National Commission on Teaching and America's Future, 2007

We have met many promising young people who have bypassed the education profession because they are intimidated by management challenges. Do a random survey. We bet you'll find the majority of people will tell you they could never be a teacher because they couldn't or don't want to "put up with all those kids." The reality is that there are typically 25+ students and only one teacher in a middle or high school classroom. A teacher can't be all things to all students all the time; but when teaching, it often feels as though she is expected to be. There are days (and not so infrequently) it seems that:

- All your students want your attention at the same time.
- All their parents want you to meet their child's individual, particular needs.
- The administration has yet another form for you to complete and hand in . . . yesterday.
- You're going to be observed by the entire administrative staff and state certification officer tomorrow.
- Your students' assessment scores are going to be published in the newspaper tonight.
- And you don't know how you can possibly get all those papers graded by tomorrow, when more will be handed in.

YOU CAN COPE! Effective classroom management can be the teacher's best defense against becoming discouraged or even giving up. In fact, well-implemented management can help make you a sane, more relaxed teacher who enjoys what she is doing; and that teacher is a better teacher.

Bottom line: The purpose of classroom management is to provide maximum learning opportunity for the maximum number of students for the maximum amount of class time. Effective instruction and meaningful learning cannot take place in a classroom where management is weak, inconsistent or non-existent. We are convinced that unless teachers can manage their classrooms and students effectively, they cannot successfully or effectively teach.

Walk down the hall of any school in America. You will come to classrooms where a mere passing glance will assure you that quality instruction and learning are taking place. Continue down that hallway. In a few classrooms, you may see a genuine struggle occurring between teachers who desperately want to teach and students who want to hinder that teacher's best efforts. Many times these instructors are first year teachers or experienced veterans suffering burnout. These classrooms, however, can change remarkably when a teacher applies effective management strategies from the first day of the school year.

Good management, of course, takes planning, practice and patience. Tough classrooms will not magically transform overnight. For example, those in education know the difficulties of taking over a classroom of students after the school year has begun. **Kay's** first teaching job began in April, two months before the end of the school year:

> *I replaced a teacher on maternity leave near the end of the year. I had little time left to develop a rapport with my students and by now their primary goal was surviving two more months. I was raring to go – I wanted to teach and I wanted them to love learning, at least for those two remaining months. As a new teacher, I knew practically nothing about quality methods of instruction, but I thought I knew multitudes about literature and grammar. I failed to realize I knew little about effective classroom management. Although this situation was difficult, my common sense and sense of humor allowed me to make it through those two months. But I'll admit – quality instruction was lacking because I was inexperienced and did not know how to establish a management framework. I learned much about teaching during that short time and about how valuable effective classroom management can be to instruction.*

Observations, internships, student teaching experiences, and education seminars are valuable; but until *you* walk into a classroom that is *yours*, until *you* close the door, and until *you* face *your* students and begin to teach, you will not *truly* know what being a teacher requires.

Teaching demands a vast amount of your time and energy, especially during that first two or three years. You want to inspire students. You want to prepare them for their futures. You want to contribute to their success. Learning to manage them effectively will make the task of teaching them gradually easier, and teaching can become one of the most rewarding aspects of your life.

II ~ Management Philosophy

PERSONAL PHILOSOPHY OF CLASSROOM MANAGEMENT

Neither of us can recall having ever been asked – as an undergraduate, student teacher, interviewee, teacher, or graduate student – to relate our philosophy of classroom management. When reflecting on our many years in the classroom, we realized that we have formulated our individual philosophies of management without a specific assignment to do so. This book is a result of our contemplation on the beliefs that have steered our classroom management and our efforts to record those beliefs, along with the strategies they have informed, for the benefit of others. Our classroom management philosophy is characterized in this section of our book and elaborated on in subsequent sections.

Upon reflection, we've recognized that our personal classroom management philosophies have influenced how we've managed our own classrooms and shaped management decisions we've made throughout our teaching careers. It is our personal management philosophies that have . . .

- given us the insight and confidence to design and apply management guidelines that benefit both our students and ourselves as teachers,
- made it possible to construct and implement frameworks that facilitate a certain degree of independent classroom operation after the first few weeks of school,
- helped us when we were faced with unique management challenges for the first time,
- allowed us to make quick decisions in the heat of the moment that have generally proven effective,
- guided our reflection on situations that have not resulted as we would have liked thus helping us become better prepared for encountering similar incidents in the future.

As you can imagine, we feel that whether or not you are asked to do so, formulating and continuously reviewing your personal management philosophy is invaluable; indeed, it's essential if you want to be an effective and exemplary teacher. Furthermore, we feel the ongoing *process* of developing, clarifying and reviewing your management philosophy is perhaps more valuable to you and your students than a "final" philosophy would be. In fact, we feel that a management philosophy is never truly "final." We encourage you to perpetually grow as a teacher throughout your career. We urge you to pursue ongoing growth in the various aspects of your teaching expertise – subject matter, educational pedagogy, creative teaching strategies and classroom management approaches. As you refine your management beliefs over time, we hope you will revise your classroom guidelines, framework, and management tactics to reflect your expanding insights and expertise.

If you are never asked to relate your classroom management philosophy, you will still be very glad that you invested the time, thought and effort into conceiving and nurturing that philosophy on your own initiative. Your investment will pay dividends for you and your students throughout your career.

WHAT IS MANAGEMENT?

A full slate of management techniques and implementation strategies are important to teachers' longevity in the profession. When the word "management" appears in presentation titles, teachers often tell us they are attracted to the session because they want to learn strategies for improving classroom discipline. To many teachers, the term "management" means discipline and behavior modification. **To us, the term "classroom management" encompasses interacting with our students, organizing our classroom framework, and choosing the materials and methods we use to generate learning.**

Effective classroom learning behavior and the role of discipline in achieving it is certainly a vital part of management and important for teachers to contemplate. However, a broad variety of management needs challenge teachers, particularly those new to the classroom. Although these additional management considerations may not immediately come to mind in all subjects when teachers think about classroom management, they are essential components of effective classroom operation; and as such can contribute to or hinder student and teacher success. These include, but are not limited to:

- Keeping records
- Planning both long and short term lessons
- Coping with the paper load and grading
- Structuring your classroom's physical arrangement for optimum teaching and learning
- Monitoring collaborative learning
- Understanding and using ever-changing technologies
- Communicating with parents

- Anticipating the inevitable turns of events that can detour the routine of any school day

Numerous tasks are frequently added to teachers' loads, often making the management of a classroom and its students seem overwhelming. We have observed that when a classroom management discussion ends, most teachers agree that effective management is *much more than discipline.* They usually feel it is a vital key to student and teacher classroom success.

STUDENT EMPOWERMENT

Student empowerment is a broad term that lends itself to vastly different interpretations. A literal interpretation may convey little substantive meaning; but when understood with its ramifications, the concept of student empowerment is quite impressive. Our concept of empowering students is an integral part of our teaching philosophy.

Teachers may hear recommendations to create "student centered classrooms," but what does that actually mean in practice? Many teachers, especially those with limited experience, may have misconceptions about "student-centered classrooms." Does each student determine her own direction? Do students determine the course of study? Does the teacher refrain from directing classroom activity? Our own classrooms would present various impressions depending upon when they are observed; but consistently focusing on student learning and maintaining clear outcome goals make our classrooms always student-centered.

In our classrooms, empowerment doesn't mean letting students dictate classroom instruction and management. We feel empowerment results from teaching students how to learn, therefore enabling them to successfully manage their own learning. Indeed, what could be more empowering than competence, even proficiency, in skills such as reading, writing, listening, computing and problem solving? Accomplishing this goal is as fundamental as teaching students to become effective readers and writers so they are able to successfully apply those skills in other classes and beyond the school environment.

Organizing, planning, scheduling, researching, and managing time are vital skills in and beyond the classroom and are considered critical in most workplace environments. Yet young people do not come innately equipped with such management skills. We want to help our students develop a broad range of skills so they will be successful in school and in the world beyond the classroom. Furthermore, we want to guide them to become independent learners so they will continue to learn throughout their lives. Most students do not have the knowledge or sophistication to develop these essential skills without teacher intervention. If they did, there would be no need for teachers. **Therefore, we advocate providing learning situations that are enhanced with guidance and coaching from dedicated, enlightened teachers, enabling our students to acquire and develop these invaluable academic and management skills.**

One strategy for addressing our outcome goals is to engage our students in learning activity that has a degree of independence. Group activities, projects, presentations and other such endeavors give students the opportunity to utilize their creative thinking; develop their planning, organization, and implementation skills; and explore their autonomy. Rather than "turning students loose," we find that providing them with guidelines, boundaries, and requirements enables them to make choices and operate independently, yet with a safety net. Only rarely do students come to our classrooms with well-developed independent study skills and mature self-discipline. We feel that part of our job is to nurture the development of those qualities. Consequently, we like to provide "guided" independent study pursuits.

Our suggestions for empowering students and centering classrooms on their learning include:

- **Treat students as learners**. Take their learning seriously, and they will too.
- **Hold students accountable** for their behavior and learning in order to empower them in their lives, now and in their futures.
- **Teach students how to learn**. If they do not practice basic study skills, teach those strategies and facilitate their application. We want our students to continue learning when they are out of our classrooms and away from school, both now and in their future.
- **Hold students responsible** for being prepared, organized, and attentive. These skills are life lessons they will use repeatedly throughout the school day and their lives.
- **Provide learning choices** to give students practice in independent learning, which they will carry beyond our classrooms. Encourage autonomy in choosing books, projects, and subjects for writing. If teachers always direct what students read or write, those students may not discover what they want to explore and express.
- **Maintain a balanced approach to curriculum choices.** Keep in mind that if students *always* choose what they read and write, they will not benefit from the wide-ranging knowledge their teachers bring to the classroom.

MANAGEMENT BASICS
A PREVIEW

Establishing and maintaining effective classroom management is hard and time-consuming work. If students initially resist, it can also be frustrating. Yet, the rewards of an effectively managed atmosphere for both students and teachers far outweigh the challenges.

When the effort is made to establish and maintain effective management, the school year will be productive and satisfying for both teachers and their students; students will respect and appreciate their teachers; and teachers' professional dignity will be intact. Set the standard; don't resort to the easiest way out at the moment.

If a school's culture is one for which effective management is the norm, establishing individual classroom management will be easier. However, we have seen schools where staff members don't know how or don't expend the effort to create an effectively managed environment. If teachers find themselves in such a situation, they can still implement effective management in their own classrooms. Granted, more energy will be required on their part; but the extra effort will be worth it. We have taught in such situations; but we were determined that our classrooms would not be "free-for-alls." In order to overcome attitudes students brought from poorly or non-managed classes, we had to thoroughly plan strategy; be consistent; endure the complaints of students; and withstand the implied resentment of some colleagues. Such fortitude is not easy, but it's worthwhile.

We have discovered that a few basic management principles strongly influence the effectiveness of instruction and the quality of students' learning:

1. **Investing time and effort into teaching and maintaining effective management strategies provides students with valuable life lessons.** Paying attention; focusing thinking; relating to others; operating in groups; and following directions will help students learn subject matter more effectively. Furthermore, developing proficiency in these management skills will pave the way for students' success when they must cope in the world beyond school.
2. **Keep in mind that management and discipline are not the same thing and management does not equal punishment.** Basing classroom management on a foundation of discipline and punishment may send the message to students that teachers expect them to behave inappropriately; under those

circumstances teachers can be assured that some students will be determined to prove them right. Prevention is more valuable for students and teachers than punishment after the fact. **Effective management minimizes the need for discipline and punishment.**

3. **Part of accomplishing effective management is basing the management plan on insight into predictable patterns of behavior.** If teachers adapt their management strategies to this concept, they will be using the natural inclinations of students to support their management process. If teachers don't acknowledge this concept in their management planning, they may be working against students' natural tendencies – an uphill battle that can sometimes be won, but more often may not.
4. **Good management is a process that requires planning.** Effective classroom management doesn't happen overnight. Hit or miss, take-it-as-it-comes management may work for the moment, but it isn't helpful in the long run. Teachers can effectively approach management as a learning process that teaches and reinforces desired management skills at all ability levels. The most challenged student as well as the most gifted can acquire and demonstrate effective learning behavior.
5. **Time on task is integrally linked to the quantity and quality of learning.** The more time spent focused on learning, the more students will learn. When teachers allow "free time" or "free days"; when students watch entertainment films unrelated to curriculum; when students squander time because of an unprepared teacher, they are not learning. When students ask for a "free day," one response might be, "When we've learned everything there is to learn, we'll have a free day; but until then, we have a lot to do."
6. **Idleness breeds disruption**. Experienced teachers will attest to this behavior pattern. When students are not engaged in learning, their idleness quickly grows into disruption as they become bored. This disruption spreads; before a teacher realizes, few in the class are focused on learning. Keep in mind that "busy work" often results in the same disruption found with idleness. When students sense (and they will) the work they are asked to do does not have genuine value, you can count on them resorting to the same non-constructive behaviors that idleness produces. Keeping students focused on *constructive learning activity* not only is valuable for them but

also helps the teacher maintain a meaningful sense of order in her classroom.

7. **Teachers' attitudes and behaviors usually generate a similar response from students.** If teachers are polite and courteous, their students will usually respond in the same manner. If teachers are curt and brusque with them, students will probably respond accordingly. What, in earlier decades, was anticipated in terms of politeness and courtesy can no longer be automatically expected in today's society. We don't assume that all students will understand and demonstrate appropriate group and classroom behavior; in some cases, students need to be taught and held responsible for appropriate behavior. Teachers can begin by modeling that behavior.
8. In addition to their speech, teachers' attitudes and behaviors convey strong messages to students. You want the conveyed message to be constructive. **Planning, preparation, and organization or their lack conveys a message to students from the first day of class.** We suggest reinforcing opening day remarks to students by demonstrating a prepared, organized, and businesslike manner. Furthermore, teacher planning, preparation and organization contribute to a classroom atmosphere that decreases the possibility for hostility or even violence to occur.
9. **We have found that a classroom with a well-defined framework is the best environment for our students' maximum achievement.** The degree of structure is something teachers will need to determine for themselves. Their personal management style and comfort level will influence the degree of detail for the framework they will establish and maintain. Our experience continually demonstrates that a well-defined framework becomes increasingly more valuable as class size increases. We keep this concept in mind: structure establishes consistency. Consistency nurtures security for students and liberates the teacher from having to continually enforce policy and procedure. When students feel secure about what they can expect of classroom operation and teacher manner, they can relax and concentrate on learning. When teachers have established and maintained consistent policy and procedures, that framework ultimately sustains independently, freeing teachers to concentrate on students and instruction. **Consequently, structure can work *for* you and students; it can support students; and it can enhance learning.**

10. **Determine and communicate behavioral expectations for students and hold them accountable for meeting those expectations.** This recommendation applies to behavior as well as academic expectations. We have found that if expectations are low, students may not rise above them. If expectations are unreasonably high, students may not be able to achieve them. Finding the appropriate level of expectation takes practice and experience. Keep in mind, though, that most students are capable of attaining high expectations for their *behavior*. However, students can't reasonably be expected to be perfect. Yet, with effective teacher **groundwork, modeling**, and **consistency** students can live up to high standards of behavioral performance.
11. Another step in establishing and maintaining effective classroom management is **holding students accountable for management policies and procedures once those practices have been taught and reinforced.** When a teacher sympathizes with a particular student's failure to adapt to procedures, this recommendation can seem difficult. Yet consistently holding *all* students accountable is essential for cementing behaviors and practices that a teacher has conscientiously taught.

Conclusion

Teachers should not resort to management by happenstance or management in response to the crisis of the moment, if they aspire to a productively managed classroom. Throughout this book we share observations, insights, strategies, and experiences collected over our numerous years in the classroom that elaborate on our management basics. As you read, notice that underlying our suggestions is philosophy that informs our recommendations. We feel the most effective management is that which is based on insight and logic. We encourage you to consider your own management philosophy as you proceed through this book.

EVALUATION OF MANAGEMENT EFFECTIVENESS
WHAT YOU SEE MAY NOT BE WHAT YOU THINK YOU SEE

What can educators expect from effective classroom management? The results of management or its lack are numerous, some obvious and others subtle.

Effective classroom management creates the time and environment for effective instruction and learning. Teachers will know if their management is working effectively from the daily functioning of the classroom, but how will others measure them as teacher managers? Assume the perspective of an administrator assigned to evaluate a teacher on a typical classroom day. Take a moment to look around the classroom scrutinizing the degree of student engagement.

- Are all or just some students engaged in learning activity?
- Are students engaged in learning activity for the entire class period or just part of it?
- Do any students have their heads down on their desks?
- Are any students off task or doing work for another class?

A classroom with all students sitting quietly at their desks is not necessarily an indicator of effective management or of effective instruction and learning, for that matter. For management to be truly meaningful, all students should be learning. Therefore, **strive for optimum *engagement* of students in learning activity for the maximum amount of time.** The result should impress any administrator.

Likewise, consider the *teacher's* activity as students are engaged in their work; be assured that administrators will notice. Are they at their desk absorbed in activity unrelated to the students' current task; or is it evident that they are fully engaged with their students and the current lesson activity? Once teachers have quickly taken roll and dispensed with required daily paperwork, look for the following:

- Do they address students in a respectful manner and tone?
- Do they circulate among students commenting and asking questions?
- Do they show genuine interest in students' learning pursuits beyond evaluation?
- Are they quick to offer reinforcement for positive learning behavior?
- Do they engage in discussion with students rather than merely asking questions?

Conscientious educators know that "yes" responses to these questions indicate effective classroom management.

Do noisy students suggest that a classroom is not well managed? Not at all. The *kind* of noise is the key. There is meaningless noise, and there is constructive learning noise. Students working as lab partners to perform an experiment should not be silent. Students working on group projects should be interacting verbally. A lively class discussion cannot occur in a drill-like manner. Performance preparation is not an isolated or silent pursuit. Peer conferencing about writing cannot occur without interaction. With close observation, constructive learning noise is usually easy to distinguish from student socializing. Administrators will be able to recognize the difference.

Early in **Patti**'s teaching career she taught drama:

One day students were preparing small group improvisations for performance during the period. As we began presenting, my principal and the English supervisor walked in. I filled them in and invited them to watch. I was proud of my students' highly creative improvisations that day. The entire class found them entertaining and responded accordingly. My visitors thanked me and left. I assumed, as a fairly new teacher, this observation was typical.

Years later the English Supervisor shared that her observation that day resulted from my principal's concern about rambunctious drama classes. After her visit, she assured him that the activity was appropriate and the noise acceptable, even necessary, for the learning process.

That was a long time ago and Patti's "old school" principal expected students to be at their desks working silently; however, this experience was an early lesson for her in the nature of classroom noise. Some types of learning require students to work independently focused on a task. Other learning activities require student interaction, discussion, and movement to be most effective. These and other instructional modes are valuable aspects of the learning process; consequently, providing students with a variety of activities results in meaningful instruction. Our guiding principle is to **keep students engaged in constructive learning activity, whatever form that may take.** Insightful administrators will recognize quality classroom and instructional management.

PROFESSIONAL DEVELOPMENT

- How can teachers continually add to their repertoire of strategies?
- How can teachers remain up-to-date with research-based best instructional practices?
- How can novice teachers orchestrate continual professional growth?

- How can committed teachers meet myriad demands without becoming disillusioned?
- How can hardworking teachers avoid the pitfalls of burnout?
- How can veteran teachers sustain their enthusiasm?
- How can returning teachers become re-inspired?

We've stayed enthusiastic professionals for many years due, in no small part, to our efforts to continually explore and consequently grow as teachers. It's important to both of us to stay current with best practices in our disciplines and in teaching pedagogy. Interacting with smart, motivated and exemplary fellow professionals has proven inspiring for us not just professionally but also personally.

Teachers who remain professionally inquisitive and make the effort to grow professionally will be much less likely to burn out. We recommend that all teachers seek out stimulating professional development experiences and take full advantage of those opportunities - even at their own expense. The rewards far outweigh the expenditures.

All these offerings fall under the rubric of professional development:

- National, regional, state and local conventions and conferences where excitement and inspiration are palpable.
- On-going institutes and workshops, like writing projects that offer valuable new methods of instruction and network membership.
- Periods of two to three days before the school year starts and selected days during the year when teachers attend lectures and workshops about the "newest buzz" from the district or engage in outdoor team building activities and such.

These staff development activities are vital for our growth and maintenance as professionals. They are particularly valuable when teachers themselves are presenters or help plan and execute the activities. PD, as it is called, can be inspiring and exciting, but when poorly planned and presented, just plain tedious for veteran teachers. For new teachers and those returning to the classroom after years away from the profession, PD's instruction and activities can be especially valuable. Below, we've presented an overview of the various types of PD offerings we've benefited from as teachers.

Conventions and Conferences/Professional Memberships

The broader forms of PD, professional conventions and conferences, are inspiring, exciting opportunities that give teachers the lifts we need. Kay's greatest regret with conferences and conventions is that she didn't attend them when she first entered the teaching profession. But during the latter years, she has become an avid convention-goer. Patti began attending conventions when a mentor invited her along, and has been active in such activities much of her career.

We will loudly proclaim that the professional conventions/conferences are, without a doubt, among the most inspiring motivational tools and the greatest modes of professional development we educators have. Attendance at a conference can send a teacher with a flagging professional commitment straight back to her classroom with newfound enthusiasm, exciting ideas, and the energy to bring these new ideas to fruition. You get out of the car or off the plane and can't wait to get back to the classroom. (Well, we may be exaggerating here, just a bit.) You're tired from the hustle and bustle of the event and the travel, but excited and inspired about the new ideas, materials, friends, and contacts you've made.

> ***Kay** remembers the first National Council of Teachers of English Convention she attended with Patti, who insisted she had to begin going to NCTE. She was like a kid with a whole new toy box! Sessions on topics she'd never heard of, exciting descriptions of all-day workshops, talks by nationally recognized authors and speakers, and chances for local evening activities added to the overall convention excitement and overflowed the massive catalog. Kay attended as many sessions and workshops as she could fit in, often dropping at day's end from delightful exhaustion.*
>
> *She met new and interesting colleagues from all over the country and the world. From the first meeting, she began to build an incredible network of like-minded professional friends – English teachers like herself – who annually come together to make new contacts, begin new friendships, and learn incredible new strategies and ideas for teaching English.*
>
> *If these perks were not enough, a vast English-teacher-shopping-mall was on site. Publishers displayed their latest wares; vendors brought exciting new materials for perusal and purchase; and "teacher freebies" like full-sized posters announcing the latest novel or poetry anthology were plentiful. A shopper's paradise offered aisles of merchandise – wonderfully specific to the*

teaching profession - with take-home gifts for colleagues and friends not lucky enough to make it to "THE CONVENTION." Every merchant, it seemed, provided the "Big Bag," emblazoned with its logo, with substantial handles for lugging mounds of accumulated goodies back to the hotel – an absolute necessity for the convention-goer/shopper.

Kay may sound like she's gushing, but attending her first NCTE Convention was an amazing professional experience. Her attitude about the career she'd chosen completely changed; she was reinvigorated.

Most national content area organizations offer at least an annual convention: National Council for the Social Studies, National Council of Teachers of Mathematics, National Science Teachers Association, International Reading Association, and many more. Additional organizations that offer "PD" include Association for Supervision and Curriculum Development, Council for Exceptional Children, and National Association of Secondary School Principals among others. Then there are specialized organizations that also offer opportunities for teachers to advance their skills: National Middle School Association, Association for the Advancement of Computers in Education, Teachers of English to Speakers of Other Languages, American Association for Gifted Children are only a few. Many of these professional organizations offer conferences on a regional and/or state level making them even more accessible. Research professional organizations that focus on your area of interest and seek out PD that they conduct. You'll be more than glad you did.

However, conventions and conferences aren't the only offerings by professional organizations. Don't overlook the fact that membership in organizations such as NCTE offers additional benefits. Subscriptions to journals, magazines and newsletters devoted to multiple levels and types of content-specific instruction are often included with membership. These publications spotlight new pedagogy, lesson plan ideas, news updates on the professions, announcements of upcoming meetings and conferences, opportunities for writers, and additional ideas and support for teachers. In addition, organizations' technology often offers instant-support web sites with chat rooms, teacher support, and book shops with member discounts on a variety of professional books and materials.

We heartily recommend that all teachers, but especially new teachers and teachers returning to the classroom from hiatus:

- Join their content-specific national and regional/state professional organizations.
- Seek out regional, state and local organizations devoted to content-specific professional development. Join these organizations,
- Subscribe to and read the journals, magazines and newsletters published by these professional organizations. What you learn in them can inspire and invigorate you and your teaching.
- Attend as many conferences and conventions as you can. Some principals or school districts provide professional development funds to send teachers to these meetings. They may ask those who attend to provide in-service to their faculties at a later time.
- Log onto education web sites and take advantage of the opportunity to talk with new teachers and/or veterans about the profession and/or individual needs and solutions to problems as well as shop and order materials between conferences and conventions.

Writing Projects

Writing instruction is now mandated across the curriculum by many state educational reform movements throughout the country. State departments of education are beginning to make student writing portfolios requirements for graduation. The SAT, now the SAT Reasoning Test, includes a writing section with an on-demand essay requirement. The ACT high school achievement and college admissions test has added an optional writing test.

Beyond the educational sector, career and employment are clearly influenced by writing proficiency or the lack thereof. Consider this data from *Writing: A Ticket to Work . . . Or a Ticket Out,* a September 2004 survey of members of the Business Roundtable, an association of chief executive officers from U.S. corporations. (www.writingcommission.org)

- "People who cannot write and communicate clearly will not be hired, and if already working, are unlikely to last long enough to be considered for promotion. Half of responding companies reported that they take writing into consideration when hiring professional employees and when making promotion decisions."
- "Two-thirds of salaried employees in large American companies have some writing responsibility. 'All employees

must have writing ability.... Manufacturing documentation, operating procedures, reporting problems, lab safety, waste-disposal operations—all have to be crystal clear,' said one human resource director."

- "Eighty percent or more of the companies in the services and the finance, insurance, and real estate sectors, the corporations with greatest employment growth potential, assess writing during hiring. 'Applicants who provide poorly written letters wouldn't likely get an interview,' commented one insurance executive."
- "More than 40 percent of responding firms offer or require training for salaried employees with writing deficiencies. 'We're likely to send out 200—300 people annually for skills upgrade courses like *business writing or technical writing*,' said one respondent."

This is only one of an increasing multitude of studies illustrating the critical value of writing proficiency beyond the classroom. It's essential for schools and teachers in *all content areas* and at *all grade levels* to embrace the essential importance of writing instruction. With this state of affairs, what can an individual teacher, especially one trained in a content other than English, do?

As school systems and universities have teamed up to offer writing projects in their regions and districts, writing projects have sprung up all over the country based on a model generated by the National Writing Project. Enthusiastic participants proclaim that writing projects will change the way teachers teach, for the better. Some project fellows even go so far as to brag that being in a writing project has been a life-changing experience. The good news is that writing projects are not just for language arts teachers. Rather, they welcome, even encourage, teachers from all grade levels and all content areas.

Each writing project is administered in a different way. Some projects have a summer institute of several weeks' duration with weekend follow-ups during the school year; teachers may receive stipends and/or university credits at the project's end. Each of the National Writing Project sites across the country and abroad operates individually. All sites, however, are links in a vibrant network of project teachers with similar goals on teaching writing in schools and colleges. Often project members and directors gather at conventions and conferences to exchange ideas, socialize, and discuss National Writing Project business. The NWP has received federal funding since 1991.

Affiliates of the National Writing Project seek to:

- improve literacy skills among students
- increase understanding of literacy assessment methods
- enhance literacy instruction at all levels, in all subjects
- recognize and promote teacher expertise in the teaching of writing and reading
- increase literacy collaboration and communication

The philosophy of the National Writing Project believes:

- writing is fundamental to learning. Summer institutes therefore involve teachers from all disciplines and levels of instruction.
- the process of writing can best be understood by engaging in this process; therefore teachers of writing should write themselves.
- teachers are the best teachers of teachers.
- real change in classroom practice happens over time.
- effective professional development programs are ongoing and systematic, (These lists are courtesy of the Louisville Writing Project Institute 2010 brochure.)

Both **Kay** and **Patti** are local writing project fellows. They heartily subscribe to the paradigm indicated in the bullet points above. They firmly believe the truth of the last statement above, and that truth accounts for the fact that they are writing to share what they've learned. They've learned much about writing from their affiliation with their local Louisville Writing Project and the NWP that has positively influenced their classroom instruction. The impact of their LWP experience has not been limited to writing instruction, but rather has permeated their overall approach with their students and in their instruction.

We can't encourage you strongly enough to apply to affiliate with your local writing project site. Most sites require teachers to attain a few years of successful teaching experience before they can submit applications. In the meantime, many sites offer mini-conferences and other professional activities that are open to all teachers. Check out the National Writing Project web site (www.nwp.org). We're confident you'll find that just as attending conventions and conferences is helpful and inspiring to new and returning teachers as well as reinvigorating for veteran teachers, so joining a writing project will be an opportunity you won't want to miss.

In-Service/Staff Development/Local Professional Development

If you're new to education or returning after a reasonably lengthy hiatus, you may have never taken part in local teacher in-service or staff development. The information and activities, which now fall under the umbrella of teacher in-service/staff development, were once the meat and potatoes of faculty meetings. In-service/staff development are additional means of professional development that local districts and individual schools have of introducing teachers to new instructional ideas and policies, and redefining policies and instructional mandates already in place.

For example, if a district mandates IEP's (Individual Education Plans) for ECE (Exceptional Child Education), all teachers may be asked to occasionally attend an IEP conference. Thus the district may in-service all teachers on policy, explaining the language of IEP's and familiarizing teachers outside special education departments about the types of documentation used in an IEP. Another example is an in-service session for faculty to work on local school initiatives, such as school safety issues or ways to deal with blood-borne pathogens. An in-service meeting more closely related to instruction might provide workshops on strategies for use with students such as writing across the curriculum or performance-based objectives.

The key to profiting from in-service/staff development is keeping abreast of what you're supposed to know and be able to do with the information and training you receive through professional development. District representatives sometimes visit schools and question teachers about procedures and policies presented through PD. Administrators may expect you to add initiatives from PD sessions to your yearly individual growth plan. During performance evaluations, principals or instructional coordinators may expect you to demonstrate strategies learned during staff development.

Be ready and keep up-to-date with what you're expected to know and be able to do by maintaining folders of both district and local materials. These materials may impact your teaching procedures immediately; moreover, at some future time this knowledge might enhance your personal evaluation.

Trends seem to indicate that twenty-first century teachers will be saddled with increasing and more complex demands. Education and those who control it, whether state legislators, district superintendents, or local school administrators, seem geared up to mandate teacher practices and continually evolving policies. It has become clear that in addition to sound teaching, educators in this century will be asked to accomplish **new**

initiatives and process increasingly more sophisticated information about their profession and their students. Our advice: do not stress over in-service or staff development. It can be valuable in helping you keep informed about that information for which you're being held accountable.

Even when it's not the most invigorating subject matter or entertaining presentation, staff development can provide essential information and training. When you have some choice in selecting in-service and staff development opportunities, we recommend choosing those sessions, which most clearly will be useful in your teaching and your students' learning.

III ~ Management Foundations

PREDICTABLE PATTERNS
WHAT MAKES TEENS TICK?

As beginning teachers we were little more than adolescents ourselves. Even though we had taken various psychology classes, we didn't have enough life experience to insightfully observe psychological principles at work or to apply what we had learned in our own classrooms. We certainly hadn't yet engaged in the reflection that later illuminated our understanding of the adolescents we were teaching.

After years of working with adolescents, we have observed that certain attitudes and behaviors appear repeatedly. When we feel frustrated by a student's behavior, it helps to remember that we have observed that behavior before. Once we realized that certain behaviors might be due to natural adolescent tendencies, our own frustrations were diminished. Additionally, once we recognized patterns in behavior, we were able to develop management strategies that anticipated those adolescent behavioral patterns. Perhaps sharing our observations will help another teacher better understand her students.

1. **Adolescents are egocentric.**

   Everything is about *them* and what they think they want. That's part of being an adolescent. Considering the feelings of others or how their behavior affects others is not particularly important to them. It's helpful for teachers to recognize this egocentricity and wear a thick skin. Don't take negative behavior or complaints personally. That's easier to do when keeping in mind that the unpleasant attitude or behavior may be a characteristic of the age group. Keep in mind that the student producing the unpleasantness will probably grow into a very respectable adult.

2. **Adolescents live in and for the moment.**

   They don't remember yesterday, let alone last week or last month. When an adolescent student sees an unsatisfactory mark for conduct on his progress report, he probably won't remember doing a single thing to warrant that mark. This is why **documentation** and *immediate* **consequences** are valuable. Likewise, adolescents do not plan ahead. They may anticipate the future – the prom, graduation, college – but actively planning and preparing for next week is quite a different matter altogether . . . and something to which many adolescents are unaccustomed. When even the best students wait until the last minute to begin a major project, don't be shocked. That doesn't imply there shouldn't be consequences for work shoddily done at the last minute. Those consequences are part of the learning process that helps adolescents grow into responsible adults. Requiring students to submit project proposals and periodic progress reports as part of their grade helps them be more responsible and organized despite their tendency to procrastinate. (Refer to the Appendix for samples of such planning and reporting tools.)

3. **Adolescents respond to immediate gratification.**

Dangling rewards far in the future probably isn't the most effective motivational strategy with adolescents. Plan rewards, however small, to coincide immediately with the behavior that earned the reward. Keep in mind that rewards are not just tangible. Praise or recognition can sometimes be more meaningful to a student than a concrete reward. A kind remark or an encouraging note on student work often means more to students than we may realize. Simple certificates of accomplishment, coupons awarded for desired behavior or performance, or the display of quality student work also provide *immediate* gratification that **reinforces** positive behaviors. By *immediately* rewarding positive behavior, a teacher lays the groundwork for a repeat performance. (Refer to the Appendix for a sample of a reward coupon.)

4. **Adolescents complain.**

This used to drive **Patti** crazy. At times she wondered if it were possible for some of her students to utter a positive word. Then one of them helped her put student complaining in perspective.

Students had returned from a senior class meeting where it was announced that heretofore the senior prom would be a junior-senior prom. My seniors were up in arms. It seemed impossible for them to recognize <u>any</u> positive aspects to such an arrangement. I shared that my prom had been a combined junior-senior event and pointed out some of the advantages.

One of my students replied, "Oh, Ms. Slagle, we just like to complain." Epiphany! At that moment I realized much of the complaining I was accustomed to hearing was probably due to adolescent patterns of behavior.

From that point, my students' complaining bothered me less. For instance, when I introduced a new project and heard initial moans and groans, I let it pass and waited until the next day. Most often, I never heard another complaint. I have learned that to change an assignment or lesson plan based on those initial complaints is overreaction on my part.

5. **Adolescents experiment with independence. This may look like rebellion.**

Growing independence is an aspect of human development. that becomes apparent as adolescents begin to mature. When teens violate their curfew or dye their hair green, they may be "trying out their wings." Making too big an issue out of harmless efforts to experience independence just makes *us* frustrated and may actually perpetuate the behavior. We measure appropriateness based on three questions:

- Does the behavior endanger the student or anyone else?
- Does the behavior express or imply disrespect for anyone?
- Does the behavior interfere with the student's or the class's learning?

A "no" answer to each of these questions indicates to us that a behavior *may* not be worth making into an issue that could divert attention from instruction and create tension between teacher and student. Of course, student behavior that meets the above test of appropriateness yet violates school policy, needs to be addressed. We recommend dealing with such situations as discreetly as possible. Like so much else with adolescents, once the novelty wears off, the behaviors generally dissipate; possibly replaced with others, but those too will usually pass.

6. **Adolescents want frameworks, even though they initially may complain about them.**

If an adolescent enters a classroom knowing what to expect and feeling confident in how to operate, he will feel secure. Sure, he may complain initially that the teacher is "too strict"; but without realizing it, he will grow to feel comfortable in the predictability of that framework. For some students, the classroom may be the most consistent order and structure they experience all day. There's comfort in that framework for the student, even though he may not consciously recognize it.

7. **Adolescents want to be held accountable, even though they may appear to resist it.**

   Holding students **accountable** communicates a number of positive messages; on the other hand, not holding students accountable communicates negative messages. When a teacher does not hold students accountable, the implied message may be that she doesn't think they are worth the effort, that she doesn't care enough, or that she doesn't think they are capable of being held accountable. Conversely, holding students accountable implies that a teacher feels students are worth the effort, that he cares about them, and that he believes they are capable of responsible performance. This action contributes to students' self-esteem.

   Continually letting students "off the hook" is not doing them any favors. Although "sticking to your guns" may be difficult when met with resistance, it won't take long for students to respond to a teacher's accountability expectations and standards once they know he is serious and **consistent**. Eventually this effort will make a teacher's life easier and will encourage students' productivity and fulfillment.

8. **Peer influence is powerful. Consequently, adolescents will go to great lengths to "save face".**

   Those who teach adolescents will quickly recognize the strong influence that peers have over their contemporaries. How others perceive them is tremendously influential in their lives, and therefore in their behavior. Ignoring or resisting this reality can make a teacher's job more difficult.

   For example, if a student is not paying attention in class, to "call him out" affects his image with his peers. It could embarrass one student, while it could result in quirky teen status for another. Either way, the teacher loses. If the student is embarrassed, he may feel the need to "save face" and respond with a smart aleck retort. Yet, if the student gains status from the admonition, he may gloat for his peers. The lesson has been disrupted and the class's **focus** has moved from instruction to the student in question . . . and the teacher has facilitated that distraction.

Before determining how to address classroom situations, consider the result in light of peer image. Without thinking, a teacher can generate a situation in which a student feels compelled to have the last word. Such scenarios can escalate into a conflagration much larger than the initial behavior warranted. Teachers can prevent such chain reactions with how they handle situations.

Our recommendations include:

- Put your own ego aside and depersonalize student behavior.
- Don't be personally insulted when a student is not paying attention.
- Acknowledge that you could have made a calculation error if a student questions a grade (even if you know the student is responsible) in order to move toward resolution.
- Don't become defensive when a student accuses you of losing an assignment.
- Don't make fun of a student even if the behavior or appearance is outlandish.
- Don't make sarcastic remarks directed toward a student even if the perfect quip is almost irresistible.
- Don't force a student to repeat an unintelligible comment uttered under his breath.

Several strategies are available for teachers to address problem behavior without blatantly jeopardizing a student's peer image. We suggest remaining calm and nonjudgmental and addressing these situations as though they were business problems that need resolving. Whenever possible, address individual student behavior one-on-one; avoid correcting behavior in front of the entire class. Moving around the classroom while teaching and directing classroom activity provides the opportunity for private intervention. Proximity can be influencing. Simply move next to the student and continue classroom business from that position. Communicating nonverbally using eye contact with an offending student can be effective in the well-managed classroom. Silence can also work to your advantage. Stop talking and wait silently and patiently until you have everyone's attention.

Initially, weighing responses may seem time consuming, and taking the time to do so may not always be possible; but contemplating responses before impulsively correcting student behavior will result in a repertoire of strategies that can be employed instinctively. When there isn't time for such contemplation, reflect on the situation; review your reactions and the resulting student response after the fact. This can help you **anticipate** future occurrences and be better prepared for handling them with a minimum of instructional interruption.

Classroom strategies suggested by these observed patterns of behavior will be discussed at more length and with detailed suggestions in various sections of this book.

TEACHER MANNER AND ATTITUDE: HOW THEY AFFECT CLASSROOM ATMOSPHERE AND STUDENT BEHAVIOR

Attitude is everything! This may be an exaggeration, but not by much. Teachers have a tremendous amount of influence over the atmosphere in their classroom and the behavior of students, even though in the beginning they may feel powerless over these things. From the first instant students enter a classroom, the teacher's attitude - both verbal and nonverbal - begins shaping students' perceptions of her and her class. Use that attitude to shape positive perceptions - the perceptions you, as a teacher, want.

Like us, Edmund J. Farrell, professor emeritus of English Education, recognizes the value of first impressions:

> "Out of emotional insecurity and an understandable desire to be liked if not loved, most beginning teachers fail to establish the academic rigor and high standards that students respect. In short, be dignified, serious, and organized from the outset; establish a tone that lets students know that you are their teacher, not their buddy, and that you hold high expectations for their performance in your class."
>
> Farrell, Edmund J., A seventy-year itch: to jettison some cargo. *English in Texas*, Vol. 32.1, Spring/Summer 2002, p. 6

Greet students at the door. We recommend using a businesslike manner, especially until you get to know them. There may be something to the old adage "don't smile until Thanksgiving", but we don't think it's a good idea to refrain from smiling is such a good idea. When to smile, the way to smile, and what generates a smile all convey messages to students. There's the nervous smile, the "let's be buddies" smile, the "I want you to like me smile," the "I don't know what I'm doing smile," the "I'm scared to death" smile and many more. Determine in advance what you want your smile to communicate and use it for that purpose. During those first couple of weeks before we know our students, we want our smiles to communicate that we respect them as learners, we're confident they can be successful, we are eager to help them achieve their goals, our classrooms are centered on learning, and we expect them to operate accordingly.

Possibly more influential than how often a teacher smiles is his tone and manner in relation to students. We try to be unfailingly polite and respectful toward students. "Please," " thank you," " sir," " Mr.," and "Miss" are heard frequently in our classrooms, because we start the very first day modeling polite and respectful behavior. Nine times out of ten, students respond in kind. If we use a polite tone and ask a student to "please" hand in her paper, she usually not only complies, but will often reply with "thank you." By combining a businesslike manner with this polite and respectful approach, we have helped our students begin shaping their attitudes and behaviors from day one. **Remember: students will most often respond in the manner in which they are addressed.**

What if a teacher isn't sure what she's doing or doesn't feel prepared? This could result from any number of probable situations like these:

- She was hired just a few days before school started.
- His teaching schedule was changed the day before school started.
- She's brand new to the profession and doesn't have experience upon which to build.
- He held a demanding summer job and didn't have time to get familiar with a new textbook.

First, do everything possible to convey confidence both verbally and nonverbally. Students can spot insecurity and uncertainty a mile away, will often interpret that as weakness, and take advantage of it; unfortunately, such behavior is contagious. Be careful, though, not to overcompensate and seem domineering and tyrannical to students. You can be assured that will be met with resistance from numerous students. Project a firm, confident tone of voice and hold your body confidently erect. Remember: the verbal and nonverbal messages conveyed to students the first few days of class will be lasting. If a teacher comes across as uncertain and hesitant at the beginning of a school year, it will be difficult to reverse that impression during the school year. Remember: be firm and definite in manner and tone. Students zero in on any hint of tentativeness, weakness, or doubt. "Firm" is not the same as "mean."

Planning is a teacher's best strategy. If she has planned and prepared, a teacher should have some degree of confidence. If time for planning is a problem, thoroughly plan a day or two at a time until getting past those first crucial couple of weeks. A teacher, especially a new teacher, does not need to have the entire year, the entire semester, or even the entire marking period planned in detail the first day of school. It is much more valuable to conduct well-organized, meaningful class sessions each and every day, even if that means staying only a couple of days ahead of the students for a while.

> Our suggestion for communicating confidence when what you really feel is far from it: Be willing to devote a considerable amount of time to the first two weeks of school. Be thoroughly prepared, even over-prepared, for the first day of classes. As such, you should be able to convey confidence about that one day. Don't think about the subsequent days while you're in the midst of teaching. Then do the same degree of planning for the second day and so on. You may have to operate one day at a time for a week or two, but if you can feel confident about each day when you're in the midst of it, you should be able to convey confidence to your students. Before you know it, you're likely to discover you're operating with confidence without consciously working to do so.

Investing time in determining classroom policies and procedures is invaluable. Keep in mind that planning how to teach classroom policies and procedures and how to orient students to those guidelines and routines requires the same kind of planning that teaching a lesson does. Regardless of her schedule, her text, or her planning time, a teacher can determine classroom policies and procedures and how she is going to teach those to her students beginning the first day of class.

Teachers, like students, will sometimes be inclined to bring personal problems to the classroom, which can compromise their normal manner and attitude. Students almost always pick up on these nuances very quickly. Thus, making a concerted effort to leave personal problems at home to be dealt with after school is our recommended policy. When your personal difficulties can't be kept at bay, several strategies are helpful.

- If a problem is overwhelming, call for a substitute. Trying to get through a day with students and the every-day demands of the classroom may be more than you need to handle.
- Share your problem with a colleague; sometimes just relaying your concerns to a friend will help to lessen their effect. A caring colleague will often appear at your door several times during the day to check on you or to offer relief for a brief period of time.
- A previously established classroom routine and procedures will make getting through a difficult day much less challenging. To further enable you to continue with instruction, have some alternative plans in reserve for a day when you may need to back off from the limelight. A generic idea tying in to whatever unit is in play in the classroom will often save the day and provide an opportunity to temper manner and attitude without totally disrupting class atmosphere.
- If comfortable and *appropriate,* share with students. "I'm having a rough day today. I know you will understand if I seem upset. Bear with me. Tomorrow will be better." With this situation, however, teachers run the risk of students inquiring about their difficulty. A firm reply, such as, "Thanks for your concern, I'll be OK," will usually stop the inquiries.

Be cautious, however, about sharing personal problems with students. The classroom is not an appropriate place to air problems, and immature students are not good sounding boards for personal difficulties. If an explanation is absolutely necessary, we recommend sharing with students only the *most general* information surrounding a personal issue. Instead, talk to a school counselor if immediate help is needed, or seek professional guidance outside of school. Return to the classroom with your normal manner and attitude fully evident to students.

Kay *remembers a day when she came to school after losing a beloved pet the previous evening. Students knew something was the matter. They inquired about her blue mood. Kay decided to share the problem (which was not inappropriately personal) with her students. They were very sympathetic, and she found that briefly sharing her grief with them helped assuage it for the time she was at school. Her students also felt they were helping to make a difficult situation easier. The next day students brought Kay cards, flowers, and a balloon – their touching way of helping her cope with her grief.*

Consistency is very important in the process of molding classroom attitude. If, after conveying a predetermined manner and behavior for the first couple of days, a teacher begins periodically spouting sarcastic comments regarding a student's behavior or "calling students out" for infractions in front of the class, he will sabotage his efforts to produce the classroom attitude he is seeking. We've all heard students say, "Mr. So-and-so 'went off' in class today," or "Ms. So-and-so 'ragged us' for half the class today." We don't want *our* students to experience that kind of teacher behavior. By establishing an attitude and manner in the first few days of class and consistently **reinforcing** it, teachers help students relax, let down their guard, and turn off their defensive mechanisms therefore making it easier to focus on learning.

> ***Patti's*** *goal is for students to say, "Ms. Slagle doesn't get mad or yell at us." I strive for even, predictable manner, tone and behavior so that students won't have to wonder every time they come into my classroom what my mood is and how it will affect them. A secondary advantage of this attitude is that when I decide it is important to demonstrate that I am upset over something that truly warrants it, I have a tremendous effect. When teachers get upset easily and frequently, they eventually are not taken seriously by their students when they do so.*

Generating particular student behavior and classroom atmosphere is a process that doesn't happen overnight. Many teachers think that their instinctive behavior will do the trick. As beginning teachers, we proceeded in that manner for a number of years but were never satisfied with the results. With experience upon which to draw, we analyzed our attitudes and behaviors in relation to our students. The more we learned about human behavior, adolescent psychology, and group dynamics, the more we realized that it doesn't "just happen." Conditioning the attitude and behavior of students takes just as much planning, guided practice, and reinforcement as developing reading or writing skills. Self-discipline is required for a teacher to consistently remember to convey the attitude she wants students to emulate. The good news is that the more it is done, the more it becomes habit.

A caution: if a teacher approaches his classes in a businesslike, organized and consistent manner, his students may at first seem critical or even resentful. Have a thick skin. That is a superficial initial reaction and will most likely change. Keep in mind that your students are adolescents and think they want the easiest path. If a teacher persists, he will find that as the year proceeds students will begin to recognize the value for *them* of that classroom approach. A few may even share something like, "At the beginning of the year I thought you were strict and hard, but now I really like the way our class runs." We hear that sort of feedback frequently. Without realizing it, students grow to recognize that learning focus, organization, consistency, and preparation not only benefit them but also make their classroom functioning easier and more comfortable.

A public service message that was once aired, demonstrates the point quite succinctly.

A young person was shown yelling at adults. You can effectively substitute "teacher(s)" for "parent(s)" in this typical adolescent diatribe:

> *"GET OFF (Okay, it may seem like I hate my parents, but I'm really demonstrating what a therapist would call 'asserting my identity,' so I can grow up to be a well-adjusted individual. Sure, I say I want freedom, but without parental supervision, I'm much more likely to smoke pot and stuff. I hope my parents don't try to act like my friends. What I really need is a parent.) MY BACK!"*

Reputation

Reputation can help or hinder teachers' classroom management. When you overhear students talking about your colleagues (and you will), be careful to form opinions based on *your own* experiences and observations. Get to know your faculty and staff before you make permanent judgments. However, be aware that you can get an idea of the influence teachers' reputations have on how students approach their classes.

- "Mr. XXXX shows films all the time."
- "It's easy to get Ms. XXX off the subject so you don't have to take the test."
- "Don't even think about cutting Miss XXX's class. She finds out every time."
- "She's hard, but she's fair."
- "If you pay attention, follow directions, and do your class work, you can do O.K. in Ms. XXX's class."
- "Mr. XXX likes the sound of his own voice and thinks he's a comedian. Get him started and you won't have to hand in your paper."
- "She forgets to take the roll most of the time, so she won't even notice you're not there."

Whether or not statements like these reflect reality, students may behave as though they do when approaching a teacher's class. The perceived reputation of a teacher by students can make her classroom management easier to implement or can make it more challenging. Perceptive teachers begin on the very first day to influence their reputations among students.

> ***Patti*** *remembers when entering the fifth grade, she was terrified of being assigned to "Mrs. Tice's" class. Based on her reputation, students feared "Mrs. Tice." As Patti stood outside the school and listened to the various teachers call out the names of their students, she became more and more tense as her name was not called. When "Mrs. Tice" stepped forward, Patti held her breath through the alphabetical reading. When the "S's" arrived, and Patti heard her name called, her heart dropped to her stomach.*
>
> *It turned out that "Mrs. Tice" had high expectations, tolerated no foolishness, and was focused on instruction. Patti was not only successful in "Mrs. Tice's" class but came to appreciate how she conducted her classroom and its contribution to Patti's success. That was her first lesson about the power of a teacher's reputation, and she's never forgotten it. She and Kay hope that Mrs. Tice's characteristics are ones that contribute to their own professional reputations.*

The first time, as a teacher, that Patti realized the power of a reputation was when she transferred to a new school. She had been at her previous school for several years and was aware that her reputation was passed on among students year after year; but she didn't realize the extent of its impact on her classroom management until she found herself in a new teaching situation. *Patti quickly recognized that since she had no reputation at the new school, how she handled her first year would influence the balance of her years in that building.* It became clear that she must concentrate on firmly establishing her classroom atmosphere, policies and routines the first year in order for her reputation to develop in a manner that positively contributed to her classroom management with upcoming students. Consequently, she set out to create a reputation that worked in her favor.

The right reputation can usually make a teacher's classroom management easier and less stressful. For instance, a reputation can minimize the frustration of being tested over and over to see if you really mean what you say. When students arrive at your classroom the first day expecting an orderly, organized, instruction-focused experience, they are more likely to behave like serious learners.

Students notice everything teachers do or don't do. The word spreads. Once a teacher has been in a school for a year, his reputation is well on its way to perpetuation. Teachers who leave their reputations to chance may find themselves judged by students' imagined reputations rather than their actual experiences. It's much more reliable for a teacher to consider what she wants her reputation to be now and in the future and make a plan for establishing that reputation. The suggestions made in this book will contribute to teachers' positive and productive reputations among their students.

> ***Kay** knows that her general reputation passed from class to class, year-to-year is that she is a "hard teacher." When students actually experience her teaching, they discover that "hard" means she has high expectations, holds students accountable and values knowledge and learning. At the end of every school year, most students have come to realize that Kay has their best interests at heart, knows what contributes to their success, and really cares about them and what they learn.*

Don't confuse your reputation with popularity. Popularity may seem fine at the moment, but for long-term effective management, instruction and student learning, popularity will not contribute much. When students arrive at your classroom knowing your reputation for high expectations, fairness, consistency, student instructional support, and reliability, your job will be easier and your students' success will be more likely.

Some teachers simply don't understand the effect *their* attitude and behavior have on students' attitude and behavior. Others may not want to exert the effort it takes to condition students' behavior and attitude. We have always considered the work put into shaping desired behavior and attitude during the first six weeks or so as an investment in the rest of the year. Sure, we work very, very hard those first few weeks, but those efforts make the rest of the school year go much more smoothly and productively. So, a few of our suggestions:

- Determine your attitude and plan how to convey it.
- Consistently model and reinforce your desired attitude, manner and behavior.
- Leave personal problems outside the school door.
- Consistently center your classroom on learning.

- Set the standard. Don't just take what appears to be the easy way out at the moment.
- Take the time and make the effort to learn from every experience. Reflect on what has been successful and unsuccessful and modify your plan accordingly

TEACHER/STUDENT RELATIONSHIPS

We feel that productive student/teacher relationships are grounded in mutual respect. Students appear in your classroom on the first day of school not knowing you (except perhaps by reputation), and you probably don't know them. How a teacher relates to her students from that very first day lays the groundwork for the relationship they will have throughout the school year. The old adage that first impressions are lasting most definitely is at play in this relationship.

Although you might think mutual respect is a given in the classroom setting, it isn't automatic. **It is critical for teachers to convey to their students they respect them as individuals and as learners.** If students do not feel respected, they will not be motivated to engage in learning activity. Consequently, they will not progress and won't be successful. It's a cycle that teachers want to avoid. Instead, respect your students as people and as learners regardless of their prior performance, reputation, appearance, class track, or anything else. Your respect will lead the way to students' motivation, performance, success, and yes, their behavior.

There's yet more to the cycle of respect. **In order to be most effective, teachers need students to respect them as someone who can facilitate their success**. But respect from students isn't automatic. Teachers can't force respect; it comes naturally as a byproduct of what they do in their classrooms with and for their students. It must be earned.

Teachers can demonstrate that they respect students by maintaining high expectations, holding them accountable, and providing thoughtful, meaningful learning activities and instruction every day. In addition, there are more subtle ways teachers can demonstrate to students that they genuinely respect them. Other practices include:

- **Honor your students' beliefs and perspectives.** Remember that you're dealing with adolescents. By nature, they can be impulsive, emotional and immature. Accordingly, they may voice opinions that you feel confident are wrongheaded. Rather than berating, squelching, or criticizing them, strive to honor their right to form opinions that may be different from yours. You can contribute to their life learning by encouraging them to seek legitimate support and evidence for those opinions. In classes such as language arts and social studies, students can practice supporting opinions with fact-based evidence as part of your instruction. When a student provides such evidence but arrives at a conclusion with which you disagree, it's important to respect their right to form that opinion.

- Along the same lines, it's important that teachers **avoid imposing their opinions and perspectives on students.** Teachers have a bully pulpit, but we must remember that we are authority figures. It is unfair for a teacher to impose his political, religious, or other subjective opinions on students that he will evaluate. Furthermore, such dogmatic behavior can get a teacher into trouble. If you impart a personal viewpoint on a timely topic and a parent is vehemently opposed to your perspective, the parent could actively object to you "forcing" your opinions on students. To protect yourself from such charges, it's much better to strive to remain **objective**. Furthermore, it's respectful and part of the learning process to encourage students to form their own opinions based on research and evidence.
- Obviously, you can't avoid expressing an opinion from time to time, and we don't think you should. Rather, we encourage teachers to **use good sense about the topics and timing surrounding the expression of their viewpoints.** Make thoughtful decisions about what opinions to express rather than impulsively spouting them. Subjective viewpoints that are inexorably tied to subject matter may actually enhance your instruction and generally shouldn't create objections. On the other hand, opinions surrounding political, religious, community, and timely issues may arouse emotions that make them best kept private. Always avoid conveying, either subtly or overtly, that you expect your students to blindly accept your opinions simply because they are *your* opinions. Respect your students' right to own their beliefs, even if you do not agree with them.
- **Refrain from telling students what to think**. Our role as teachers is to help our students learn to draw *informed* conclusions and form opinions based on *evidence*. The teacher who tells students what to think – whether it is an interpretation of a literary selection, an analysis of the impact of an historical event, or numerous other situations that typically arise in a classroom – is robbing students of the opportunity to learn to think critically. When we respect our

students as learners, we recognize that a more productive approach is to coach students to use information, facts, examples, and evidence to draw their own inferences and come to their own conclusions. Telling students what to think is not only disrespectful of them as learners, it is also the very lowest level thinking skill. In fact, it's hardly asking them to think at all. Guiding students to draw evidence-based conclusions is a higher order thinking skill that respects their abilities, and one we feel teachers should foster.

Patti *once had a student teacher who fancied himself an author. He thought he had all the answers – at least in literary matters. As Patti observed him teaching a contemporary novel to an honors class, she heard him repeatedly say, "This is what the author means." After the lesson, Patti asked him if he had read the author's explanation of his intent or had communicated with the author in order to know his underlying motivations. He had not. When she asked the basis of his pronouncements, he replied, "It is generally accepted in literary circles." The conversation continued along these lines:*

Patti: What is the value to students of sitting and listening to you interpret a novel for them?
ST: They'll be more well read.
Patti: What will happen when they read something, and you're not there to interpret it for them?
ST: They're bright. They'll figure it out.
Patti: Do you believe there is one and only one interpretation of a literary work?
ST: Some interpretations are more legitimate than others.
Patti: Is that to say that a student's interpretation is not valid?
ST: Well, what do they know about writing?

At this point, Patti threw up her hands abandoning her attempt to help the student teacher gain insight into the inquiry process of instruction and became his teacher:

"It's important to encourage students to practice the skill of reading and drawing inferences based on the text. Then it's important to value their interpretations as legitimate. If we want to motivate students to engage in such evaluative thinking, it's important to honor their interpretations."

Unfortunately, the student teacher didn't alter his methods and continued to dictate what he wanted students to think.

Interestingly, when school started the following year, he had not been hired.

We believe that if there is not mutual respect between students and their teacher, limited productive learning activity can occur. Building and nurturing that respect begins with the teacher. If he truly respects his students and demonstrates that respect with thoughtful classroom attitudes, behavior and instruction, his students will follow his lead.

Ever since you decided to teach, you may have heard various stories about teacher-student relationships and their maintenance. Advice runs the gamut: "Don't get too close to your students. Students need role models and mentors, not friends. Don't be cold with your kids; let them get to know you as a human being." The truth is that all of this advice rings true to some degree.

An essential aspect of the relationship challenge is how to engage students in the teaching learning process while maintaining a healthy, professional relationship with them and earning their **respect**. Another part of this challenge is how to accomplish those goals, and at the same time, get to know your students and let them get to know you. Over our long careers, we have found ways to engage students by getting to know them better, and thereby maintaining a reasonable balance in our relationships.

Let's examine the many-faceted ways you can come to know your students and how they learn as well as let them get to know you and how you teach. At the beginning of each school year, how we communicate becomes extremely important. In our classes, we discuss the value of open and honest communication. Then we talk about how we communicate in our high-tech world.

Kay *mentions her concern to students that media tell us the art of personal letter writing no longer exists. Then she and her students explore the differences between e-mailing, telephoning, and texting compared to writing and sending personal letters. During the first week of school, Kay asks students to compose personal letters introducing themselves to her. She tells them she wants to know who they are, what they care about, what they hope and dream, and what they want to accomplish this year in her class.*

In turn, she writes a letter to her students. In her letter she tries to tell them the same things about herself that she wants to know about them. Because she cannot write individual letters to each student, she personalizes each greeting by hand ("Dear Jessica" "Dear Kevin") and then carefully signs each letter individually (e.g. "With hopes for a great year, Ms. Twaryonas"). She distributes her letters and collects one from each student.

Their letters are written on store-bought stationary often with flowers, dolphins, or cats with various child-like stickers attached; "serious" stationary with computer-generated monograms; plain white, unlined paper; even lined notebook paper. She relishes reading each one, and she gives students classroom credit for their letters. The points accrued from letter writing make nice "gift-cushions" with which each student begins the drive toward that coveted "A".

Through these letters, she learns a great deal about these new young people with whom she's going to interact for the next nine months – information to which she might never be privy without these letters. What young people have to say is often interesting, sometimes amusing, and occasionally poignant.

***Patti**, too, uses letters to learn about her students. She especially remembers one student who seemed surprised that her teacher was interested enough to ask her to write about herself. This student took the initiative to express to Patti, "It was so nice of you to ask us to write you letters about ourselves. I think that's one of the nicest things a teacher has done."*

Teachers' attention to their students' tastes in popular culture lets them know that their interests are valid and their opinions matter. Even though we may not share our students' interests, we listen to what they have to say and respond in an atmosphere of open, friendly give-and-take. These interactions engender respect between teachers and students. Shared interests often serve as links to continued mentoring opportunities after graduation.

Additionally, seemingly insignificant gestures may be valuable in securing good relationships between teachers and students. Positive comments ("Great video with your project, Denise. I was really impressed.") can make a student's day. A wish of good luck to an actress ("Hey, break a leg – it's opening night.") or athlete ("Go for the win, Mike. Good luck.") may be remembered for a long while. *Genuine* interest in a student can be a meaningful way of establishing good feelings ("I hope you're feeling better, Hannah, we missed you last week.") or healing sore ones ("I'm glad we're on a more positive footing, Josh. It feels better to me. I hope it does to you, too.") In the frenzied heat of a teacher's day, it may seem as though it takes all her energy to manage from one class to the next. But as teachers, we have endless small ways to promote good teacher-student relationships, and the nice part is that being thoughtful, interested, or kind is easy and not very time-consuming.

Simple gestures that teachers perform for friends and acquaintances outside school have the same enduring effect when extended to students. Handwritten notes convey to students that a teacher takes interest in them. Efforts such as thank you notes for gifts/holiday cards or notes of congratulations for accomplishments or achievements are uncomplicated ways to provide individual student attention.

Patti keeps a collection of note cards in her desk allowing her to easily compose personal notes to students when the occasion arises. Asking a student about the meaning of a slang term he uses, complimenting her on a new hair-do or piece of jewelry, inquiring where she found a certain item of clothing or unusual school supply, all demonstrate a teacher's interest in students as individuals. Students, like all of us, want to be separated from the crowd and recognized for who they are as unique individuals. Teachers can provide this affirmation for students with these simple considerations.

Very early in her career, ***Patti*** *taught a young man who played cello with the local youth orchestra. She expressed to him her interest in classical music, and he subsequently invited her to a recital he was giving on a Sunday afternoon. She attended because he was her student, but she may have gone anyway because the music was something in which she was interested. In the twenty-five or so years since, he has become principal cellist for the local symphony. Whenever their paths cross, often at concerts, his twinkling eyes and grin indicate his delight in still telling others that she was his teacher.*

However, students may sometimes misinterpret interest, thoughtfulness, and kindnesses. As teachers eager to get to know our students, we must remember that "kids are kids." **They may not recognize appropriate limits for personal interactions.** When we become too familiar with students, especially in aspects of their personal lives, or they get to know us and our personal lives in a less-than-healthy way, we put ourselves in a compromising and unprofessional position. Offering ourselves as personal confidantes, mother-confessors, or sounding boards may result in late-night phone calls, tearful confessions, or unpleasant harangues. These entanglements could have possible legal repercussions.

Because our students are adolescents and, as such, sometimes emotionally volatile, relationships which become too personal or too important can grow to overshadow the learning focus which should take center stage for all parties. These same students whom we might wish to counsel and help with personal issues are the ones we must manage and assess in our classrooms. Charges of favoritism about grades and conduct, or undue personal attention to a few select students can compromise a teacher's relationship with *all students* in her class. Let counseling about difficult personal matters take place in the school's counseling suite or in professional centers whose qualified personnel are trained to work with students who need attention with these kinds of problems. **Keep your relationships with your students friendly, but keep those connections**

confined to the arena of intellectual, mutual interest issues; stay away from personal, more intimate concerns. Things are different today from what they were in the past. Associations and interactions that may have passed muster when we were teaching 15-20 years ago, today raise eyebrows, questions, and even criminal charges.

We've all known or heard about the teacher who has been accused of taking inappropriate liberties with students. If the news media gets wind of the accusation, a teacher's whole life can be disrupted. Even if absolved, a shadow hangs over accused teachers for the rest of their careers. We cannot emphasize strongly enough how vital it is for teachers to conscientiously avoid putting themselves in situations where they are vulnerable to such accusations, even if their motives are innocent.

Popularity

Often teachers want to be popular with their students. Some teachers want to be their students' buddies. Other teachers want to be their confessor. We don't recommend any of these roles. **We aspire to be respected and eventually appreciated by our students**, and we are rarely disappointed. A teacher is not her students' pal, parent, or confessor. We are their teachers, and our charge is to teach them reading, writing, computing, speaking, listening, and thinking. That challenge in itself is a huge job. Besides, teachers can't *make* popularity happen. In fact, students often laugh behind the backs of teachers who seem wrapped up in seeking popularity with students. As one of our colleagues has said, "Popular is something you want to be in high school. As a teacher, you want to be **respect**ed." We couldn't have said it better. Rather than wasting time worrying about how students perceive you, spend that time planning, preparing and responding; the rest will take care of itself.

Teachers should also limit their extra-curricular associations with students to school-sponsored events and school-related functions. If a movie with a close tie-in to a book being read in English class, for example, is showing only on Saturday night, send a note home to parents requesting their permission to meet their sons and daughters at the cinema for a class viewing of the film. Refrain from meeting one or two students for the film and then going out together. Stay away from inviting one or two students to your home to help them with a special project. Instead, send parents a note about plans to meet their kids at the public library or some other public venue for special assistance with the work. Always get permission for special functions in writing and file them. You'll save yourself difficulties that might arise later about "a clandestine meeting at the library." Stories can be embellished and go viral very quickly, and being on the safe side in all situations is to a teacher's professional and personal advantage. Keep parents informed about any classroom related activity outside of school and traditional school time slots.

We don't let these cautions keep us from being friendly, understanding educators; rather, we use our good professional judgment. As their teachers, we will bond with many of our students in a variety of ways. We must keep those ways focused on the educational mandate we've been given as professionals – to teach and oversee student learners.

During our long careers, we have been fortunate in maintaining contacts across the years with many of our **former students**. Because we have taught upper classmen for much of our careers, these connections are easier to cultivate. Seniors return to high school, especially the first few years after graduation, eager to keep teachers posted on their college work, personal successes, and new careers. They sometimes continue to visit, send letters and e-mails telling of new jobs, marriages, children, graduations, awards.

Social networking web sites have added to the means by which former students can keep us apprised of their adult activity and successes. Previously, teachers often had to take on faith that they played a positive and significant role in their students' development. Technology now makes it more possible than ever for teachers to discover the impact they may have had on their development. Teachers deserve that affirmation more than ever. The amazing variety of information we learn about former students makes us proud to be teachers – a worthy profession having its own special rewards.

Often, graduates provide feedback about their high school years and the roles we played in them; most always, we are filled with pride. We're sure most of them would never have spoken so freely when they were our "official students." Some confess that even though they were often distressed about the heavy work load we assigned, or the weekends and late hours they "slaved over papers and projects," what they learned has helped them become confident college students, successful workers, and productive people in their personal lives. We thank our students for letting us know that we have been successful and valued as teachers. **Respect your students, get to know your students, and remember your mission.** Classroom memories last a lifetime.

TEACHER EXPECTATIONS
The power of the self-fulfilling prophecy

In our years of experience we have found that the overwhelming majority of students *want* to learn and *can* learn. Students that some teachers have "written off" have performed like seasoned learners in other's classes. Although the teacher may make the difference, **it is often the teacher's expectations for students that motivate them to perform.**

The **self-fulfilling prophecy** is one of the most significant means that teachers have to influence student performance. If teachers genuinely believe students can and want to learn, they will usually live up to those expectations. Conversely, if teachers believe students don't care about school and don't want to learn, they won't disappoint.

Patti learned about the relationship between self-fulfilling prophecies and student performance after she had been teaching only four years:

> *One summer our inner city district was merged with the suburban county district for court-ordered desegregation. Our student body demographic was to change drastically. During professional development to prepare for the anticipated changes, I learned about the concept of the self-fulfilling prophecy.*
>
> *That I distinctly remember the presenter introducing the idea and explaining how our students would live up – or down – to our expectations attests to the impact the concept subsequently had on my approach to instruction and management. Years of trial, error and reflection have demonstrated to me how the self-fulfilling prophecy manifests itself in the classroom setting. After many years as a teacher, I realize the self-fulfilling prophecy has been the most significant conceptual influence on my teaching approach.*

Teachers face many daunting challenges. Among those is how to make state or district curriculum requirements relevant to students. They also must generate student confidence in their ability to achieve proficiency in that core content. To most effectively achieve this goal, teachers must first believe in their students' capacities for success.

When **Patti** was teaching in a program for her school's lowest academically achieving students, a substitute in her classroom shared an astute observation with Kay who, in turn, shared it with Patti:

> *The substitute commented to Kay that a week earlier, she had some students that were "wild" and "bouncing off the walls"; yet she was surprised to find some of those same students in my*

classes behaving like learners. The difference? I believed that all of my students could be successful. I had high expectations, which I communicated; furthermore, I taught everyone how to achieve them. When I genuinely believed they could meet those expectations, my students did also and were proud of themselves.

In that same program for academically challenged students, a social studies instructor was placed on the team:

He generally showed videos -sometimes related to social studies, usually not – while he read the newspaper. He frequently dozed off. Initially, students liked this easy approach; but after a while, class became boring. Finally one of the students tearfully approached ***Patti*** *saying, "I want to learn something so I can graduate and get a job." The social studies teacher had labeled this student as one who "doesn't want to learn anything" and "doesn't care about school." She was one of Patti's* <u>*successful*</u> *students. Teacher expectations, respect, and support made the difference.*

The self-fulfilling prophecy applies equally to high-achieving students as another of **Patti's** experiences illustrates:

Early in the year my advanced sophomores approached literature study superficially, seldom immersing themselves in the material thoughtfully. They revealed to me, "We've never had to read the whole book before." These bright students relied on paying attention, using commercial guides, and answering scores of study questions to pass objective tests with respectable marks. Evidence of critical, inferential, interpretive, and analytical thinking was missing.

I informed them there would be no study questions; that commercial guides wouldn't substitute for reading the literature; and that higher order thinking was expected. Students complained, but I knew they could rise to the challenge of my expectations.

After a few weeks, the complaining subsided and my students "knuckled down." Later a parent commented that her son liked English for the first time. What better testament to the power of positive expectations!

We certainly don't want to dwell on *negative expectations*, but they must be mentioned. **When teachers expect students to misbehave, underachieve, shirk responsibility, or show disrespect, they probably**

will. Such negative expectations do not give students a reason to behave or perform differently. When teachers try to warn us about former students who are coming to our classes, we won't let them tell us anything negative. We want to meet our new students with *positive preconceptions* only. By focusing on positive expectations for students, we believe the chances for their constructive behavior and performance increase substantially.

Kay remembers several students for whom her expectations and encouragement paid dividends.

> *After finishing a writing project, I was inspired about teaching writing and eager to try new techniques. My small group of low achieving students seemed less than eager to write. When I introduced journals, they were reluctant. "When are we gonna' do English?" "What do you mean by 'do English'?" I inquired. "Work sheets," they replied. Many had not written in years, spending their days doing work sheets, canned questions, multiple choice exercises and spelling lists – they had not been challenged.*
>
> *I chose a different approach saying, "I think each of you has a story to tell. When you write in your journal, tell stories you want to share with others." I wrote with them sharing my stories and asking them to respond to my writing. Soon students had become excited by writing and were seeking feedback from each other. They read their stories in our "writer's chair" and they enthusiastically placed their work in our Writer's Corner. They, indeed, had become writers. Because I believed they could become writers, they were able to rise to my expectation.*

Books on writing abound with techniques and projects to get students writing and loving it. But the high expectations of the teacher accompanied by encouragement and guidance are key prescriptions for the self-fulfilling prophecy. The positive power of teacher expectations is demonstrated in **Kay's** account:

> *One of my newfound writers wrote stories from childhood memories. His tale about the silliness of wearing bow ties and his account of embarrassing relatives greeting him by pinching his cheeks amused his classmates with colorful details. This twenty-one-year-old senior who had never been expected to write, crafted touching pieces. I wanted to recognize his accomplishment at the senior awards ceremony.*
>
> *He had to make special arrangements at the garage where he worked as a mechanic to attend the ceremony. He arrived in his*

work shirt with his name on the front and his fingernails covered with grease. When his name was called for an English award, he proudly approached the podium and picked up his certificate. His mother, through tears, said to me, "This is the only award my boy has ever gotten and I can tell he's proud. I've read his journal and you're right, he is a writer."

We expect the best from *all* students. Consistently, we believe they can meet goals and utilize talents they might not realize they have. Maintaining positive expectations for students and proceeding in a manner commensurate with faith in them, not only results in their success but also provides professional and personal fulfillment for teachers.

FRAMEWORK FOR MANAGEMENT

A classroom framework provides structure that maximizes time focused on learning and minimizes time spent on mundane housekeeping and bookkeeping tasks. To some, structure implies students marching in line, sitting silently waiting for the teacher to address them, and reciting only when called upon. In *our* classrooms students may be working in groups, discussing a concept, presenting a skit, partnering on an assignment, or each doing something different; however, they are learning while engaged in these activities because a classroom framework has been established and maintained from the first day.

We base our classroom frameworks on plans with rationales, not merely structures for the sake of order. The first several years in our careers were spent learning from experiences, observing others, reflecting, and planning. After a number of years, we could consider classroom structure based on our numerous and varied experiences and observations. We eventually perceived how much and what kind of structure was appropriate for most of our students and for our teaching styles. We regularly make adjustments to accommodate differences in administrations, students, class size and accountability requirements.

We feel classrooms must have an underlying framework or havoc may result. Instead of relying on a plan to fall into place and take care of itself, we recommend devising structures to fit your needs and the needs of your particular students. It is important to take stock every year and with every new class relying on professional judgment to determine the kind of structure that works best. We share some principles below to guide your consideration of the nature and degree of structure teachers may decide to implement in their classrooms.

A classroom framework can create a comfort zone for students. When they know expectations and procedures, students can enter a classroom with confidence that the teacher will address their particular needs and that they will know how to proceed. Structure helps students feel that success is attainable; consequently, they can relax and concentrate on learning. For some students, classrooms may provide a needed framework for a part of their typical day that they won't experience anywhere else. Classroom structure gives students not only a genuine opportunity to learn, but also offers them a respite from possible disorder in other parts of their day.

A classroom framework can minimize distractions and diversions from learning. Once students have learned classroom policies and routines and the teacher consistently observes these, non-instructional minutiae can be handled without consuming much instructional time. Taking attendance, dealing with make-up work, collecting field trip money, and signing absence slips and permission forms need only divert a minimum of a classroom's instructional focus.

A classroom framework can minimize volatility and potential eruptions. When students observe policies and procedures in a learning-focused classroom, they tend to forget such things as hallway insults or petty grievances that, in other circumstances, might spill into the classroom and generate distractions from learning. With a classroom framework, students may forget to "play around," "goof off," or "get off the subject." Those behaviors can precipitate escalating situations that often become disruptive; classroom structure and management can deter such occurrences.

A classroom framework can create an environment that allows, even encourages, creativity and imagination. An interview with a filmmaker noted for his imagination that we once read, indicated that his considerably ordered environment freed him from the mundane allowing him to focus on creativity. Order, organization, structure - whatever you call it - make quick business of mundane minutiae generating more time for and creating an environment where imagination can flourish.

A classroom framework can make a teacher's life easier and less stressful. Teachers cannot best serve their students if they are stressed, frustrated, and exhausted. Teaching can quickly result in those nonproductive states if teachers don't have some strategies to offset them. Even with up to thirty or thirty-five students in a class, a single teacher is held accountable for *each* student's learning. Although the teaching day may be six hours; for every hour spent in instruction, a teacher could easily fill several hours with planning, grading, and following up. A normal person may have difficulty accomplishing this seemingly superhuman feat.

Structuring the classroom will help considerably. Once students know and are held accountable for routines, policies, and procedures, much of the desired behavior and activity occur regularly without teacher direction or intervention. Consequently, teachers are freed from many management tasks which saves time and lowers stress levels.

Imagine this classroom scene: Five students were absent yesterday. Three were absent yesterday only, one was absent for two days, and one for a week. All return to class today. Each approaches the teacher for make-up work. She remembers what the class did yesterday, but has difficulty recalling specific details about what was done the day before and before that. Pulling make-up assignments for each student, she gets confused and frustrated. The class waits for instruction to begin, some talking, laughing, and a few wandering. The room gets louder and louder. One student gets so overcome with a classmate's humor, that he rolls out of his desk laughing and showing off.

This scene is possible, but not inevitable. When students have been taught and held accountable for a classroom framework, this scene could be quite different. **Imagine again:** Five students were absent for the same durations. All students enter the classroom, read the warm-up writing activity on the board and begin to respond to the prompt in their learning log notebooks. Former absentees circulate the class notebook to secure information about their make-up work. Each former absentee writes a note to the teacher requesting specific make-up work. She can use the notes to pull the make-up work while the class is working. The teacher takes roll from her seating chart then organizes her thoughts and materials. In a few minutes the teacher announces instruction will begin shortly. A few moments later, the teacher begins interacting with students. She is relaxed and focusing her energy on instruction.

Although this scene may read like a movie script, we know it can occur with *all* students. This scenario could have been one of Kay's advanced groups or one of Patti's challenged classes. When we discovered the practicality of classroom frameworks, we were less stressed and did a better job of teaching.

An ordered classroom environment creates a framework that allows teachers to concentrate on best instructional practices and helps students achieve to their maximum capacity. Considering their teaching styles and comfort levels along with their students, individual teachers determine how their classrooms are structured. Yet, a few principles seem universal:

- Effective classroom frameworks are planned and thoughtfully implemented; they don't just fall into place.
- Students are taught the classroom framework.

- Students understand the reasons for classroom routines, policies and procedures.
- Teachers model consistency by following their own framework.
- Students are held accountable for observing classroom policies and procedures.

IV ~ Management Guidelines

STUDENT ACCOUNTABILITY

Preparing students for the world beyond the classroom includes not only developing their academic skills but also teaching them self-discipline and organization. Assuming responsibility for their actions and decisions is an invaluable life lesson for students. By allowing students leniency in matters of self-discipline, organization and responsibility, teachers do them no favors

When teachers model accountability themselves, they can more effectively hold students accountable. Students may complain when expected to be responsible because some may not have much experience with accountability. Sometimes students are experienced at talking teachers (or parents) out of holding them responsible for their actions and decisions. If they succeed, they can be expected to try again.

Once teachers employ accountability expectations, they may find their jobs easier. Students become accustomed to expectations and many will not consider deviating from them. Meanwhile, they still may behave irresponsibly in other classes, if those teachers have not established a pattern of accountability expectations.

How do teachers get students to accept responsibilities in their classes? Some of our methods may prove helpful.

1. **Teach classroom rules and procedures.** Post them prominently. Give a quiz over them. Then consistently hold students accountable for following them. If classroom rules/procedures/expectations have been effectively taught, students will know how that classroom operates and will usually comply, possibly with grumbling; but for the most part, they will eventually adapt to the teacher's expectations, if she consistently adheres to them herself.
2. **Reward accountability**. When students have demonstrated accountability for required work, we sometimes reward them with bonus opportunities. For instance, Patti's students can earn bonus points on their learning logs and assignments, but only if they are handed in on time. When students finish all of their class work, they can read independently for bonus points; but they do not have this bonus option if their class work is incomplete or unsatisfactory.

3. **Reward/give credit for appropriate learning behavior**. For example, we have reinforced positive learning behavior using a learning performance grade. To provide an incentive for students to focus on learning and accept responsibility for their own learning, they can even sometimes earn bonus credit for this grade component.
4. **Be sure there are consequences if you decide to allow less than full accountability from a student or a class; otherwise, this reprieve will be expected time after time.** Although a teacher may want to help out an individual student, she must consider the fallout with the rest of her class when making her decision. For example, when a teacher decides to accept a major assignment late, consider communicating with the student that full credit will not be received. Otherwise, students who handed in the assignment on time could feel affronted
5. **Designate a location in the classroom where students can always find upcoming due dates, deadlines, announced quizzes and tests.** This practice places responsibility on students and eliminates opportunities for claiming lack of awareness when deadlines arrive. Don't rely on verbal announcements alone for conveying this information to students.
6. **Review, remind, reiterate, repeat, and reinforce** thereby giving students every possible opportunity to assume their responsibilities as learners.
7. **Require students to keep a record throughout each grading period of *all* grades.** Patti provides a form for doing so and a folder for storing their graded work. Kay uses school planners that often provide sections to help students keep records of their graded work. When students ask what assignments they are missing, send them to their personal records to determine that for themselves.
8. **Consider requiring students to average their grades for their own information at the end of grading periods.** This is valuable for their awareness and to double-check the teacher's calculations. This process shows that their grade is determined by work they've completed and/or have left undone. It is also a reminder about earlier work that a student failed to complete, but has managed to forget in the intervening weeks.

***Patti** provides a worksheet she calls a **Grade Review Sheet** for this process, counts it as an assignment, and gives bonus points for prompt return with a parent signature. If a student has not kept his own record complete, Patti does not relate those grades to him during class. Instead she gives such students the option of returning after school to get their grade information. In this manner, students experience the consequence of inconvenience generated by their lack of accountability.*

9. **Use rubrics to help students complete their work and be accountable for its quality.** Rubrics inform students of the expectations for assignments from the outset. Each rubric spells out assignment demands in clear, unequivocal terms. Initially, read rubrics with students answering questions about the assignment, thereby minimizing later misunderstandings or complaints.

   In some instances, teachers may expect students to guess their grading criteria or change assignment expectations after students have begun or submitted work. Neither of these teacher behaviors is productive. Rubrics discourage these practices and provide teachers and students with clear scoring guidelines. Carefully constructed rubrics eliminate many of the potential pitfalls associated with assessment and keep teachers accountable to their students.

   In other instances, you might want to guide a class in creating an assessment rubric when an assignment or project is introduced. When students participate in creating the assessment standards, they are much more willing to accept personal responsibility, if they do not meet those standards.

10. **Encourage students to reflect on their grade**. Patti accomplishes this by assigning a learning log prompt that asks students to reflect on factors that determined their grade, to establish strategies for improvement, and to set personal goals for the upcoming grading period. Teachers can provide the impetus for students to reflect on their grade in any number of ways.

Students arrive in class with varying degrees of personal responsibility. Teachers cannot assume that all students understand the concepts underlying accountability. Therefore, overtly teaching the value of being personally accountable and how that responsibility works may be helpful. Teachers use numerous methods to teach accountability. One of **Patti's** strategies is a lesson in decision-making.

> *She reminds students: "Any time you make a decision, there will be consequences. Failure to decide is a decision having consequences. Make decisions thoughtfully and be prepared to accept the outcome – positive or negative." Her example is, "Not doing an assignment is your choice, but you will be choosing to take a loss of points that will impact your overall grade." She doesn't harangue if students don't turn in an assignment; rather she reminds them they have made that decision.*

When students do not meet their responsibilities, often their first reaction is to make **excuses**. This is natural, youthful behavior. However, if excuse-making is accepted, teachers will not only see it repeated but will also find its practice spreading. When this occurs, teachers can acquire a reputation as an "easy mark"; and they will become increasingly besieged with student excuses. Once the practice has proliferated, it is even more difficult, perhaps nearly impossible, to break the pattern of excuse-making.

When teachers are confident they have provided ample opportunities and support for student accountability, we recommend they should strive to avoid succumbing to excuses. If teachers have effective management in place, make themselves clear, and monitor student progress, students have few legitimate reasons for failing to be accountable. Accepting responsibility and being accountable is a life skill that teachers can help their students develop. Established classroom tone, practices, and routines that discourage excuse-making support teachers when it's in students' best interest to experience the consequences of their choices rather than accepting their excuses.

An effective defense against excuse-making is to anticipate possible situations that lend themselves to excuses then utilize classroom policies and procedures to help students avoid scenarios that tempt them to fall back on excuses. When a teacher has posted deadlines, provided ample reminders, even required periodic progress checks, students are supported in their efforts to be responsible and the teacher is well within reason to decline excuses. Teachers who manage effectively, utilize specific policies, and follow through with those policies the first time an excuse is offered help students recognize the consequences of not being responsible. These teachers will find excuse-making held to a minimum in their classrooms.

When, despite a teacher's routines and reminders, a student still fails to meet his responsibilities and resorts to offering excuses, a teacher can review the numerous opportunities and reminders that were given. The student, as well as his classmates, will often recognize the teacher's efforts on behalf of students. When a teacher, against her better judgment, gives in to excuses often enough, other students will try the excuses ploy. On the other hand, when a teacher has been conscientious, an offending student will often acknowledge his lack of accountability and the teacher can encourage him to practice more productive behavior in the future. Handled carefully, teachers can use the situation as a "teachable moment" to remind students that when they plan ahead, prepare and don't wait until the last minute, they won't need to resort to excuses.

Most methods for holding students accountable for classroom performance are effective with all but the most recalcitrant students. In some cases, however, accountability expectations and measurements may vary depending on students' academic competence. Flexibility in establishing those measurements is particularly important when considering student accountability for *academic* pursuits. In our efforts to hold *all* students accountable, we recognize we must be accountable for making expectations reasonable, clear, consistent and fair.

> ***Kay** has taught students at all academic levels. She often makes complex instructional demands of advanced students, based on the sophistication of some assignments. Long term projects or independent studies could require submission of work at varying intervals. Although she maintains accountability expectations for challenged students, she may not make the same academic demands at this level of complexity for them.*

Teachers can become frustrated when faced with situations that challenge their efforts to maintain student accountability. When this challenge occurs, think through the circumstances and devise a plan to avoid letting such a situation control you and your classroom. **Patti's** experience illustrates the value of this approach:

> *Our advanced and honors sophomores annually mount an elaborate Renaissance Faire which requires numerous students to miss class at various times. The first year I didn't know what students to expect in class on any given day, and students who had missed class interrupted my other classes to request missed assignments or to turn in work. Collecting one assignment could drag on for a week; giving missed quizzes and tests was nearly unmanageable and students who missed class were not prepared with the following day's assignment.*

Determined not to let the Renaissance Faire compromise instruction or management the following year, I began planning well in advance. Because I supported this valuable learning experience, I adjusted lesson plans on days when large numbers of students would miss class. Yet, I didn't want English class progress to suffer. I required Renaissance Faire participants to sign a contract that stipulated students who missed class were responsible for:

- *Handing in assignments on time. If they need to miss class when an assignment is due, they will send it with another student.*
- *Being prepared with the next day's assignment*
- *Taking all quizzes and tests after school the day of or the day after*
- *Refraining from interrupting my other classes*
- *Using my planning period or staying after school to get assignments, material, and information as well as make up quizzes and tests.*

Students received photocopies of their signed contracts. Once they realized I would adhere to the contract guidelines, they were conscientious about taking care of class responsibilities.

These clearly articulated expectations prevented the chaos of the Faire's first year for both students and me. In operation, these guidelines helped students keep up with their class work ensuring that learning proceeded in tandem with their worthwhile interdisciplinary endeavor.

Students and I were pleased with how smoothly things went. They worked collaboratively to secure assignments or hand them in for one another. Upon reflection, I realized my students learned about time management and personal accountability, both skills that will benefit them beyond their classroom experience.

When we prepare students for their future by teaching and reinforcing accountability and responsibility, we provide them with a body of skills that will work on their behalf throughout their lives. They may not remember all of the content information imparted in their many years of schooling, but well-developed habits of self-discipline, organization, and personal responsibility are lessons they will remember and employ to their benefit throughout their lives.

CLASSROOM ATMOSPHERE

One of the most apparent results of effective management is the atmosphere it creates in a classroom. Inexperienced teachers may aspire to close relationships with their students or a casual classroom atmosphere as seen in Hollywood depictions of schools. Unfortunately, these images are not very realistic. Each class will assume some of its own identity as teachers bond with their students. Curiously, the time of day each class meets will influence a class's tone. From the very first day you meet with them, conveying **respect** for your students while demonstrating that your classroom is a learning place is, in our experience, the most reliable approach for establishing an atmosphere in which positive ambiance can develop and in which students and teachers can flourish.

A classroom will be more consistently positive if students are clear about the teacher's **expectations** from the outset. Telling students once and expecting them to understand, remember and implement expectations is unrealistic and ineffective. **A teacher must instruct students in expectations using some of the same strategies she uses to teach subject matter**: teach, review, repeat, remind, reiterate, and **reinforce**. Then stick to the stated expectations and allow students to experience both positive and negative **consequences**. Remember: if a teacher has taught how her classroom operates and students know the consequences of ignoring those procedures, they will most often comply.

***How* a teacher enforces rules and procedures influences atmosphere in the classroom.** We feel that **consistency** is the place to begin. Letting one student slide on Monday and penalizing another student for the same infraction on Wednesday generates resentment and gives the penalized student an opening for belligerence. This inconsistency doesn't contribute to a productive classroom atmosphere. Furthermore, a teacher's tone and manner shape the classroom's atmosphere. "Sit down! Don't sharpen your pencil now!" in an accusatory tone generates different student attitudes than "Please do not get up and sharpen your pencil while I'm talking to the class." – stated firmly, yet politely. Which manner will contribute to the cumulative effect you desire in your classroom?

We try to avoid blatantly telling students they are wrong. This doesn't foster an exploratory atmosphere for learning. Instead, we have developed a reservoir of reinforcing and encouraging responses such as "Good effort.", "You are on the right track.", "You're in the ballpark." or "Your response shows that you are thinking." Heard frequently, such reactions will eventually help put reluctant students at ease. We use open-ended questions more often than single-answer questions. When students feel there's not one and only one acceptable answer, they are more comfortable about responding and contributing their ideas. Such questions require use of higher order thinking skills, which teachers want their students to practice and develop anyway. If employed regularly, these teacher behaviors and others like them contribute subtly, yet powerfully, to shaping a classroom atmosphere that positively influences learning.

One student can alter classroom atmosphere that a teacher has worked hard to build. Any time a new student is placed in a class, the dynamics change. This is not to say they change negatively, but they *do* change. It will take a few days for the class to find and settle into its new "feel."

Unfortunately, one student with a particularly negative attitude can contaminate an entire class's tone. Once in a while a teacher may have a student who is continually surly or even palpably resistant regardless of what she does. This behavior may have nothing to do with anything the teacher has said or done (at least consciously.) Such students often bring "baggage" with them when they enter the classroom:

- A history of bad school experiences
- Parents who are quarrelling or divorcing
- An overly strict parent causing a student to rebel against any kind of authority
- A student who didn't want to attend your school
- Abuse
- Friendship feuds
- Neighborhood issues

The possibilities are virtually endless.

As soon as a teacher recognizes a pattern of non-constructive behavior, enlist the aid of the school's support staff. Ask the counselor about the student. Check with the assistant principal to see if the student has a record of school infractions. Look up the student's schedule and ask other teachers what they have experienced with the student. Often it helps to know you are not the only recipient of the student's attitude. If the attitude and behavior persist, a teacher will eventually need to communicate with the parent(s); but be cautious. Collect as much background information as possible before making that initial parent contact. Parent-student conflict may be the source of the problem or the parent may have accumulated school resentment from prior bad experiences. It helps for a teacher to know what he may encounter.

In the meantime, orchestrate as many positive experiences in the classroom for the student as you can. The sooner he begins associating positive experiences with a class, the harder it will become to sustain a negative attitude and behavior. If the source of the problem is prior unpleasant school experience, once the student accumulates a number of positive experiences he may begin to let down his guard. If he is tremendously insecure about reading or writing, providing non-threatening opportunities for success will help him lighten up. If the student's appearance (green hair, numerous piercings, brazen tattoo, etc.) has generated negative reactions from parents, administrators, previous teachers, and even other students, knowing that you value him as a person and don't judge him based on his appearance will build an alliance.

Patti once had a student in her junior English class who wore black leather, chains, outlandishly spiked hair, piercings, and tattoos long before they came into vogue:

"Chad" experienced daily aggravation from his parents, administrators, other teachers, and his classmate based on his appearance. Needless to say, he walked around with a chip on his shoulder and constantly on his guard. His defensiveness radiated from him during class. One day when I overheard some of my students badgering him yet again before class, I decided it was time to intervene.

I initiated a class discussion on identity by asking various students what aspect of their identity was uniquely their own and most valued. Then I asked "Chad" if his leather, chains, and piercings were his way of asserting his unique identity and making a statement to the world that he was an individual unto himself. He was almost awestruck as he realized an adult actually understood his motivation. I shared that I, just like everyone in the room, had the desire for unique statements of my identity.

I then segued into a lesson on the responsibility we assume when we choose to be obviously different. I solicited anecdotes from numerous students about experiences when they had made such choices as well as shared some of my own. We acknowledged that such decisions could often be counted on to garner lingering stares, adult/authority figure displeasure, and stereotyping. I tried to help my students realize that we all have moments when we wish to exert our particular individuality, so we should strive to accept those efforts on the part of others. Conversely, I helped my students see that when our need to express our individual identity is strong, we must anticipate the reaction, and accept the responsibility for our choices.

We concluded by writing about identity in our learning logs. By then the period was over, and I had to junk my lesson plan for that day; but as a result, "Chad" no longer experienced harassment (at least in my class) and our classroom atmosphere was increasingly more accepting. In fact, when students worked on group activities, his group mates seemed oblivious to his eccentric appearance focusing more on his creative ideas as they delved into their project.

Kay had a senior English class that enjoyed jokes, puns, and double entendres. She recognized the potential for negative effect in the classroom:

"Nick," in particular, enjoyed cracking up the class with his frequent "remarks" about everything from poetry to vocabulary. Every time he commented, the class lost two or three minutes of time in giggles and laughter. I was aware that "Nick" just wanted some attention. He was a bright young man with little interest in school, but he was trying to be a part of the class "in his own way."

I found most of his input clever, so I decided that rather than allow the remarks to be disruptive, I would try to find a way to acknowledge them and keep them from taking up unnecessary time. I knew that if the students realized I wasn't flummoxed by "Nick's" antics the class would react less to him each time he performed.

I chose to allow "Nick" his role as class "humorist" which often lightened up the lesson and kept him and other students from controlling the atmosphere of the class. I learned to anticipate when he would perform: I would look over at him and say, "Yes, 'Nick'?" He would add his "input" and we would continue with class. Occasionally, I have to admit that he was very funny and right on target with a pun or a joke connected to our lesson.

As he was encouraged to respond, his interferences became less disruptive and he began to enter into our class discussions in positive and academic ways. Eventually, the whole class, including me, was pleased with "Nick's" responses and his new interest in class, still able to enjoy his occasional joke or pun.

Some of the saving graces teachers must cultivate are a sense of humor and an ability to recognize it in students. Often a bit of classroom humor is just the prescription needed. Of course, if any students persist in off-color remarks or inappropriate humor, teachers must intervene to quell that kind of disruptive behavior from the first instance. Failure to act on disorders will give students the message that it is acceptable to disrupt class for any reason.

STUDENT ATTENTIVENESS

We cannot teach students until we have their attention. Likewise, students don't achieve effectively until they are focused on learning.

Our goal is to focus all students on their learning for the majority of each class period. This objective doesn't mean they will sit quietly and listen or do seat work an entire period. In some instances, each student might be performing a different task; students might be working in groups; we might be working with a group while others are reading; or one student at a time might conference with us while others are writing and revising. What matters to us is that every student is engaged in productive learning activity.

Learning to focus and practicing attentiveness are life lessons that will serve students well once they are away from the classroom. For example, focus is necessary when a driver is being given directions. Attentiveness is essential when a worker receives on-the-job training. When a supervisor is giving technical information, focus and attentiveness are vital for the employee to successfully utilize that information. Students may be more receptive to teachers' expectations for attentiveness if they understand the rationale for and value of concentration-related skills.

Engaging a full class of students in learning activity does not happen automatically. Understanding group dynamics and utilizing group process strategies will contribute to teachers' expertise in focusing everyone's attention on learning. Over the years we have developed numerous strategies that moved us close to our goal of maximum student focus on and attentiveness to learning. Perhaps some of our strategies will work for you.

1. **Start class on time.** Engage students in learning activity before they have the opportunity to become distracted. By **consistently** initiating the learning process as soon as class begins, a teacher signals to her students that she is serious about their learning and that her classroom is focused on instruction. Furthermore, it prevents students from becoming distracted from the task at hand – learning. Once students' focus has moved to something else, it becomes increasingly difficult to refocus them on your lesson.

   Exceptions to this recommendation will arise – the office may call, an unforeseen announcement may come on the public address system, or an administrator may walk into the room with a request. Numerous interruptions may keep a teacher from starting class on time. Persevere. A few cautions:

- Don't begin class by calling roll.
- Don't allow time for students to begin individual conversations of their own.

- Don't turn your back to the class and write on the board, allowing students to do as they wish until you finish. Instead, write board information prior to class.

If teachers overlook these few simple cautions, they may spend precious learning time regaining both management and focus.

2. Engage students from the moment class begins.

   - If the teacher herself will not be students' focus, be prepared with an activity for students to begin immediately. A strategy we have found exceedingly effective is starting class with a writer's notebook or learning log entry that engages students in thinking and writing thus signaling that it's time for learning to begin. It's important to have prompts ready for students the moment class begins. Furthermore, we recommend having a specified time limit and encouraging students to complete the task for homework if they need more time. With students on task, the teacher now has time to take attendance and complete business essential to the start of class. Resume your lesson for the day only when all writing notebooks are stowed away. Otherwise, some students will continue writing and fail to focus on the next activity.
   - On Mondays, teachers could begin class by explaining the week's schedule and plan for work. We suggest requiring students to write down the schedule or at least make notes. Each day's beginning can then be based on the activities that were outlined for that week. Different plans may call for varied beginnings. How will teachers start, for instance, if they are going to show a film? What if they have scheduled a test? Eventually teachers will learn the ways that work best for them and their situations.

Students will quickly master routines if teachers demonstrate consistency. As in all kinds of planning, the levels at which students operate will determine how much structure and assistance students will need to adapt to pre-set routines. A teacher will learn quickly the needs of each class.

***Kay** varies her routine for her advanced classes as some tire of the writer's notebook or log entries every day. She tests students' tolerance for certain routines and plans accordingly. For example, if her students are engaged in collaboration, she expects them to come into class, quickly form their groups, and begin work. Kay recognizes the necessity of teaching these kinds of behaviors.*

3. **Teach students to refrain from irrelevant activities when they need to be focused on directions, information, or learning.** Some students are notorious for getting out materials, writing personal notes, or sharpening pencils rather than focusing exclusively on the teacher's instructions or information. Teachers can discourage such behaviors with straightforward methods:

    - Announce what materials students should get out and have ready when instruction begins.
    - Clearly indicate that instructions and information will only be explained at the outset. Anyone who isn't focused will have to get information from another source. Announcing that you will not explain information to students who weren't paying attention while it was being presented to the class – and sticking to it - applies a consequence to inattention.

      When applying this strategy, it's important to be very sure that you have given students every opportunity to clarify and ask questions before you move on. Be sure to repeat, review and invite questions when giving those instructions and explanations to be sure that students who *are* listening with concentration will understand.

      It's also important to be sure that students have access to an alternate source for the information, in case they see the error of their ways.

Adhering to announced guidelines is critical for reinforcing student attentiveness. Although it may seem strict to require inattentive students to seek information elsewhere, a teacher's tone of voice and manner when enforcing such consequences can influence the student's reaction. This instruction can be polite and uncritical, yet firm and definite. When a teacher maintains her guidelines, she'll soon discover that previously inattentive students will become more focused.

4. **Help students give their full attention and concentration to information or explanations provided by the teacher.** This

process becomes especially important when the teacher knows it will be essential for students to understand and remember the information for future success.

- For instance, if the day's assignment is on the board, some students will work on that instead of concentrating on what the teacher is explaining. To offset inattentiveness, cover up board information until ready for students to use it.

  ***Patti** begins many periods with the day's learning log prompt already written on the board. But when class does not begin with that prompt, she covers it with a screen preventing students from writing their responses when they need to be listening to or focused on something else. Putting prompts on PowerPoint slides makes it simple to reveal them only when you're ready for students to begin their writing.*

- Wait until you have the entire class's attention before addressing the group. Patti waits patiently and quietly until students get the point. We've seen teachers talking "over" some students who needed to be listening. This practice is difficult for the teacher, limited in effectiveness for those who are trying to listen, and useless for those not paying attention.
- Don't give students material that can be read, if you want them to listen. Everyone has seen this scenario: a speaker is doing fine until he distributes written information. Participants shift their focus away from the speaker to the sheets as they begin reading them. Thoughtfully plan when to distribute handouts to the class with the knowledge that their focus will shift from instruction to the printed material as soon as it is in their hands. Another method is to plan guides that present the basics of information being taught, so that students can follow along even inserting their own notes. Sometimes Kay and Patti make outlines or graphic organizers that students can use as note-taking sheets to engage them with the teacher's instruction. This strategy reinforces focus and attentiveness.

5. **Hold students accountable for listening and paying attention**. One strategy is to give daily learning performance points for demonstrating *learning* focus. The consequences for students who do not demonstrate appropriate and adequate attentiveness is reduction or loss of their learning performance

points. Read more about learning performance grades in the "Managing Behavior" section of this book as well as in the Appendix.

6. **Do not lose the class's focus while addressing one student's particular need.** While a concept is being explained, a student sometimes may ask a question applying only to him. If a teacher stops to address that one student's particular need, she could lose other students' focus. Simple presentation strategies can help avoid this situation.

> *Before starting detailed directions,* ***Patti*** *sometimes asks students to hold individual questions until a designated time. She suggests they jot these down, if necessary. Often Patti's planned remarks address the concern, so asking a student to wait may lead to his discovery of the answer even before the question has been asked.*
>
> *In other situations, she may ask an individual student to wait until the class is working independently. Then she makes sure to address that student's question; if she doesn't, students in the future will be less willing to wait.*

- It's not unusual for students to cluster around the teacher's desk or lectern wanting immediate attention for their particular instructional needs. When this occurs, a teacher could jot down each student's name and assure them she will take their questions in the order received when the class is working independently. If a student demands attention, he could be asked to write a note describing his need. The act of note writing helps the student address his concern while freeing the teacher to go on with class.
- Early in the year some students are prone to call out the teacher's name every time they want attention thereby distracting the class's focus. In our first-week orientation, we tell students to raise their hands until we can get to them. With a little work, a class can be taught this procedure that makes the teacher's one-on-one assistance more efficient. Often when a student must wait, he finds his own answer, a learning process in itself.

  It's easy to fall into the pattern of attending to the most persistent students first. When a teacher succumbs to this behavior, she is rewarding and therefore reinforcing inappropriate behavior. Teaching students to raise a hand and wait patiently for their turn makes it easier to deal with students in turn rather than attending to the most persistent first. The teacher's responsibility is to continually scan the classroom so as not to overlook students patiently waiting for assistance.

- This situation suggests another management concern. While students are working independently, teachers might be taking attendance, signing absence notes, or getting out make-up assignments. If students raise their hands, teachers should not feel compelled to assist them *instantly* on demand. By doing so, the teacher may not finish his task, leaving record keeping incomplete or students without requested materials. Asking students to wait a moment before you respond is acceptable. Most students will cooperate as long as teachers are certain to get to them in the order requests were received and do not let more assertive students preempt them. This lesson in group process is one that students need to learn for their future outside the classroom.

7. **Practice the fine art of giving directions until it has been mastered.** Giving directions that students can understand and follow is not automatic. Actually, effectively giving directions is a learned skill that merits thought and practice.

   Sometimes when students do not perform according to a teacher's expectations, the cause may be traced back to the teacher's inadequate directions. Directions that are complicated, sketchy, poorly organized, or piecemeal contribute to students' inability to satisfactorily complete an assigned task. Teachers should not assume that students will automatically know what questions to ask in order to clarify their understanding of the teachers' directions. Likewise, students may not even realize they don't understand directions until work is returned with an unsatisfactory grade. As teachers, we want students to learn from the lessons and activities that we assign. Therefore, we have a responsibility to provide clear and complete directions and assure that all students understand them before asking students to perform a task, especially when it is one that will be graded.

   Frequently interrupting the flow of informational directions to answer individual questions is only one of the difficulties in helping every student in a class understand. This practice interferes with the stream of thought necessary to process the sequential nature of most directions. Generally, most questions that a student would be inclined to ask spontaneously are something the teacher is planning to address, if she thoughtfully planned her directions. Suggestions that we have found make giving directions more effective include:

- **Divide directions into segments**, go over a segment, repeat it and call for questions; once students are clear on that segment, move on to the next one. Practicing this procedure consistently teaches students to listen attentively throughout the directions-giving process.
- **Encourage students to make notes as directions are given.** Help them understand they are more likely to remember the full set of directions if they have written something to which they can refer. Even suggest what they might include in their notes. As well as being useful when students are trying to implement directions, this note taking practice is a learning activity itself.
- **Provide written as well as oral directions whenever possible**. Written directions provide a reference once students are away from the classroom. Furthermore, when written directions are available, students who do not pay attention to oral directions experience the consequence of becoming solely dependent on the written directions or any help a classmate will give.

When students don't follow directions, teachers' jobs become harder and processing their papers takes longer. Once teachers are confident they are giving and explaining directions effectively, they can (and we feel *should)* hold students accountable for following them.

8. **Use proximity and eye contact to help students maintain their learning focus.**

If teachers are always in front of the classroom or at their desks, students find it easier to divert their focus from learning. Circulating and commenting on student work, interacting with individual students, and answering questions are all valuable instructional strategies. The additional benefit of placing yourself in close proximity to students is that it encourages them to stay focused on their learning task.

If a student is writing a personal note, you can move to that student's side and stand quietly until she shifts attention back to the learning task; often no words need be exchanged. The same effect can often be achieved with eye contact. When a student is inattentive during instruction, the teacher can stop talking, focus on the student and wait silently until that student's attention has been regained.

To maintain student attention and focus, ***Kay*** *may walk around the room, stop for a while and move on. The lesson's activity will determine the pattern. She keeps three stools in the room with a lectern at the front. She circulates according to the variable moods of the class and the needs of the daily lesson. Her "perches" provide a multitude of options for achieving varying management needs.*

The need for moving around the classroom when teaching is illustrated by an experience of **Kay's:**

One semester, a student teacher assumed responsibility for a rowdy junior English class. I had modeled strategies to head off inattentiveness and student disruptions with this class for the student teacher and demonstrated how to refocus student attention by circulating. "When students aren't paying attention," I said, "move closer to them making direct eye contact. Let them know you will stay close until you have their attention." I thought she had grasped the strategy.

However, one day she sat on a stool at the front of the classroom. As she was teaching her lesson, pockets of noise began to surface near the back of the room. I resisted the urge to intervene and eliminate the problem before it escalated. She continued "teaching away," cemented to the stool, seemingly oblivious to the growing problem. She was quickly losing the attention of increasing numbers of students.

She had numerous opportunities to quell what started out as talking and finally ended as almost complete loss of student focus, dooming the lesson. This student teacher came to realize that she couldn't teach a lesson until she was able to manage her students and focus their attention on learning.

Teachers must get students' attention and focus it on learning. Routines that are taught and which students are required to follow can make each class begin smoothly. Maneuvers that teachers practice to maintain class attentiveness will pay off in smooth classroom operation and enhanced learning. The central premise for student focus and attentiveness is built on the underlying purpose of all classroom management: to provide optimum learning opportunities for all students for the maximum amount of class time.

MANAGING BEHAVIOR

Teachers have a considerable amount of influence on their students' behavior, although it sometimes feels quite the opposite. Anyone who has tried to teach thirty unruly middle or high schoolers will acknowledge that concrete strategies for managing behavior are essential. **In order for every single student to have an optimum learning experience, individual and group behavior must be managed.**

Behavior management does not just occur; it is the result of *consistently* applied well-thought-out strategies. We *teach* students appropriate and expected learning behaviors; not merely *announce* what is expected. Our first steps are to **model** behaviors that we want to see from students: respect, manners, punctuality, preparedness, and organization. We do not assume that students recognize good manners or understand that they are appropriate and expected in a classroom. Likewise, we avoid assumptions regarding all behaviors. Some students may not know what good organization, respectful behavior, or punctuality look like in practice. Beginning the school year by teaching desired behaviors using strategies similar to those used in teaching content is, we find, a valuable investment for our students and for us as teachers.

One of the most important behaviors we consistently model is *respect*. If a student suspects that a teacher does not respect him as a person or as a learner, why should he cooperate with that teacher? Why should he conform to that teacher's behavioral and instructional expectations? On the other hand, if a student receives respect from a teacher, he will most likely strive to meet that teacher's expectations. Respect must be genuine; students may easily detect feigned respect. Teachers can be respectful toward students without conveying weakness or abdication; on the contrary, relating to students with respect conveys that a teacher has the confidence to do so. Often teachers who are insecure in their behavior management skills relate to students as an authoritarian who demands respect from her students. This manner may work for the moment, but it does not lay a foundation for the long term.

Another behavioral management tool is *feedback* - immediate feedback. Adolescents may not remember yesterday, let alone last week or last month. It is not effective to wait until the term's end conduct grade to address behavioral issues. Upon receiving a lowered conduct grade, a student may not remember contributing misbehavior that occurred early in the term. Address inappropriate behavior when it occurs, deal with it, and move on. Don't hold the misbehavior against a student for the rest of the term; such action will engender resentment that inhibits cooperation. In order for a particular behavior to improve or change, students must experience *immediate* consequences and feedback.

Yet another essential element in managing behavior is *consistency.* If teachers *consistently*

- Maintain their established manner with students,
- Model expected behaviors,
- Relate to students with respect,
- Observe and enforce classroom rules and procedures,
- Address misbehavior at the time it occurs,

they will find that students will also begin to assume this consistency. Eventually most students will demonstrate that same behavioral consistency.

Be aware that classroom rules and/or procedures will be tested; be prepared to persevere. If the teacher doesn't relent, she will pass the test in students' eyes and will not have to repeat that dogged adherence – at least too often. Unfortunately, one student may force the teacher to make him an example of her consistency. If the teacher allows him to persist, this challenge will most certainly be repeated.

The following scenario illustrates the above concept in practice:

> ***Patti*** *teaches classroom procedures at the beginning of the school year. Activities and a quiz help students internalize those procedures. One rule is that students must be seated when the tardy tone sounds or experience the consequence of unexcused tardiness and the school policy regarding such. Knowing this will*

probably be one of the first rules tested, Patti emphasizes and reinforces it daily.

Eventually a student will test her consistency; if Patti lets her "slide" with a warning, subsequent students will expect the same. If such lapses continue without enforcement, the rule would become meaningless. Likewise, when she decides to apply consequences, the affected student would be resentful for experiencing consequences that numerous students before her have not.

Although appearing strict at the moment, applying immediate consequences illustrates that the teacher enforces her rules and demonstrates consistency. Students know the rule from her classroom orientation, so the action is viewed as fair. After that, Patti generally has minimal problems with unexcused tardiness.

Giving students **positive experiences** in a classroom can build good will and create bonding that often discourage negative behaviors. This positive approach can also help generate and reinforce a secure, constructive atmosphere in the classroom. When students are in an environment in which they feel reassured, the need to act out is diminished. Accomplishing this atmosphere is uncomplicated and fulfilling for the teacher. Compliment students, particularly choosing the most unlikely students for praise. This might be praise of an attractive shirt, a neatly done assignment, or a well-executed basketball maneuver in last night's game. Don't necessarily limit praise to instruction; students are touched when teachers notice and comment positively on aspects other than class work. Be careful not to overlook quiet, introverted students; they need compliments too. However, praise doesn't need to be public. Although some students may thrive on public attention, teachers need to sense who is comfortable with public praise and who would prefer private acknowledgement. Keep in mind that shy students may need private compliments.

Along those same lines, provide opportunities for students to help with simple tasks or errands. Even though middle and high school students may seem to physically resemble adults, they still feel the same warm tingle they experienced in elementary school when the teacher asked them to do something for her. We create numerous opportunities for *all* students to experience that tingle. We are mindful to choose both genders and from all representative ethnic groups. In fact, we make it a point to ask the most unlikely students from time to time. Asking students for assistance conveys trust. If a specific student or students from a particular group are never chosen, they may sense a subtle lack of teacher trust. Students may assume favoritism if teachers always choose in the same manner; consequently, resentment can fester erecting barriers to both management and instruction. Selecting students thoughtfully to carry out tasks or errands fosters trust, which contributes to positive behavior and supports management.

Additionally, a teacher can discourage negative behavior and reinforce positive experiences by developing an awareness of students' activities and interests. We don't feel it is appropriate (or advisable) for teachers to insinuate themselves into students' personal problems and relationships; however, discovering and casually discussing with students interests such as musical tastes, hobbies, or sports activities can promote student/teacher rapport.

> *Because* ***Kay*** *loves music, she is interested in students' musical tastes and encourages them to share their favorite kinds of music and artists. Often students bring her recordings of their music. When she fails to appreciate some singer or type of music, she asks the student to explain its appeal. When appropriate, she shares some of her musical favorites. This dialogue connects her to the adolescent world and its ever-changing culture. Such interaction shows students that she values their ideas and interests.*

Building earned rewards into the classroom framework can positively reinforce behavior that teachers want repeated. We make sure that rewards are truly earned; doling them out indiscriminately without actual student effort does not contribute to desired classroom behavior. In fact, doing so could interfere with behavior management. Keep in mind: if students receive rewards one day for doing virtually nothing, why should they make effort another day to *earn* a reward?

We build several methods into our classroom frameworks for administering rewards earned for appropriate behaviors that contribute to learning. Our students understand that:

- They can earn extra points on regular classroom activity such as learning logs or vocabulary exercises when they exert exemplary effort. They must satisfactorily meet requirements before they can earn the rewards for additional effort. This framework component encourages and rewards attention to recurring classroom activities.
- They can earn bonus points by reading a predetermined book of their choice once they have completed all class work. This procedure not only rewards staying on task but also positively rewards reading activity.

- Sometimes bonus assignments will be available when students complete required work satisfactorily and on time. They must be present to benefit because no make-up of bonus activities is made available. This opportunity rewards good attendance as well as focuses on learning tasks.
- Coupons for bonus points are awarded from time to time. Students may receive coupons for behaving appropriately with a substitute, returning a sheet with a parent signature promptly, or turning in required work early. These coupons are tangible rewards that encourage conscientious behavior. See the Appendix for an example.

A cornerstone of **Patti's** behavior management plan, the **Learning Performance Grade**, is a tool she developed, refined and has utilized over many years. This strategy employs immediate consequences, positive or negative.

Patti often teaches students who struggle academically. She wants those students to recognize that their learning behavior makes success attainable. Patti helps students understand they have control over their Learning Performance Grade. Only through their efforts can students earn the rewards that this plan makes possible.

Daily learning performance points encourage students to regularly assume positive learning behaviors since a student cannot hurriedly accumulate numerous points at the end of a grading period. A significant part of this plan design is to teach students to behave and perform like seasoned learners on a daily basis. For more detailed information about Patti's Learning Performance Grade procedure, see the Appendix for this book.

This approach for managing student behavior can work with all academic levels, as Patti's experience will demonstrate:

*After teaching a full schedule of academically challenged classes, **Patti** was assigned two advanced program sophomore classes. Reasoning that advanced program students were motivated and skilled learners, she thought they did not need a learning performance grade.*

Patti discovered these academically bright young people were still adolescents and many of them would do little more than that for which they were held accountable. Furthermore, they were young enough to become distracted from a learning task, often taking every opportunity to create those distractions for one another.

Once she implemented learning performance grades, their attitude and learning focus improved considerably. Most of them earned an "A" for learning performance, but the incentive kept them focused on learning and instruction for the balance of the school year.

Kay uses another method of reinforcement of positive learning behavior:

***Kay** awards Scholar's Bonus points at the end of every grading period for students who have modeled outstanding scholarship. The criteria include: perfect attendance, timely submission of all work, exemplary conduct, class participation, enthusiasm, and a positive attitude toward academic challenges – behavior characteristics of highly motivated students. These last three categories are subjective and at the teacher's discretion, but remember this is a bonus. After introducing the Scholar's Bonus rubric, Kay tracks participation, making notes of her observations, checking for perfect attendance and tracking work submission records. The title Scholar's Bonus is popular with older and advanced students because it connotes distinction and importance. Reflecting a measure of extra student effort, it can augment a grade. The recognition identifies students as particularly motivated and provides an academic incentive.*

If teachers decide to build similar rewards into their classroom framework, they will want to devise a variation with which they are comfortable. Initially, we recommend keeping the plan simple and straightforward. *Be sure to document.* As teachers refine their methods and perfect their plans, they may want to layer on more detailed documentation; or they may prefer to keep their notations as basic as possible. Discussing intentions with administrators is a good idea to ensure that they are comfortable supporting this aspect of grading, if the need should arise.

In conclusion, remember that teachers cannot count on desirable classroom behaviors occurring automatically. Indeed, a plan with specific strategies is the most effective route to the behavior teachers desire from their students.

MANAGING DISCIPLINE

When many people address classroom management, they think of discipline. Our perception of management is much broader. Although discipline usually comes into play at some point, we feel it should not be the cornerstone of classroom management, if that management is to be most effective. A reasonable goal for teachers is to manage their classrooms so that discipline is minimally needed and only as a last resort. **Effective management can minimize the need for discipline.**

Some educators think of discipline as punishment; others think of it as a form of self-control. Perhaps it would be helpful to think about what discipline should *not* be, in order to be most effective. In our experience, discipline for discipline's sake is not particularly effective. Discipline meted out in the heat of the moment because a teacher is frustrated or angry is not advisable. Discipline that is the result of impulsive emotional reaction doesn't have positive lasting effects.

Discipline can have positive enduring effects; unfortunately, it can also have long lasting negative effects. *How* teachers handle a situation that requires discipline will have ongoing effects that can help their classroom management or can deter and stifle the management, atmosphere, and relationships that they have worked to establish. Our suggestions encourage the former. Thinking about discipline before needing to implement it, determining the ongoing effects desired from discipline, and having some preplanned strategies are the first steps toward making discipline work *for* teachers rather than *against* them.

Prevention is much more effective than discipline after the fact. Regardless of how effectively teachers apply discipline, they are still administering a negative consequence. We feel it is desirable to keep all negatives, including negative consequences, to a minimum. Everything teachers do to

- determine their management philosophy;
- organize their classroom procedures;
- plan management training of their students;
- prepare for the first weeks with them;
- prepare and implement their lesson plans;
- and monitor their attitudes, behaviors and modeling

will help them prevent the need for administering discipline. Furthermore, the framework, expectations, and consistency that they continually maintain in the classroom contribute to preventing the need for discipline. We have observed that without thought and planning, a classroom can easily become an environment where behavior and actions requiring disciplinary measures can arise frequently. Teachers can establish and maintain a classroom environment where problems don't arise – at least not very often.

Idleness breeds disruption. Student behavior is inexorably tied to a teacher's instructional planning. If a student is not engaged, she quickly becomes restless. Restlessness is contagious. Once several students become restless, others are distracted from their learning. It doesn't take long before few students are engaged in learning as the class becomes rowdier and rowdier until eventually it can be out of control. It is best to quell idleness before it can spread. Better yet, prevent any students from becoming restless in the first place. Overplanning is better than not planning enough. If a teacher must delay or even delete part of a lesson plan, she can make adjustments for the next day. It is prudent to keep bonus enrichment assignments or activities on reserve. When students are focused on and engaged in worthwhile learning activity, they usually forget to misbehave. It's really as simple as that.

Allow students to experience consequences – both positive and negative – of their actions, behaviors, and decisions. This is a life lesson. The foundation of our "discipline" is consequences. Allowing students to experience the natural consequences of their decisions, actions, and behavior is a discipline preventive as well as reinforcement - sometimes positive, sometimes negative. Consequences are not the same as punishment; they are generated by a student's own choices thus making them powerful lessons. In a thoughtfully-structured and well-managed classroom, students will often experience consequences without the teacher administering them, hence removing him from the continual role of "bad guy."

Positive reinforcement is more powerful than punishment. Understanding how **reinforcement** works and using it constructively gives teachers considerable leverage in their classroom. Both positive and negative reinforcement can be employed to meet a teacher's needs; but in our experience, **positive reinforcement** is more powerful. Every time a teacher rewards desired behavior with positive reinforcement, the recipient will want to repeat that behavior. Teachers cannot give out too much positive reinforcement as long as they reserve it for truly deserving acts and behavior. Its power comes from the pleasure of affirmation combined with the self-esteem it generates. Recall how it felt when a teacher praised you for effort you had exerted. Didn't that make you feel proud as well as make you want to exert such effort again?

Positive reinforcement is particularly effective when a teacher acknowledges a student who consistently seems to "drop the ball." When that student finally hands in an assignment on time, be sure to acknowledge him with a genuine compliment and a smile just for him. Be careful to avoid the tendency to sound sarcastic by saying something like,

"Good for you. You *finally* turned something in on time!" Even slight sarcasm can defeat the purpose of the desired effect. Also avoid handing out praise indiscriminately by being sure that affirmations are actually earned. We're not suggesting that compliments surrounding classroom efforts should be reserved only for monumental accomplishments. On the contrary, what seems like a small accomplishment to a teacher may have required considerable effort on the student's part . . . effort that the teacher would like continued. If you're going to err in this arena, we suggest you err on the side of abundance of affirmations.

Teachers may assume that **negative reinforcement** will serve as a deterrent to future exhibitions of the act that prompted it. Be alert to a number of cautions associated with negative reinforcement. Without careful administration, negative reinforcement can alienate a student rather than address only the behavior in question. Remember: as teachers we want to negatively reinforce the undesired *act*, not the *student* himself. For students who don't get much attention in the course of their day, negative attention can be better than no attention. This sad state of affairs can override a teacher's goal in using negative reinforcement.

Negative reinforcement does not need to be emotional or public to achieve the desired effect. In fact, publicly administered negative reinforcement could compound a teacher's problem rather than stifle it. We keep in mind that adolescents need to "save face," especially with their peers; so reprimanding a student in front of the entire class could generate a retort that the teacher would find inappropriate and would feel the need to address. When she does so, the student could feel compelled to react thereby escalating the incident. This cycle could continue until the situation becomes blown well out of proportion to the original act. We recommend administering negative reinforcement privately whenever possible; however, a student may blatantly act out to the extent that a teacher needs to address the action so that other students will not replicate the undesired behavior thinking it tolerable and acceptable. When this is the case, make the decision to publicly apply negative reinforcement a conscious one, not an impulsive act; moreover, try not to react out of frustration.

Negative reinforcement can be as straightforward as lost points for an assignment turned in late. In fact, if a student does not meet all of the criteria a teacher has outlined in an assignment, project, or test, she should not receive credit equivalent to those who met all of the criteria. Doing so would positively reinforce behavior that a teacher does not want continued.

Patti's rule of thumb: if a student's failure to follow directions or meet outlined expectations creates extra work for her, that student experiences negative consequences.

For instance, if a student hands in an assignment late, extra time and effort are required to deal with that paper separately from those that were turned in on time and together; therefore that student will not receive full credit. If a student fails to put the required information at the top of her paper (name, date, class period, etc.), additional time must be spent determining what assignment it is, whose paper it is, or from what class it came. The student compensates for that time by forfeiting points; this will usually jog her memory the next time she is preparing class work. When a student hands in his learning log late, time must be found - separate from the time allotted to grade his class's logs - to grade his. He loses grade points and forfeits the opportunity to earn bonus points.

I make sure to inform students of the consequences for failing to follow directions as part of our classroom orientation as well as when making assignments. Doing so preempts charges of unfairness when the consequences occur. Make no mistake, a student might utter, "That's not fair," when a paper with reduced points is returned, but that utterance will more likely be expressing frustration with himself. In my opinion, it's often best to let such utterances slide by.

Inconvenience can serve as a subtle, yet effective, form of negative reinforcement. For example, if a student has not kept her personal grade record updated as instructed and needs the teacher's help in sorting out the information, provide help on "her time" such as after school. If a student did not secure learning log prompts for make-up work upon returning from an absence, a teacher could provide access to them "on the student's time." In this manner, students are never denied assistance or resources; they are just required to work a little harder than if they had followed directions or classroom procedures. A teacher does not need to complain or even admonish under these circumstances. The negative reinforcement of the inconvenience often serves as a deterrent in the future.

For major projects and assignments that carry considerable weight on students' grades, we present written guidelines, expectations, and consequences when making the assignment. For particularly major assignments, we require students to sign contracts, which outline the guidelines, expectations, and consequences surrounding that assignment. We sometimes even require a parent signature. These are kept on file as documentation that students were informed of the requirements and consequences from the outset. In this day and age of challenges and charges, teachers can never document too much.

These examples are given to illustrate principles and strategies for negative consequences. While we don't consider consequences relating to class work to be discipline as such, the need for discipline can quickly arise from situations emanating from class work requirements and grading. Without class work guidelines and grading procedures in place, what begins as a problem with class work can quickly escalate into a discipline problem.

Punishment is a form of negative reinforcement. At some point a teacher may decide that punishment is necessary; but be sure to do just that: *consciously* decide rather than impulsively doling out punishment in the heat of the moment. It is helpful to contemplate punishment before finding it necessary to administer. Consider the purpose of punishment: to associate negative consequences that will deter further exhibitions of an undesired behavior. With that recommendation in mind, it is valuable to reflect on some experiences with punishment. Perhaps you have witnessed punishment that provided emotional ventilation for the person assigning the punishment; or maybe you have observed punishment that was grossly out of proportion to the misbehavior that generated it. Both of these are behaviors for teachers to avoid, if punishment is to be most effective. If teachers use punishment to vent personal frustrations and/or give punishment out of proportion to the misbehavior, the recipient will probably become angry or resentful. That anger and resentment may not wane overnight; in fact, it can remain as a dark cloud over the teacher's relationship with that student or even with an entire class. With these considerations, the value of contemplating the concept of punishment, the long-range effects of punishment, and constructive variations of punishment *before* finding yourself in a position to assign punishment to a student becomes clear.

The **tone, manner, and behavior** of teachers while administering discipline or preventive discipline will have significant influence on how effective they are and in how students react. **Patti's** experience as a teacher new to her school before the administration knew her, is an example of how she was able to handle a discipline situation to her advantage. How she handled the incident served her well not just at the moment but also for the rest of the years she taught at that school.

> *A student "went off" in my class when he received an "F" on his progress report. Forget that there was absolutely no doubt whatsoever that he deserved the "F;" he still acted shocked by yelling and cursing at me. I quietly let him hang himself and simply sat and recorded everything he said word-for-word (including the curse words). Then when I turned in a discipline referral, I stapled the documented quotes to it.*

The assistant principal couldn't wait to recount what happened when he called the student in. He merely showed the student what I had recorded. The AP just loved telling me (and others) that the student looked dumbfounded and said, "I can't believe she wrote down everything I said!" From there it was clear cut for the assistant principal because there wasn't much the student could say in denials or defense of himself.

Of even greater value was the regard I received from the assistant principal; who, by the way, went on to become the principal. Furthermore, the indignant student repeated the story over and over to his buddies, so word got around not to go off on Ms. Slagle. I'm sure that one instance deterred many future incidents that might have occurred with disgruntled students.

Don't make a threat unless fully prepared to carry it out . . . sooner rather than later. If a teacher is not fully comfortable and confident with carrying out a threat, he sets himself up to warn and warn and warn until the moment of truth when he can't stand it any longer and ends up making someone an example. This scenario creates a multitude of undesirable consequences. First of all, warning repeatedly is a waste of valuable instructional time, not to mention wearing on the teacher. He will either get pushed to his limit or get sick of the situation and feel compelled to enforce his threat or back down and sacrifice his credibility as the manager of his classroom.

If he finally enforces the threat, the affected student will feel victimized since numerous other offenders have escaped with only a warning. That student can become disenchanted and classmates will probably feel sympathetic toward him.. The victimized student may become disenchanted quietly, but it's likely she will feel that she has been treated unfairly and will act out in response. The teacher has actually created yet another problem that needs resolving. Keep in mind: nothing seems to incense students - and parents – quite as much as the feeling that a student has been treated unfairly. If such a situation results in confrontation with the student or even a parent, count on being accused of "letting lots of other students get away with it" and "picking on" the student in question.

Sense the classroom atmosphere this whole scenario generates. Is this an environment that best supports learning and instruction? Consider the long-term effects when a teacher makes a threat that he is not comfortable carrying out immediately, if necessary. After a chain reaction of events such as that described above, how effective do you think that teacher's next threat or pronouncement will be? He has abdicated some of his classroom control, management, and supervision by his own actions. He set himself up. A solution? Thoughtfully plan management strategy to avoid making threats as much as possible. If it's necessary to make a threat, do so thoughtfully and carefully, mindful of the long-term effects and definitely not in the heat of the moment.

We recommend some basic principles and procedures that rarely let us down.

- **Do what you say you are going to do.** Count on being tested. If teachers adhere to what they have said, they won't be tested too often. If they don't, they can count on challenges becoming a pattern.
- **Don't say it unless you are prepared to do it.** A few illustrations:

  If a teacher tells a class that no one will be allowed to go to his/her locker under any circumstances, he can expect a situation to arise where someone wants to go to her locker and it actually serves the student's and teacher's best interests. What will that teacher hear when she later denies another student permission to go to his locker? Better to avoid blanket prohibitions unless you are fully prepared to adhere to them consistently.

  Don't tell a student or students that they will be put out of class for a certain behavior unless you actually have the authority and administrative backing to do so.

  Avoid telling students that a paper won't be accepted if they don't adhere to certain directions unless you are willing to do so with every student and know with confidence that the administration will back that decision.

Teachers can make classroom pronouncements on which they cannot possibly follow through because of school rules, and most students know this. Count on a student taking advantage of this knowledge and using it against a teacher. Why become a target?

The teacher can escalate or defuse situations involving discipline. *How* a teacher handles a situation can determine if it is concluded quickly or if it drags out and escalates. For instance, if a teacher "calls out" a student in front of the entire class, that student may talk back; but if the teacher quietly and privately admonishes that same student, the situation may very well be over. To avoid undermining your authority, reprimand students' undesirable behavior respectfully and considerately, yet firmly. Doing so provides a much greater likelihood of ending the incident with that reprimand. When delivering correction, keep in mind that adolescents often respond in the manner in which they are addressed. If a teacher yells, "Go to Tardy Hall!" when a student enters class late, the chances of that student making a derogatory remark on the way out are much greater than if that teacher says, "I'm sorry, but you'll need to go to Tardy Hall because the tardy tone has already sounded." We have discovered that when the tone and manner in disciplinary situations is kept dispassionate and nonthreatening, the disciplined student will generally be less volatile.

If an agitated student *does* act out, responding in an emotional manner can escalate the student's heated behavior. We recommend never, never engaging in argument with a student. The teacher will lose in the long run. If a teacher extends the argument trying to come out ahead, he will escalate the situation. If the teacher persists until he prevails, he'll acquire that student's resentment. Adolescents can generally "out argue" anyone, including teachers; so don't fall into the argument trap. **Patti's** story illustrates the pitfalls of engaging in conflict with a student:

> *A new student entered my class in the middle of the semester. From the beginning, all he wanted to write about was being "kicked out" of another high school because he "beat up" a teacher. After reading his interpretation of events in various writing assignments and meeting with his father on conference day, I could formulate a pretty good picture of what transpired.*
>
> *According to the student, he and a buddy arrived to school late and were sent to "Tardy Hall." The student maintained that the monitor insulted his friend and he came to his pal's defense. When he did, the monitor supposedly said something that offended my student. One thing led to another with exchanged words leading to exchanged blows until the administration broke it up and had the student arrested.*
>
> *I suspect the two students swaggered into Tardy Hall with chips on their shoulders, which the monitor took personally. When words were exchanged, the monitor fell into the trap of one-upmanship rather than letting it drop. Both students and the adult put their egos on the line and refused to be the one to "give in."*
>
> *This incident never had to happen. The monitor would have been better off not to personalize the students' manner, behavior or comments. Furthermore, he could have refrained from getting caught up in the one-upmanship trap. He needed to recognize the students' escalating volatility, drop the argument (without concern for "saving face" on his part) and resort to alternate means for dealing with the students. Unfortunately, I suspect this incident*

> *resulted because the adult could not put his own ego needs aside. Consequently, he escalated a situation that never needed to reach the point that it did.*

Teachers cannot expect students to do what they ask simply because they are teachers. Likewise, teachers cannot always count on parents to reinforce their disciplinary measures at home. Due to this reality, it is vital for teachers to utilize well-thought-out disciplinary measures. In addition, it is critical for teachers to **document conscientiously**. A teacher cannot depend solely on her memory. Patti keeps a pad at her lectern making it quick and easy to jot down behavior and discipline notes when the occasion warrants. When a parent challenges a teacher's disciplining of her child, pulling out written documentation of dates the student committed the offense(s) and measures already taken can be a teacher's best ally.

Patti's experience as a beginning teacher taught her the value of documentation early in her career:

> *A student in my homeroom was frequently absent and brought obviously forged excuse notes. After a few weeks, I wrote a discipline referral that resulted in a parent conference. The parent was hostile from the beginning of the conference. The mother asked for the exact dates when the student gave me these allegedly forged notes and for proof that they were forged. Since I hadn't kept the notes or a record, I had to depend on my memory which was not very convincing. The best the administrator could do was give the girl a warning, and that was it. I could just feel the mother's and the girl's smirks as they left the office. As you can imagine, my relationship with the student was strained throughout the rest of the school year.*
>
> *Fortunately, my assistant principal helped me reflect on the incident and used it as a teachable moment to illustrate the value of documentation. Throughout my career, I observed or heard about situations where teachers had to rely on their memories to defend their actions, whether with a discipline, grading, or academic situation. Having learned from that incident, when I am now called upon to justify my actions or decisions, I am relieved to have documentation to back me up. Often just presenting the documentation resolves issues with students or parents.*

Providing documentation can almost assure administrative support. If administrators know a teacher can be counted on to document interactions with students, they will be much more willing to provide blanket support when needed. Likewise, if administrators know a teacher goes to great lengths to prevent classroom discipline problems and to handle them when they do occur, she will usually be able to count on unwavering administrative support when the need arises. However, when a teacher writes discipline referrals indiscriminately and regularly hands a fistful into the administration daily, she had better actively solicit administrative support before a parent conference. Writing discipline referrals as the first line of defense in disciplinary situations limits their effectiveness with students as well as with administrators.

Another pointer: consider the ramifications before putting a student in the hall as a discipline measure. Often those students get bored or act out their boredom or frustrations in ways that disturb other classrooms thus alienating your colleagues. In addition, don't overlook the mayhem a student could perpetrate such as setting off a fire alarm or other potential dangers. Putting a student in the hall only addresses the need for that very moment; it doesn't resolve the source of the initial problem. Actually, putting a student in the hall may be playing right into his hands. He may have wanted to get out of the classroom because he didn't have his class work or because he has a buddy in the class across the hall. If a student is disrupting a class to the extent that the teacher needs to remove him, send him to the office and forward a discipline referral via an aide or trusted student. In severe cases, call or send a message to the office asking for an administrator or security guard to escort the student out of the classroom. Sometimes in middle school teams, it's tempting to move a difficult student to another classroom; but doing so often merely transfers your problem to another teacher. We suggest not using this strategy unless you have made prior arrangements with a colleague(s).

We can honestly say that we can each count on one hand the number of times in our lengthy teaching careers that extreme measures were necessary. Conducting a well-managed, structured, learning-centered classroom has precluded such disruptions except in the most severe situations and these were generally due to factors over which we had little, if any, control.

TEACHER BEHAVIORS THAT IMPACT CLASSROOM MANAGEMENT

What may seem like inconsequential behaviors in some cases, can significantly impact teachers' effectiveness. Some basic behaviors can enhance teachers' relationships with their students as well as maximize their instructional effectiveness. However, teachers sometimes sabotage themselves without realizing it. They demonstrate behaviors that make it easy, even encouraging, for students to test them. Some behaviors prevent students from taking a teacher seriously. Others allow students to contribute to a teacher's already-high stress level. Yet other behaviors interfere with positive teacher relationships with colleagues and administrators. A few relatively simple practices incorporated into a teacher's routine can enhance her classroom effectiveness and help her avoid generating undesirable outcomes.

Modeling

Becoming accustomed to modeling behavior you expect from students not only facilitates the conditioning of student attitudes and behaviors, but also provides added security for the teacher as well. An administrator will more favorably evaluate a teacher who is prompt, organized, and reliable. Furthermore, it is advisable to avoid doing anything that will not hold up under scrutiny. Letting something slide "just this one time" may be the time it catches up with you. Keep in mind that in the public press, educators are generally perceived as though guilty until proven innocent, when something occurs that hits the news. Even if a teacher is exonerated, she must live under the cloud of suspicion. Consequently, it is important for teachers to continually strive to maintain their reputations in the classroom, their school and their community.

> *We once taught with a teacher who transferred to an elementary school. Some years later she had to endure public scrutiny in the local media because an aide had reported to parents the she had yelled at a child in her class, grabbed him, and generally mistreated him. We never knew the particulars from her point of view; but using our teachers' perspective to read between the lines of the numerous media reports, we suspect that she had done nothing outrageous in dealing with this apparently difficult and uncooperative student. Nevertheless, her reputation and image were tarnished. She received a few days of unpaid suspension from the board of education for verifiable acts of which most any teacher could be found guilty at some time or another and retired at the end of the school year. Her pleasure in retirement was diminished because of this incident.*

Wiggle Room

When a teacher makes it a regular practice to *clearly* tell students what his **expectations** are, what the **consequences** of not meeting those expectations are, and what the rewards for achieving those expectations are . . . and sticks to them, "**wiggle room**" is eliminated. When students sense "wiggle room," they will try every angle to "wiggle out." Such student maneuvering makes management and instruction more difficult and adds a layer of stress to an already demanding pursuit.

Whether orienting students to a new project assignment, preparing them for a field trip, or giving them directions about missing class to attend a meeting, eliminating all "wiggle room" makes it easier for them as well as for the teacher. Students don't have to guess about the teacher's expectations then take their chances with the outcomes. Just a few of the many situations where students could take advantage of "wiggle room" might include:

- Upon turning in a project, a teacher doesn't want a student to be able to say, "But you didn't tell us that you'd count off if it wasn't typed."
- When taking students on a field trip to see a live theatre performance, a teacher doesn't want one of them to distract the actors or the audience by getting up in the middle of the first act to get a drink then distract everyone again by returning to his seat. Teachers especially don't want to hear his explanation of, "But you never told us not to get up during the play."
- Teachers don't want students to miss their class in order to hear a speaker in another classroom, if they haven't been given prior notice. You really don't want a student to be able to say, "But you said what we were doing in class today really wasn't that important."

Develop the practice of **anticipating** student behaviors and responses. Then be sure to address those possible behaviors and responses when orienting students, whatever the occasion. Eliminating "wiggle room" in this manner will save teachers time as well as relieve them from stress and frustration. In addition, such orientation will help students develop responsibility and accountability.

Ending Class

One way that teachers create "wiggle room" for their students is in the manner in which they conclude classes. We're all familiar with it. The bell rings and as students gather up their supplies and materials and begin to exit the room, the teacher is calling out the next day's assignment. What happens the next day? Several students have not done the assignment claiming they did not hear the teacher make it . . . and they really may not have. The teacher is frustrated, even angry, and may need to spontaneously alter that day's lesson plan because so many students are unprepared. This teacher sabotaged herself. If that happens, make sure it only happens once or at least once in a great while.

Condition yourself to remain conscious of the time and stop activity about five minutes before the end of the class period to make an assignment or give directions. Once students become accustomed to the pattern, they will often remind the teacher that class will end in a few minutes and they need to know their instructions. This is particularly helpful if a teacher becomes oblivious to the time, perhaps working with an individual student. In this manner students and teacher subtly become a learning team, an atmosphere that is not only constructive but also satisfying.

If a teacher has very important homework instructions or other essential information to relay to students, try doing it at the beginning of class; if it's not too disruptive, take a small amount of time in the middle of class to weave in a homework assignment or a farewell message. Kay suggests that if these strategies seem too intrusive on class time or "out of synch," be sure to pace yourself and check your watch so you're not barking instructions as students are on the move out the door.

After numerous years in the classroom, ***Kay*** *has become convinced that many teachers have a working pace which they develop, an amazing ability to pronounce the last word of instruction or sing out the last chorus of a homework assignment just as the bell rings. Some students remark on her ability, referring to it as one of "Ms. T's talents." But even with a talent for ending class, the well-organized teacher must insist that the class does not spring to their feet when the tone sounds. Kay tells students at the beginning of the year that the teacher, not the tone, dismisses the class. A cheery closing – "Have a nice day," Thanks for a great class," or "See you all tomorrow" – is the signal that class is over and students may leave. Kay sees this gesture as one of the built-in courtesies teachers should expect, and she tells her students so. However, when she uses this dismissal procedure, she is always careful to end class quickly to avoid making students tardy to the* *next class. Students and colleagues will be upset if this small courtesy infringes on their brief class change time.*

Saying "No"

It is acceptable for teachers to say "no" to students. "No" may be a word some students haven't heard too often, but there are occasions when it is appropriate. "Can I go get my book out of my locker?" If a teacher has clarified in his classroom orientation that this is not allowed, a simple "no" that allows for no "wiggle room" may be all it takes. In such scenarios a student might be so surprised to hear a definite "no," that he may turn around and return to his seat almost stunned. Of course, keep in mind that the manner and tone in which the "no" is delivered will impact how a student reacts. We choose a polite, yet definite tone. That's effective most of the time.

Asking Students to Wait

It is easy for students to escalate a teacher's stress level, but teachers have some defenses against that occurring. Keep in mind that by nature adolescents tend to be self-absorbed and want immediate gratification. That explains why a student wants the teacher's assistance *now* when she thinks of a question or hits a snag and expects him to drop everything and rush to her side. That is why students will surround a teacher's desk as soon as they enter the classroom vying for his attention to their individual needs. This adolescent behavior can pull teachers in numerous directions at once, preventing them from completing their own tasks, and generally heightening their level of stress. Teachers don't need to let their students control them in this manner.

Remember: *you're* the teacher here; you call the shots. It's O.K. to ask a student to wait for a moment until the current task is finished before helping her. In fact, many times a student will figure out what she needs if required to spend a moment or two thinking about it. Persist on doing only one thing at a time. If students try to interrupt, politely yet firmly ask them to wait. This is a lesson in good manners. When multiple students want your attention at once, ask them to wait their turn. You may want to jot down students' names in the order in which they made their requests. As you help each student, thank her politely for waiting. In addition to keeping yourself sane, this is modeling a useful life lesson since students cannot expect instant attention in the larger world outside of the school setting.

*In fact, **Kay** has learned that at a national bookstore chain, the rule for staff is to finish whatever task in which they are engaged before moving on* *to another – even if that means asking a customer to wait a moment for service. The managers know that diverting from a task increases the risk of not returning to or completing it. Asking students to exercise the same consideration is another of those life lessons.*

Students Leaving the Classroom

Then there is the issue of students in the hallways. Bottom line: don't let your students wander the halls. Generally students seem oblivious to the notion that concentration and learning are occurring in classrooms as they pass by. Even the best students may wave or even pantomime messages to their pals in a classroom with an open door. Students mindlessly run their hands down the line of lockers, talk loudly, bounce a basketball, even call to their friends in the classes they pass as they saunter down a hallway where classes are in session. Anticipate that students will take the longest and slowest route to and from their destination unless the teacher has specified differently. There is the potential for a student to disrupt the entire school by pulling a fire alarm. A teacher doesn't want that to be one of his students; especially one that he has needlessly allowed to leave the classroom. Teachers may think that "good" students wouldn't behave in such a manner, but what if there is a big test for which a student is not prepared and wants to avoid? No matter how bright or how conscientious a student, he is still a "kid."

When students ask to leave the classroom to use the telephone, go see the counselor, etc., ***Patti*** *suggests they leave five minutes before the end of the period or once the class is working independently on an assignment. Students usually agree to this. In fact, they often forget the original request, especially if it was not for a genuine need. This strategy not only helps weed out students without legitimate needs, but also prevents students from missing valuable instruction and helps the teacher avoid having to repeat what occurred while they were out of the room.*

Keep supplies in the room that will prevent students from needing to leave. Band aids, safety pins, cough drops, tissue, wet wipes, antiseptic hand cleaner, needle and thread, saline solution and tweezers are just a few of the items that prove useful. Every time a student makes a request to leave the classroom to secure a particular supply, Patti adds that to her collection, if feasible. We do not suggest giving medication such as aspirin, Tylenol, or Midol to students because if they experience an allergic reaction, the teacher could be liable.

When a student asks to leave the classroom, you could tell him that it will be recorded as an unexcused tardy and subject to school penalties. Often the student will decide it's not worth it. When a student doesn't have paper or pencil, she can't work and will often become disruptive; but sending her out of the room to secure materials isn't a constructive solution. Save paper and pencils/pens that are left in the room, on the floor, or in the hallway. When a student doesn't have the required supplies, provide paper (which may bear a footprint or some doodling) or a pencil that might be a stub, complete with teeth marks, or missing an eraser. The student will have adequate materials to do the day's class work and will be more likely to bring her own, more desirable supplies in the future.

Although these seem like relatively minor issues, it's the little things that influence professional relationships. Perhaps students that a teacher has allowed to leave her classroom have repeatedly disturbed a colleague's class but the offending teacher doesn't know about it because the colleague has been quietly seething. Then the offending teacher plans a stimulating field trip to an art museum that will last most of the day. Will the seething colleague readily sign permission forms for the offending teacher's students to miss her class, or will she remember all of those times that a student from that teacher's class wandered the halls interfering with her instruction?

In today's society, knowing the whereabouts of all students for which a teacher is responsible is an even greater concern than it was just a few years ago. If a teacher needlessly allows students to leave his classroom, and those students engage in vandalism, other mischief or even violence or are the victims of such, that teacher may be held accountable and could be called upon to defend his action. A worthwhile goal: **be able to account for the whereabouts of *all* students assigned to you at any given time.** This shouldn't be too difficult because most, if not all of them, will be in the classroom the greatest majority of the time. **The implication of frequently allowing students to leave the room is that the classroom activity isn't that important.** Is that the message you want to convey to students, their parents, and the administration?

Nevertheless, there will be occasions when it is necessary for a student to leave the classroom or when it is instructionally valuable for a student to be able to go somewhere else in the building. Teachers should **anticipate** potential difficulties and guard against them by giving *specific* instructions to students before they leave the room:

- "You have five minutes."

- "Go straight to the office and come straight back with no detours."
- "Have a staff person in the Media Center sign your pass and write the time that you arrive and leave on it."
- "Do not disturb any other classes while your are away from our classroom."

Be sure never to let a student (including student aides) leave the classroom without a pass that states in writing the name of the student, his destination and the time of departure. Teach students that one of your expectations is that they are responsible for securing the signature and time of departure from the person they saw (counselor, librarian, assistant principal, another teacher, etc.) Many schools have a pass policy and procedure. The teacher's job is easier if that is the case; but if it is not, establish your policy and procedure and teach students to follow it. Proceeding in this manner assures that your procedure is not burdensome. Before she taught in a school that had a procedure, Patti made her own passes:

Using 3 x 5 index cards, I generated a variety of passes for different uses: to the restroom, to the library, to the counselor, to the office, and for student aides. On the front I wrote:

- Office Pass or Restroom Pass or Library Pass
- Date: ________________________________
- Student: ______________________________
- Time: ________________________________

*On the **back** I wrote my expectations:*

- Go straight there and come straight back.
- Take the most direct route to and from your destination.
- Do not disturb any classes.

When a student truly needed to leave the classroom, I just pulled out the appropriate pass, filled in the information, and she was on her way. Then I collected the pass from the student upon her return.

Over time as the need for documentation became more serious, I employed a 5" X 8" card in the same manner but left lines for a number of student names. As each card was filled, I filed it as ***documentation*** *of where my students had been at various times when they weren't in my classroom and started another card. If this seems like too much trouble, perhaps it may not be vital for students to leave the classroom or perhaps too many students are leaving your classroom frivolously.*

Regardless of the nature of the hall passes you use, be *very* conscientious about collecting *all* passes, including those used by student aides, when students return to the classroom. Otherwise, students could use your pass for activities you have not sanctioned.

One of our personal rules: **never throw any documentation papers away until after the close of the school year.** This includes admit slips, absence notes, requests for make-up work, hall passes, etc. An easy way to manage such papers is to maintain an easily-accessible folder for each class. Throw the items, including passes that have been retrieved when students return to the classroom or other teachers' pass notes, into the appropriate class's folder as students enter or return to class. This will provide access to documentation if it ever becomes necessary. There's no need to organize the items in the folder; but they are there, if ever needed for verification.

Student Aides

We have worked with colleagues who do not recognize their responsibility for supervising and monitoring student aides. Their attitude appeared to be that if they didn't have tasks for their aides, the aides could do as they pleased. This attitude frequently resulted in aides wandering the hallways disturbing the classes of others.

Kay *remembers a student aide that she "adopted" because he was always roaming the halls and visiting other classrooms. His teacher seldom felt responsible enough to give him work to do. Occasionally, the young man would be locked out of the room because his teacher forgot to tell him she had work to do in another part of the building or she was leaving school early.*

If teachers assume the responsibility of student aides, be certain to teach them to be responsible workers, whether the teacher is monitoring them or not. Do not allow aides to have special privileges which violate school rules. Aides and student office workers may or may not receive grades or credit for their work; regardless, they should be expected to be serious about their job. We have suggested to student aides that they include their aide responsibilities on what may be scant resumes. Able to cite their work habits and reliability, we have eagerly written letters of recommendation for numerous student aides. Of course, the student will only be serious about aiding if the teacher has rules and expectations for her to follow. If an aide has no work to do or finishes tasks early, he should be expected to work on class work or relax quietly with a book or magazine.

Liability

When she was a new teacher, an assistant principal taught **Patti** some very valuable lessons:

> *Among those lessons were the potential for liability and the value of documentation. She eventually became my principal (one of the first women to achieve this role in our district), and in that capacity she hammered home how vital it is to never leave our classrooms lest we become liable for student injuries. She reinforced that it would be difficult for her to support us in the event of such an incident, if we had not been in our classroom.*

We have been astounded when we have observed teachers mindlessly leaving their classrooms unattended to get a cup or coffee or soda, use the copy machine, visit with a colleague, or even leave school early. Besides returning to a class that has shifted focus from learning activity to socialization, those teachers have no defense if faced with irate (or worse) parents whose child was upset or injured in her absence. Our personal rule of thumb: never leave class without securing another certified staff member to monitor in our absence. The very act of securing a proxy will help support a teacher's case in the unlikely event of an incident. Teachers diminish the possibility of liability issues when they are always in their classroom while students are present.

A teacher is liable if she leaves her classroom and an unforeseen event takes place. In the school climate we hear about in the media, anything – a sick student or a sudden fight - can very quickly affect the atmosphere in the classroom. If the teacher has left the room for whatever reason, the consequences for everyone could be disastrous. Our bottom line is this: a teacher who is absent from a classroom full of students for whatever reason is a teacher who is missing instruction time with her students. Period.

Unpleasant Encounters

Teachers cannot depend on all encounters and experiences with students and parents to turn out satisfactorily. This is especially true when a teacher doesn't have a bank of past experience upon which to draw; but even the most capable and experienced teachers will have an unpleasant, unsatisfactory experience from time to time. Don't spend time berating yourself when this happens. Turn it instead into a constructive learning experience. Analyze the encounter in retrospect and develop strategies to avoid such situations in the future. Often an unpleasant occurrence can be the genesis of a management technique that can be incorporated into routine classroom functioning. If a teacher has limited experience, check with veteran teachers and ask some of their methods for avoiding or handling such situations. Chances are they have been there, if they've been in the profession for very long.

Patti once received a phone call from an irate parent who proceeded to lambaste her for a comment she had written in a student's reading log:

> *The parent ranted about how the entire family had become so upset they had cancelled weekend plans to go out of town. The parent felt I had challenged her daughter's integrity when I wrote, "Did you write in your reading log while reading at home?" The parent misinterpreted the comment to mean I was implying her daughter did something she was not supposed to do. Since the parent didn't know the context of my comment, she immediately became inflamed.*
>
> *All became clear. Because the student's entries were quite sparse, my comment questioned if the student had recorded in her reading log, <u>as she was supposed to do,</u> when reading at home. The irony is that I had phrased my comment as a question in order to avoid accusing the student of not doing what she was assigned to do.*
>
> *The parent replied, "Oh. Well, then goodbye." No apology. Although I had done nothing wrong, I became much more conscientious about trying to avoid ambiguity in future written comments.*

Teacher Knowledge

Teachers don't have to know everything or be right all of the time to be effective. In fact, if a teacher insists on such unyielding attitudes, she may put a barrier between herself and her students.

No one reasonably expects a teacher to know everything about her subject. The more we teach, the more we learn; learning along with students can be a satisfying as well as instructionally-productive experience. We don't recommend announcing to students or their parents that you don't know anything about a particular topic; but as questions arise, don't be reluctant to acknowledge that you don't know the answer but will search for it alongside your students – and then do so. Patti recalls teaching Dickens' *A Tale of Two Cities* for the first time to advanced program students:

> *Somehow I had never read the novel in school, so I was reading and studying it for the first time in order to teach it. Since I had a number of new preparations that year, I didn't have a great amount of lead-time to read the book and prepare detailed lesson plans. With Dickens' dense style, it's not a book that even an English teacher can zip through quickly, so I found myself reading along with my students staying just a few chapters ahead of them. Although I was uncomfortable with this state of affairs, I realized that I was making discoveries_about the novel right along with my students and we mutually shared the excitement of those revelations . Although I don't recommend this approach as a matter of routine, when faced with a similar situation, it is not without its merits.*

In another instance, **Patti** once had a student teacher that thought he knew everything because he had worked for a number of years as a substitute.

> *He felt there wasn't much that she or her students could teach him and conveyed this attitude in his daily manner. While assigning a project, he told students to go to an art museum and take photographs of some artwork. Two students interjected that their art teacher had told them photographing works of art in a museum was not allowed. He insisted he knew what he was talking about and persisted in the assignment. Patti paid a visit to the local art museum and confirmed what she had suspected – he was wrong. Ultimately he had to rescind his assignment and the students gloated. It's not hard to imagine the lack of rapport he had with the students for the balance of his student teaching experience.*

Teacher Errors

Some teachers think that admitting to students they made a mistake makes them vulnerable. Actually, admitting error can work in a teacher's favor. If teachers insist on always being right, some students will make it their quest to prove them wrong. Why give them that opportunity? We're all human; and teachers must daily deal with up to, perhaps, 150 or so students plus the paperwork they generate in addition to tasks assigned by the administration. It's unrealistic to think that a teacher won't make some mistakes. Frequent and continual mistakes will leave a teacher vulnerable, so build double checks and safeguards into processes to minimize errors. However, when that occasional error occurs, accept responsibility. In doing so, a teacher will be modeling accountability for students.

Patti's Grade Review Sheet (See Appendix.) that her students complete at the end of each grading period serves this purpose and many more.

> *I explain the value for students of the Grade Review Sheet in this manner: "This Grade Review Sheet will give you the opportunity to see your grade before you receive your progress report. Furthermore, it will let you see exactly what determined that grade. Keep in mind that at grade time, I must calculate 149 other grades in addition to yours. Although my accuracy is very good, from time to time I may enter the wrong number into my calculator, read a grade from my grade book incorrectly, or inadvertently enter it into the computer incorrectly. This Grade Review Sheet is your way to double check my calculations."*
>
> *After students complete their Grade Review Sheets, I collect them to verify the grade at which they arrived against what I have calculated in my grade book. If there is a discrepancy, I review my calculations. Usually the student has made an error, but from time to time I am the one who has erred. This method allows me to catch and correct those errors before I turn in grades to the office and before parents receive progress reports. Students appreciate my willingness to acknowledge that I am not infallible. They also appreciate the security of knowing they won't suffer as the result of a teacher error that goes undetected. This contributes to their growing respect for and confidence in me as the year progresses.*

Kay also knows from experience that students respect a teacher who is forthright.

> ***Kay** recalls several times when she made calculation errors in figuring a student's six weeks or semester grade. She always advises her students that if they find an error, they should make her aware of it immediately. When that situation occurs, Kay sits down with the student and together they re-average the grade. If error is found, Kay graciously changes the grade and apologizes to the student. She remembers several times when the grade change was not in the student's favor. Together they discuss the need for accuracy and fairness. Usually the student leaves sadder, but wiser, for the experience. She always remembers to call the counselor or clerk to report the grade change. She also jots a note on the grade report so that parents will be aware that the teacher made the grade change.*

Continually strive for maximum accuracy and precision, but don't be afraid to admit mistakes when something slips up on you; just remember to be courteous and fair when resolving and correcting such errors..

Collegial Relationships

A teacher's relationship with his colleagues as well as his administrators can be a valuable asset, but should not be taken for granted. Teachers will need their colleagues' assistance and administrators' support at some point. Build positive relationships *before* the need to call for assistance and support.

Don't forget hallway "neighbors" when making management decisions. A teacher's neighbor colleagues will appreciate his consideration.

- Make sure students do not disturb any other classrooms if sent into the hall to practice a skit or work on a project.
- Exercise consideration when showing a video by not turning the volume up so high that it bleeds into the room next door.
- Close the door when the class is engaged in noise-producing activity.
- Don't allow students to cluster in the doorway before it is time for class to be dismissed; they can spill out into the hall and disturb others who teach the full period.
- Do not allow students to leave class early. Again, this disturbs others, creates hallway problems, and stimulates students in other classes to badger their teachers (your colleagues) to do the same.

Likewise, the value of a positive working relationship with administrators can never be underestimated. Continuously strive to develop a good working rapport with your administrators. They particularly appreciate efforts such as those suggested above as well as attention to details that directly affect them.

- Make it a point to submit all requests from administrators such as insurance paperwork, emergency contact information, substitute requests, etc. on time.
- Consistently observe school policies and procedures. For example, perform all steps and submit appropriate documentation on time when organizing field trips.
- Apprise administrators of your efforts to preempt potential controversies or problems. For example, share parental permission letters with administrators.

Administrators will take notice if you're conscientious and dependable; but they will notice even more quickly if you must be reminded time and again.

Teacher Attire

"A graduate student friend of mine, asked me how I managed to have such good evaluations from my freshmen English composition classes when I was so hard and so strict (that's what he said). He wanted a relaxed atmosphere but they (his students) never listened. I told him to stop letting students call him by his first name – 'you must draw the line in the sand somewhere,' I said, and also to take a look in the mirror. He wore a striped sleeveless tank top and what looked like underwear over some kind of latex bike pants and shower shoes. You are the teacher; look and act like one." Dorgan, Virginia (2002, Spring/Summer). Top 10 things every beginning teacher should know. *English in Texas*, 32.1, 12-15

Teacher dress can convey messages to students, colleagues, and administrators. If a school does not have a teacher dress code, don't mindlessly wear the first thing pulled out of the closet each morning. Give some thought to the nonverbal messages attire conveys and the effect that may have on school relationships. What teachers wear is a factor in the image they project, and the image they project can influence their classroom management either positively or negatively. Which would you prefer?

Generally, business-like dress conveys a business-like classroom atmosphere while exceedingly casual dress conveys a casually managed classroom. We are a society of more casual dressers than we were just a few years ago, so men in ties and women in dress-for-success suits may not be the school norm anymore. However, teachers can dress in a casual, yet businesslike manner, and convey professionalism.

If a teacher's attire appears too similar to her students, she may find them relating to her more as a peer than as a teacher thereby making her management task more difficult. Likewise, the administration may subtly perceive her as more adolescent than adult therefore making it more difficult to establish herself as a knowledgeable, skilled professional. A parent's impression of a teacher as a professional may be subtly undermined, if that teacher is dressed in an ultra casual manner during a parent conference.

We choose businesslike dress for all of the above reasons and also to model appropriate business attire for students who will be engaging in job interviews before too much longer. We recommend keeping your attire simple and nondistracting. Something to consider: if the school dress code does not allow students to wear jeans, what effect will a teacher have if he wears jeans? Could such seemingly benign behavior subtly breed resentment that could grow into hostility? It's something to ponder.

Sense of Humor

Be willing to laugh at yourself. This puts students at ease and helps them let down their defensive guard. If a teacher constantly takes himself and his job too seriously, some students will make it their mission to "trip him up." Why help them out? When a teacher inadvertently does something amusing, join in the fun. Patti recalls an occasion when a necklace she was wearing spontaneously broke and little beads flew everywhere. It was funny. She laughed along with her students, then they voluntarily gathered up the little beads.

*One morning, while dressing in relative darkness, **Kay** made the mistake of wearing two similarly styled but differently colored shoes to school. Throughout the morning, she noticed students' strange glances and quiet snickers. At the end of second period, several students approached her: "Ms. Twaryonas (they grinned), do you realize you're wearing two different shoes?" Thinking very quickly on her differently clad feet, she remarked, "I was wondering how observant my students were, so this morning I decided to put them to the test!" The students rolled their eyes and Ms. Twaryonas' unannounced "test" provided laughs all day long. A sense of humor shows your humanity and perhaps your "cleverness," too.*

We're all going to have those experiences when we drop a stack of folders that we're carrying, the bottom falls out of the box we're moving, or the books all fall off the shelf. Rather than let such occurrences ruin the day, use the opportunity to create goodwill in the classroom. If you do, students will laugh *with* you; but if you persist in taking yourself seriously all of the time, they will laugh *at you* when those inevitable mishaps occur.

People who make presentations or conduct workshops know that humor breaks down resistance and builds rapport with an audience. That's why they so often begin with humor. The same effect can occur in a classroom. Students like to laugh. Why not make them feel good before starting instruction or while teaching a lesson? Teachers don't have to be stand up comedians for this to work for them. They can reap the benefits of humor in the classroom by sharing an experience they had growing up or as a student. One of Patti's sure-fire anecdotes fits in very nicely when she is teaching about sensory details.

> *I relate my experiences as a child at my grandparents' dairy farm emphasizing the odors. I start out by describing the odor of silage (which I have to define for my urban students), go on to the odors in the muddy holding pen, and climax with the odors in the milking barn. I use all of my descriptive powers, employ my best sensory detail technique, and, yes, even embellish some. I can count on my students to find it all very amusing, especially since most of them have spent their lives in the city far removed from the countryside. After a good laugh by us all, they eagerly proceed to develop their own sensory detail anecdotes following my model.*
>
> ***Kay** often shares a humorous saying, a short funny poem (Ogden Nash garners either chuckles or furrowed brows), a cartoon, or curriculum-related "English ditty" (like a tongue twister or a palindrome) at the beginning of class. She offers these amusements only occasionally, as she does not want them to become expectations. She scours newspapers, magazines, and books for class starters. Sometimes she notices that students are writing her opening contribution down in their writer's notebook. Once in a while a student asks for a copy of that "funny thing you shared with us yesterday. My dad would get a big kick out of it."*

Humor keeps a classroom and the relations between students and teachers human and real. As with any good thing, however, operate with moderation in mind.

In addition to his classroom routines and instructional preparation, practically every behavior a teacher exhibits in his classroom and throughout the school will impact his ease or difficulty in managing his classroom and instruction. This may seem like a burden. You might be thinking that you can't orchestrate every single action. Of course, it's unrealistic to think that a teacher can choreograph her every action and behavior. We recommend concentrating on your attitudes toward learning and your students. Formulating your personal philosophy of classroom and instructional management is a valuable practice that will prove very instructive as you're faced with decisions. If you have firmly-established, constructive attitudes and maintain them consistently, you'll find they inform your decisions and behaviors.

INSTRUCTIONAL AND TIME MANAGEMENT STRATEGIES FOR STUDENTS

Just as teachers must use thoughtful management strategies and practices, students also benefit from effective ways to manage the job of being successful students. As teachers, we should not assume that our students – even the best of them – are employing the most proficient learning practices. Whole books have been written about student success, but here we'd like to offer a few techniques that we've taught our students to help them become more efficient learners and, thereby, more successful students.

The phasing out of the lecture method as a teaching strategy in secondary schools seemed to bring the demise of student **note taking**. In earlier times student notes over a teacher's lecture often served the purpose, among other things, of aiding students in spouting that same information back on a test. Although this teaching approach is rarely seen in today's middle and high schools, proficient student note taking is still of value. Moreover, many students still face lectures by college professors, often in large groups of several hundred. They may sink or swim on their note taking ability. We shouldn't forget to further our students' development of that important skill.

Another valuable form of note taking, **reading notes**, is one of the most effective methods of learning from a textbook or other reading material. With a teacher's guidance, today's students can make valuable use of learning logs and reader's and writer's notebooks to comprehend material and be able to work with it more effectively. These same students may need to struggle through dense and difficult college texts; their reading assignments may be long, and they will need to read and understand material in record time. Mnemonic devices and other memorization techniques may be shortcuts for remembering large amounts of information; but using a textbook wisely and taking complete reading notes are the most effective ways to cope with large reading assignments and difficult concepts.

We should not assume that students, even the most advanced, have well-developed learning skills. If they are aware of these methods, they may not practice them until their teacher makes it in their best interest. Teachers will be doing a giant favor for their students if they take the time to teach secondary students effective strategies to use when tackling daunting academic demands.

A guide for helping students to use **textbooks** effectively appears in the appendix to this book. As teachers, we should not assume that our students know how to garner the maximum benefit from their text. Use a guide such as the one we've provided as a "getting to know your textbook" mini-lesson on the first day students bring a new book to class. This procedure may seem unnecessary to some teachers, but when students ask on which page a certain reading begins, you can be sure they're not in the habit of using a table of contents.

> ***Kay*** *has found that many students do not know how to effectively use tools appended in books. They may skip over footnotes and definitions in reading assignments. They often fail to notice sidebars and extra material presenting related topics. They pass up maps and illustrations, seldom studying them or reading captions. Students also fail to use tables of contents and indexes to help them locate a reading. They overlook glossaries and other material in appendices, which enhance learning. Consequently, at the beginning of each year or beginning a new unit or supplementary material, Kay takes time to introduce students to their books and to help them get to know their tools. This practice assures her that they are aware of the many helpful aides within their materials.*
>
> ***Kay*** *urges students to use self-stick notes in their textbooks to point out important information that needs further study. She also suggests they use these notes to jot down questions for which they want answers, and post the notes at appropriate places in textbooks. If students cannot write in state-owned textbooks or class sets of novels, then self-stick notes become an ideal device by which to annotate pages or sections of books.*

If students' lack of familiarity with their books bothers you, wait until you see their panic when they're asked to make **oral presentations** or give talks in front of their classmates.

To ease students' anxieties, another skill ***Kay*** *teaches early in the year is how to make effective oral presentations. Such presentations are difficult for many students, especially those who lack self-confidence, who are shy, or who previously have been unsuccessful when presenting orally. That is one of the reasons it is important for students to develop their oral presentation skills when they have the support of a caring teacher. Kay models a presentation for the class, reinforcing the guidelines she has suggested. (See guidelines in the appendix for this book.) She demonstrates both practices which enhance good presentations and those which students should avoid. Try coaching your students in effective strategies and best practices. You should see the results very quickly.*

When we coach our students to use the practices which will make them successful students, we are doing both them and ourselves a favor. We have the satisfaction that with practice they'll become better readers, speakers and presenters. They have the satisfaction of using newfound confidence and skills to succeed in classroom situations, which may have been their worst nightmares. Furthermore, students will experience the long lasting developmental value of such essential learning skills as they proceed through college, training programs and to the workplace.

In addition, teaching **time management strategies** to our students enhances their possibilities for success as students and workers. Urging them to improve poor attendance records and get to school and class on time are parts of the time management sequence. But what can we do to help them survive and prosper in their current job – being a successful student? What other strategies do we need to introduce to students to assist them to become better organized and consequently more successful?

Many schools provide student **organizational planners** as a part of a back-to-school regimen, along with ID cards and locker assignments. Often these school planners are district-specific and contain basic information about the school. The most useful feature of these planners is the day-by-day calendar to help students organize their time and work.

Each Monday as ***Kay*** *begins class, she allows about five minutes to summarize the week's schedule. "Today we will be covering . . . Don't forget your narratives are due on Wednesday . . . We'll have a peer-editing session the last part of the period on Tuesday . . . Vocabulary practice is due on Thursday." At the beginning of each week students know the class schedule. Kay has just made them* ***accountable*** *for what they are expected to know and do, and when* *they are expected to have the work completed. Information in the class log reinforces the student planners. (More later on class logs as organizational aids.) It is a backup for everyone, especially absentees. When you have students use planners and logs, don't forget to announce schedule changes when you make them: "Because of Friday's assembly, we'll need to have the vocabulary check-up quiz originally scheduled for Friday on Thursday. Please change that date in your planner and in the log."*

Take note, however, that some students are natural organizers; they organize without coaching. Seek out the laggards. Find students who are not using their planners and explain how time management strategies and planners will help them work more efficiently. If your school doesn't provide student planners, consider making them a requirement for your class. Inexpensive organizational planners can be found most anywhere that sells school supplies. Students will soon see the advantages of using them in your class, and those advantages will carry over to other classes. Other tools that students might find useful can be found on personal computers: notetaking formats, calculators, calendar-makers, etc.

All of us, teachers and students, can be great **procrastinators**. When students put off doing long assignments until the night before they're due, the quality of the finished product suffers, not to mention the learning value of thoughtfully executing the assignment. Teachers can manage their classrooms and assignments to discourage student procrastination. Consider some of these strategies:

- Emphasize to students that quality of work is of paramount importance.
- Urge them to set time tables and goals for long assignments.
- Require periodic progress reports to spur students into action.
- Suggest they leave their work for short periods so they may return to it with a fresh attitude. This practice may determine whether a student enjoys and learns from a particular assignment, or merely finds it burdensome.
- Create early submission dates with added bonus credit, which encourage students to avoid waiting until the last minute.
- Check long-term work at intervals.
- Ask to see the work.
- Have students submit work reports outlining what they've accomplished and require them to submit their plans for completion.

When students are personally invested in a project, work reports become important to them. Require a work report as part of a brief conference. In this way you can check on problems students may be having, and thereby become a partner/consultant in their learning. Interventions, such as conferences, take time and planning; however, they are effective strategies for teaching time management and accountability. Moreover, helping students approach long-term tasks in this manner will increase the learning they experience from engaging with the assignment. Models of forms that can be used to assist students in successful project completion can be found in the Appendix of this book.

A final word about time management strategies. Occasionally, two or three students always lag behind when completing tests. A mini-lesson in **test-taking strategies,** including managing test time, may offer suggestions for dealing with the common problem of "test stress." Students will appreciate your mini-lesson when they face that first exam, and the many that will follow.

We offer the following test-taking suggestions that may be helpful for students:

- Look over the entire test before you begin in order to determine what you'll have to do.
- Read all directions, making sure you understand them. If you don't, ask for explanations before testing begins.
- Notice the point or percentage values of each section of the test. (Teachers can provide this information on the test paper or write it on the answer sheet or chalk board.)
- Do not feel compelled to work the test in order, unless instructed to do so. You may want to tackle weightier sections first, so they will not be left until the end of the test, when you may be running out of time or getting tired.
- Read each section or question carefully and determine the specific action you are being asked to take. Operative words, such as "compare," "discuss," "list," "order" "give examples," etc. are keys to determining how to respond to each question or section of the test. Attention to these key words increases the possibility that you will do what the test is asking.
- Wear a watch on test day, so you can check how much time remains to work on the test.
- Ask your teacher to keep students apprised of the time remaining for a test by writing it on the board or providing a clock in the classroom.

- Be sure to have enough paper on your desk. Interferences like sharpening pencils or getting more paper may compromise your concentration as well as eat into your test-taking time.
- Save a few minutes at test's end to check for errors and possible changes. In haste at the end of a test, you can leave out answers or fail to make changes, which end up costing points on the exam.
- Be sure to hand in your test before you leave the classroom. (This advice may seem ridiculous, but we've seen this scenario more than once. A student inadvertently sticks test papers in her binder in her haste to exit and head to the next class. When she realizes much too late that she still has the test in her possession, the results of her error are most unfortunate.)

Although some teachers may think teaching management techniques unnecessary, we can help our students greatly by showing them ways to become more successful. Furthermore, this preparation benefits our students as they move on to college or even the job application process where testing is often required. Upon entering the workforce, the prospect of our former students' success in entry-level jobs can be enhanced with well-developed organization, time management, listening and speaking skills. Finally, having successful students helps make our jobs easier, not to mention more satisfying in the end.

V ~ Daily Classroom Management

GROUNDWORK & GUIDELINES

Every situation in which groups function co-operatively requires training for individuals so they can function efficiently and effectively as a group. Think about it. Individuals must be trained in driving procedure so that millions of drivers can function safely. In football, basketball, soccer, in fact, in all team sports, individuals must be trained so that the team can function successfully. Any job requires training so that individuals will work constructively, often as part of a hands-on team. This training applies to everything from work in fast food restaurants to law enforcement or medical work. Even in work that does not actually occur in group settings, individuals are trained in policies and procedures so they can function for the good of the whole. Classrooms are no different.

In one-on-one teaching situations a minimum of training is necessary; but the larger a group of learners becomes, the more valuable training is to the individuals as well as to the group as a whole. **Training makes it possible for the greatest number of students to receive the greatest benefit from the classroom experience** even though there may be only one teacher for thirty or thirty-five students.

Patti's standard procedure illustrates one approach for training students to be successful while simultaneously building a learning environment that is nurturing, encouraging, motivating and challenging.

The first week or two of my school year focuses on instruction on my expectations, classroom policies and routines. After that, the nature of training shifts somewhat, but it is training nonetheless: training in active reading strategies, training in the writing process, training in revision. You get the picture.

First, I present analogies to which students can relate to illustrate the value of policies and procedures. I begin by pointing out that if they were the only person on the road, there would be no need for driving rules; but as soon as there is one more vehicle, the need for a few driving regulations arises so they won't run into one another. The greater the number of drivers and pedestrians becomes, the more driving regulations become necessary. When we live in groups, we sacrifice some of our individual freedom so that we and everyone else can function well. The smaller the group, the less we must sacrifice; the larger the group, the more we must give up. Think of a small village compared to a large city. Then I ask students to provide examples of situations where people give up individual freedom so they and others can function effectively and efficiently.

I am straightforward with students: "We will spend the first week engaged in active training in how to be successful in Ms. Slagle's class." I ask how many of them have jobs; many of them do. I ask them to describe the training they received in their job and the operating manuals for those jobs. Many delight in describing the huge and detailed manuals that accompany their employment. After all, how else can a Big Mac be the same throughout the country? I share my operating manual – our school's Teacher Handbook - to demonstrate that I, too, have policies and procedures that must be followed. I describe some of the training I received as a new teacher and as a teacher new to that school. In other words, I establish a ***rationale*** *for the policies and routines in my classroom, as well as for the training they will experience in order to learn these policies and procedures.*

These analogies help students understand that classroom and school rules do not exist merely to inconvenience them. Students begin to see that asking everyone to head his/her paper in a consistent manner makes it possible for the teacher to spend more time considering the thoughts expressed in each student's work when she doesn't have to devote time to sorting through papers trying to figure out what's what. They begin to realize that there are penalties for deadlines not met so that everyone can have equitable consideration.

What if we don't have classroom rules, policies, procedures, and training? In society that would result in anarchy; the result is similar in a school or classroom. Consider the underlying effect on students of no rules, procedures, or training. Without policies and routines students are left to guess what is acceptable and what is unacceptable. If they guess incorrectly, they experience unpleasant consequences. With rules, policies and procedures students are not left to guesswork that leaves them vulnerable to the teacher's reprimands. Without rules, policies, routines and training in them, students are left to read the teacher's mind about her expectations. Thought of this way, it's not hard to see how the absence of rules, procedures and training is clearly unfair to students.

Some teachers dive right into content instruction at the beginning of the school year expecting students to read their minds about expectations for student behavior and performance. Others may distribute a list of rules the first day and expect students to adhere to them diligently, meeting the teacher's standards for performance. When students who have five, six, even seven classes a day forget a rule in one of those classes, they may suffer that teacher's ire. Is it not better for everyone concerned to spend a few class periods training students in rules, policies, procedures, expectations, and consequences for that particular classroom? Keep in mind that some classes will need more extensive and concentrated training than others. As with so much else, all groups of students are not the same. It's part of a teacher's professional judgment to determine how much training is enough, how much is too little, and how much is too much.

Think about the steps in training for any endeavor such as a sport. First there is instruction in concepts and rules, then there is modeling followed by guided practice. Perhaps there is some form of mastery measurement, which may indicate that reteaching or additional practice is called for. Sound like the process for teaching skills? Not a coincidence. Training in policy and procedure takes the same form as training in any skill development whether it is on a playing field, in a laboratory, in the workplace, or in a classroom.

As a consequence of thoughtfully planned training, students can function confidently thus enhancing their self-esteem and improving their attitude. Teachers can function efficiently preserving valuable time for instruction. Everyone can focus on learning in a constructive, productive atmosphere for the balance of the school year.

Rules

An integral component of orienting students is introduction to and instruction in class rules. Rudeness in our society carries over to our schools. Lack of consideration for others has become prevalent. Among other functions, rules maintain the decorum of a classroom. We remember the days when "the rules" meant enforcing the policies of:

- No chewing gum
- No visiting the wastebasket without permission
- No turning around to talk with your neighbor
- No sleeping in class

Infractions of these rules drew innocuous punishments, like staying after class to "do the teacher's bidding," standing in the corner until class ended, or writing one hundred times, "I will not tease my neighbor ever again." Those punishments seem old-fashioned now. Infractions these days can involve detention, in-school suspension, the summoning of local authorities, or even permanent expulsion. Classes function better when students know the class rules and the penalties for breaking them.

Kay *goes over her rules at the beginning of the year every day for the first week. When infractions occur, she repeats the rules. She keeps the rules simple and has as few as possible. Students receive written copies of the rules to keep in their class notebook. She writes the rules on the chalkboard where they remain for the first several weeks. She finds that students will tend to abide by a short list of simple rules rather than long lists of rules that are irrelevant or that will likely be forgotten.*

Teachers must enforce their rules immediately and consistently. Students notice and take full advantage when a teacher does not consistently and/or fairly apply the rules. A few essential rules will work in most cases. These work for **Kay** in most classes:

- Be on time: in your seat ready to begin class.
- Be sure you have all needed materials: book(s), paper, pen.
- Be respectful of fellow classmates and the teacher.
- Stay on task during the period to get your work done.

Kay's rules are basically management tools that keep the classroom functioning efficiently on a daily basis. She also keeps procedures such as late work, make-up work, and handling tardiness as straightforward as possible. The more straightforward the rules, the more likely they will be remembered and followed. Keep in mind that different classes call for different sets of rules. As situations arise or patterns occur, adapt rules accordingly. When students are on task and know and abide by the rules, they are more productive. (See "Rules for Success" in the Appendix for this book.)

At semester's or year's end, update rules where necessary. Continual reflection about the rules for your classroom is vital in order to address specific needs in an evolving environment. When guidelines are established and groundwork is laid, the prospects for a productive and satisfying school year for both students and teachers are very likely.

ORGANIZATION

Grade Books, Plan Books & Seating Charts

Teachers cannot live up to their potential if they are not well organized. Likewise, organization can help teachers cope with the numerous demands made of them without leaving them feeling overwhelmed. Each teacher is faced with a variety of organizational decisions that can help or hinder her efficiency. Establishing some organizational structures at the outset of the school year will lay groundwork upon which a teacher can build throughout the year.

Throughout much of our careers the three main organizational tools have been a **grade book**, a **plan book**, and a **seating chart** grid. As new technologies emerge, these tools may take different forms; but we're willing to bet that teachers will continue to rely on each of them in some form or another. Although most new teachers will take these tools for granted, the effective use of each is vital for smooth and efficient classroom operation.

Believe it or not, we have known teachers who did not use these essential tools; or at the very least, used them ineffectively. Apparently, they were not aware of how these tools could make their lives easier as well as enhance their management and instruction.

School districts typically provide grade books and plan books for each teacher, either hard copy or electronic. The styles of these books often match the district's latest educational trends, so their design may be changed from time to time. As teachers' management techniques evolve, they will probably develop their own best methods for keeping records of instruction and student activity. For new teachers, however, a few guidelines could be of value.

Grade Books – Never put your grade book in the hands of students or give them access. Take it with you or lock it up when you leave the room, especially when students (your own or another teacher's) are present, during assemblies, or at night when you leave school. If your grade book exists in an electronic format, be sure to employ safeguards so that students cannot access your grade records. Furthermore, keep alternate copies of your electronic grade records in the event that your computer should crash. **Never leave your grade book for a substitute.** With your grade book in someone else's hands, you have no way to monitor how it is used. A student's grades are of no importance to a one or two-day substitute. A student's grade is a private matter; a substitute could inadvertently show a student's grades to another student without realizing he'd done something wrong. Furthermore, a substitute may not appreciate the gravity of protecting the grade book. In some schools, teachers are told to take their grade books with them during fire or other disaster drills; occasionally, administrators check to see if teachers are following the rules. Remember, your grade book is the official record, often of student attendance as well as classroom activity and student work that is evaluated. If you lose it . . . well, let's just say, don't lose it . . . ever.

Additional precautions also concern grade books. **Do not let students calculate your grades**. This task is one that is strictly reserved for teachers – the professionals. You might allow a trusted student aide to grade certain types of papers, to sort and staple student papers, and perhaps even file graded student work; but all work relative to student grades is the responsibility of the teacher and no one else. Trust and friendship can often clash when grades are the subject. Your district, your school, your students, and their parents hold you responsible for accuracy, privacy, and timely reportage. Take this role seriously. A tidy grade book where student scores and attendance are kept is considered the mark of a successful teacher. In some schools, administrators frequently check grade books to see that the teacher is accurately recording student work and keeping proper records.

At the beginning of the school year, be prepared to keep grades and attendance on temporary grid sheets (An example is included in the appendix of this book.) If you fill in the grade book during the first week of school, students may have schedule changes and your grade book can quickly become a disaster. So hold off recording students' names for a few days, even weeks, until it's clear that all enrollment adjustments have been finalized. Sure, you'll have students enter in the middle of a grading period or between quarters/trimesters/semesters, but adding one or two students to your roll book is easy compared to restructuring the chaos which can result if you are too anxious to fill out your grade book before class changes are complete. The grade book is the teacher's most essential tool. Keep it in good order.

The increasing proliferation of electronic grade recording has eliminated some of these concerns, but there are still compelling reasons to keep print records of student attendance and grades, even if those records are more informal than an official electronic record. As school districts embrace technology, electronic grade books will, if everyone is mandated to use them, require their own set of rules. Until these new ways of recording student work become realities in your school, keep your traditional grade book orderly, updated, accurate and secure.

Plan Books - - We couldn't operate each day without a plan book. It's the map for daily, weekly, and semester "trips" in the classroom. Plan books are very personal. Some teachers fill the little blocks with page numbers only. Others use a system of microscopic shorthand to record all the activities they wish to accomplish during a specified time. Some plan books are messy; some are carefully color-coded. We've even seen empty ones. If you don't use the plan book, use something. **It is impossible to be an effective teacher as well as meet all of today's expectations and mandates without planning.** We've yet to see a teacher who can *effectively* plan completely in his head. The plan book is a teacher's **documentation** of the quality of planning effort he makes. Be alert – just like grade books, administrators in some schools check plan books and/or lesson plans on a regular basis.

Some publishers now provide electronic and even online lesson planners. These can be timesavers if a teacher has compatible computer access in her classroom and at home; changes become much easier when accomplished electronically. Some administrators require teachers to record appropriate state standards with each daily lesson plan. Publishers' electronic planning tools may be correlated with state standards, which could make this chore less cumbersome. If electronic planners accompany the texts for your classes, don't overlook their possibility for facilitating at least some of your personal planning process.

Planning is an important key to successful management, so we can't put too much emphasis on doing it faithfully.

***Kay** usually fills out her plan book on Thursday or Friday afternoons. She checks carefully to make sure she's prepared for the week to come. Did she run off those handouts for Tuesday's peer review? Did she design the PowerPoint slides she needs for Monday's lesson? Kay also uses the plan book at the beginning of every week to apprise her students of the upcoming work. When she changes plans, she tells students immediately, so they can change their personal planners; and she changes her plan book accordingly. Interruptions of the best laid plans are inevitable. Often she won't finish a lesson as she had thought she would, and will have to carry a part of it over to the next day. She notes the change in her plan book. If an unscheduled assembly is announced or a weather crisis interferes with plans to view a video, she scratches out the plans and inserts new ones or sometimes draws an arrow to a different day. Sticky notes can be used as extensions of the plan book.*

However you choose to plan your lessons, use your plan book and keep it updated. Just like Kay's grade book, she does not usually make the plan book available to substitutes. She plans several weeks in advance, and the loss or misplacement of it would be a disaster for her.

***Patti** keeps her plan book in pencil. She is surprised how often changes must occur and erasing keeps her plan book efficiently useful. Patti also uses her plan book to keep herself organized. The moment she receives notices of assemblies, counselor class visits, faculty or committee meetings, office paperwork deadlines, etc. she records them in her plan book thereby diminishing the possibility that she might forget or overlook an important event or deadline. In this manner, she uses her plan book as her central clearinghouse not only for her instruction but also for all her school-*

related calendar data, making it much more likely that she will be consistently efficient.

The plan book is a handy place to note details specific to each class period. When teaching multiple sections of the same class, it's difficult and not necessarily advisable to keep each class period in lockstep with the others. Yet it's difficult to keep such details in your head. Patti notes in her plan book any stopping points, carryovers or other details specific to each class period for future reference.

The plan book is not only a map of where a teacher wants to take her classes but also a record of where they've been. Accordingly, Patti makes sure to update her plan book at the end of each day to reflect any changes or deviations that may have occurred. If you're asked a question about a specific day, class or lesson, it's much easier to refer back to your plan book than to attempt mining your memory. Besides, referring to your plan book when organizing future lessons on the same topics is very helpful.

Teachers must process a mountain of information every day and continually remember numerous details. Maximizing the many functions of the plan book, whether in print or electronic format, can relieve a teacher from the stress of trying to store volumes of information in her head as well as contribute to her efficiency.

Seating charts provide numerous values, especially when a teacher is facing a group of unfamiliar students. Perhaps the greatest merit of seating charts is the message they convey to students from the initial class meeting: this teacher is organized, knows what she expects, and is serious about the business of learning. Some of the specific advantages of seating charts include:

- They help teachers learn the names of students more quickly.
- They help teachers identify students before they know each one.
- They facilitate roll taking.
- They help substitutes.
- They allow teachers to separate easily-distracted students from one another.
- They allow teachers to seat new students, ESL, or ECE students next to helpers.
- They assure that particular positioning of students with physical needs - close to the front, near the board, etc. – can be achieved with a minimum of attention drawn to that student's needs.
- They can economize the returning of graded work.

Seating charts are essential whether you use an alphabetical seating arrangement, seat students in some prescribed order, or allow them to choose where they wish to sit as long as they behave and remain attentive. Keep in mind that it's easy to rearrange seating or to let students do so, but once they have seated themselves without some sort of seating consistency, it's very difficult to switch to a consistent seating plan. Once students are seated, make a record of the seating assignments. Be sure to update every time a change is made.

The greatest value of a seating chart is, perhaps, at the beginning of the class period. A consistent seating arrangement encourages students to move into the classroom, take their seats, and begin their learning activities while it allows the teacher to efficiently take roll. The use of a seating chart does not suggest that students stay locked in their seats throughout the entire class period. Once your class has begun and students are focused on learning, some students might move around the classroom to access resources, shift position for group work, or move to learning stations. Active learning is just that – active. Yet the use of a seating chart establishes an order and routine that carry over into all of a class's activities.

Taking attendance should require little class time and need not interfere with instruction. Be sure students are on task and then quickly take roll. A glance at a seating chart and a quick look over students is generally all that is necessary to determine absentees. In other places in this book, we have discussed effective ways to begin class and offered suggestions about taking attendance and handling other housekeeping chores. Seating charts can contribute considerably in this regard.

Seating charts are also essential for substitutes or anyone who manages your students during your absence from the classroom. For maximum effectiveness, be sure to keep your seating charts up to date. If a student leaves your class or is added to your rolls, revise the chart to reflect these changes. Using a prescribed order for seating will alleviate many problems when you're absent. More information about seating charts, their value and specific suggestions can be found in the sections of this book titled "From the First Day and Beyond" and "Time Management."

Effective management requires thoughtfully handling what may seem like small, insignificant tasks. The time spent addressing these organizational details is an investment that teachers will want to make in order to assure a well-managed classroom.

MANAGING PHYSICAL SPACE

Another of the numerous facets of teaching is organizing the physical space of the classroom. Some aspects of organization are a headache, but attention to those areas which bring a classroom alive for teaching purposes, such as displaying student work and fitting out a room to make it academically inspiring, can be exciting. Furthermore, physical layout can contribute tremendously to instructional organization and diminish teacher frustration if thoughtfully considered. This attention to physical space includes seating arrangements, extra furniture, bulletin boards, displays, decorations, equipment storage, and any other physical need that impacts the optimum use of the classroom and its contents by both the teacher and her students.

Oversized spaces (e.g. cafeteria, auditorium, etc.) as well as cramped spaces offer challenges for teachers. Typically, though, teachers never have enough **space**. At the top of many teachers' wish lists, after more time, would be more room. Administrators could assign them to an old gymnasium, and some teachers (including us, probably) still would not have enough space to accomplish the myriad tasks and activities that occur daily in a typical classroom. Teachers' classrooms need to accommodate activities as diverse as individual student work; group work; presentation practice; lab activities; conferencing; project creation and display, and more. Furthermore, classrooms often need to provide book and supply storage; learning stations; classroom library; secure, locked storage; teacher workspace; computers, and more.

The first challenge teachers face with their rooms is assessing the physical space and transforming it to accommodate its multiple functions. Often classrooms where non-lab classes are taught are on the small side. Large classrooms frequently are reserved for science, art and computer classes. At the least, we hope there's room for a teacher desk, at least one general-purpose table, individual student seating (In most secondary classrooms that means 25-30+ student desks or tables that each accommodate 4-6 students.), filing cabinet, bookshelves and other furniture to store materials and supplies. If your school happens to be planning a renovation, inquire about the opportunity for teachers to offer design input. Two outstanding needs most teachers express are lots of storage space and running water.

*Don't scoff at the opportunity to teach in a nontraditional classroom. Over the course of her career, **Patti** has had the pleasure of teaching English in a science lab with lots of storage cabinets and running water as* *well as a music room equipped with riser seating, practice rooms for group work, and running water.*

***Kay** remembers several incidents when she was teaching in a science room with sinks, gas outlets, running water and a group of less-than-well-behaved sophomores. Use your imagination about the scenarios.*

With materials, equipment and resources to fulfill a myriad of instructional needs, there may hardly be room left for much movement. The addition of desktop computers to classrooms that were not designed for them just compounds the challenge. Even desks are being made larger to accommodate growing students, particularly in high schools; but the classrooms are not necessarily expanded or the class sizes reduced to accommodate the larger desks.

What is a teacher to do? How can he work within the confines of a small classroom to manage the varied activities he wants and needs to do, such as speaking, presenting, experimenting, performing and collaborating? How can she manage the space for the larger groups of students schools continually need to serve? The first step is to forecast what types of activities you will ask your students to engage in most often, and then choose an arrangement which best allows for that activity.

Kay's Classroom

For example, Kay's room is a rectangle, longer than it is wide. She has placed her desk with tables and a podium at the front of the room. She has an extra table at the back of the class for multiple uses. She will often station herself there for certain types of monitoring, such as that done during tests; and the back table is the place where she keeps class logs and other student resources. She conferences with students at that table and small groups of students will often meet there for some purpose.

Bookshelves, magazine racks, two sets of encyclopedias, and various storage containers line most of the wall space in Kay's classroom. She tries to keep permanent audiovisual equipment on carts so that it can be moved around the room for ease of use and stored wherever space permits. Student desks, all 31 of them, are arranged in three long rows on each side of the room facing each other; about 15 desks on each side are arranged three desks deep. It is a tight fit and a difficult space in which to operate. A long space cuts down the middle of the room, like a runway, where she can walk up and down and stand and address the class. She has a podium at the front of the room; more often than not, she feels isolated from students when she's sitting there. Consequently, she keeps three stools in various locations around the room for use when she needs a perch to get off her feet. She likes interacting with her students from these stools in different parts of the room. They fit her style of teaching.

Patti's Classroom

Patti has found that placing a long table perpendicular to the room's entrance provides multiple advantages. Classroom notebooks can reside on this table for easy student access; students can sit at the table to copy information from the class notebook; papers for students to pick up as they enter or exit the classroom can be placed here; the teacher can conference with students using the table; and it discourages students from congregating at the door just inside the classroom. Additionally, Patti's room needs space for a five-drawer filing cabinet (one drawer for each class) with student access, student-accessible files for writing folders, classroom library, and Patti's active trays (See the Time Management section of this book for a description of how these trays are used.). She also likes to have a table beside her lectern for separately stacking materials to be used with each class. Although she doesn't teach from behind her lectern, it's a good place to keep materials like her grade book, plan book, seating chart, student notes, and papers to return easily accessible.

In plotting the arrangement of her classroom, Patti likes to cordon off a corner or section to function as her "office." She uses filing cabinets or other furniture including the teacher's desk to isolate this "office" portion of the room. This arrangement facilitates her planning by keeping supplies and materials close at hand. Furthermore, it allows her to make teacher-only items less accessible to students. Kay concurs with the value of at least a small amount of private space for the teacher.

All of these preferences require **furniture** and classrooms don't necessarily come supplied with what an individual teacher wants for her particular set-up. Our best advice: scavenge. Keep eyes and ears open and don't be afraid to ask. Patti once asked the librarians about shelving she was seeking, and for years afterwards they kept her in mind when discarding shelves. Custodians and maintenance personnel generally move all over a school building; consider asking them to keep an eye out for an unused piece of furniture for you. Some schools or school districts have a discard room or warehouse where unused furniture items are stored or are waiting for disposal. Don't be afraid to rescue a dirty or broken piece of furniture and clean or repair it yourself. Patti spied a once-lovely library table shoved in a corner of the school's basement when she was there for a disaster drill. She rescued it, refinished it, and ended up with a lovely wooden table for her classroom. Resourcefulness is a teacher's best trait when it comes to furnishing a classroom.

The **physical set-up** of a room should meet student needs according to numbers and the teaching/learning style a teacher uses most often. Physical space can always be altered for special projects and additional needs. Classes should work within the set-up that is most useful and comfortable for everyone's needs.

***Kay** has had colleagues call her room "cluttered." On the other hand, she has had students come in and say, "I like this room; there's so much to see." Once when a district administrator visited, he remarked, "I can tell there's a lot of work and learning taking place in this classroom." Those last two comments reinforced Kay's sense of pride in her room. She says, "My room may be busy and overloaded, but everything's here, student work is displayed, and it's evident that teaching and learning are in progress." Never again did she worry about her "cluttered" room.*

Teachers try to stay organized; but the more "things" kept in the classroom, the more challenging it is to **organize** them. Plastic organizer drawers on wheels in which to keep supplies are a great help with this challenge. They're inexpensive and movable; they can hold pens, note cards, sticky notes, scissors, markers, tape, paper clips – all the necessities for an everyday working classroom. Since they're on wheels, it's easy to roll them to different classroom locations as instructional situations vary.

Supplemental Reading Materials

We like to provide current magazines, public service booklets, book reviews, and other **periodicals** on small racks and shelves that are accessible to students. When students finish an assignment or test early, they have something meaningful, even entertaining, to read. Bring your used magazines (only appropriate titles, of course) for students to peruse; just be sure to blank out your mailing address on subscription labels. Many newspapers and magazines offer special rates for educators. You can discover some of these by searching studentmags.com. We think you'll be surprised at the interest some students exhibit for what may seem commonplace to you. We've taught numerous students who didn't have access to magazines in their homes, so our classrooms provided an enriched environment they may not have otherwise experienced. Such real world publications make our classrooms a richer, more meaningful, and more interesting resource for our students.

We're big fans of the **classroom library.** Regardless of your subject matter, students can benefit from access to books in your classroom. Make it a quest to find titles that relate to your content – even remotely. Take advantage of books from library sales, auctions, second-hand stores, flea markets, and yard sales. Before adding them to a classroom library, assess their appropriateness for students. Be sure to set up a workable system for checking books out. Otherwise, books may not find their way back to your library. One possibility is to recruit a reliable student to serve as the class librarian. We suggest you search for additional ways to make reading materials noticeable and available for students to use. When extra reading materials are available in the classroom, the message is sent that reading is important and can be a pleasant pastime, not just an academic necessity.

Brick and plywood shelves can hold a wealth of books. Occasionally stores that are going out of business have paperback racks and other display furniture available for the taking or for a small price. Take advantage of these finds. When teachers retire, they're often willing to part with some of their classroom items.

Once at a professional conference, **Patti** was chatting with a publisher's rep near the end of the exhibit period. As the rep started to take down her display, she asked Patti if she'd like to have the book display rack that had been used for that conference. Never one to turn down anything for her classroom, Patti naturally accepted. That rack turned out to be a great way to display books in Patti's classroom library. Just another advantage of attending professional meetings and conferences!

Enrichment Materials

In addition to collecting and displaying books, we like to enlist students' help in procuring other forms of classroom inspiration that will serve all students that pass through our rooms throughout the school year. Quotations, cartoons, articles and the like discovered by both the teacher and students can enliven a classroom as well as point out real world connections to your subject matter.

*As an English and humanities teacher, **Kay** collects quotations about specific books, poetry, poets, fiction, reading and writing in general. Many great little books about writing, in particular, are available which quote the famous and the infamous concerning the writing life. Some offer tips for writers and readers. Similar books are available for scientists, artists,* *historians, mathematicians, etc. Kay compiles lists and students create hanging mobiles for the room using these quotations. Some of their artistic endeavors show considerable creativity and amusing slants in their interpretations of the quotations. These mobiles are always popular and many of Kay's colleagues have emulated this idea. The mobiles, which hang from the ceiling, "jazz up" any classroom and often provide necessary inspiration for blocked writers and daydreaming readers.*

We, of course, owe this idea to sculptor Alexander Calder; Kay uses the mobiles for instruction by providing a mini-talk about Calder showing pictures of some of his work before students begin to make their own mobiles. She's used them for the study of mythology and literature, too. Teachers in any subject matter can use student-made mobiles to spotlight aspects of their curriculum. Your classroom might provide opportunities for other forms of student expression such as wall murals, window painting, etc. Be sure to secure administrative permission before undertaking projects that result in permanent changes.

Patti, *a language arts teacher, places quotes about reading and writing above the long chalkboard in her classroom. From time to time, she observes a student pondering one of the quotes, indicating that students do take notice of them. As part of her introduction to reading and writing instruction, she encourages her students to discuss some of these quotes. She then asks them to choose a quote and respond to it in their learning logs. Their choices and related comments are illuminating. Without fail, multiple students will choose "Red" Smith's quote, "There's nothing to writing. All you do is sit down at a typewriter and open a vein."*

A similar effect can be achieved with **posters** on bulletin boards, doors or any open wall space. Use prints, purchased for a reasonable sum in museums or art stores, or borrowed from the art department or the media center to decorate the room and inspire creative thinking and writing. Catalogs and special "teacher stores" which carry educator supplies are sources of ready-to-use materials and decorations of all kinds that add visual interest to our classrooms. Some bookstores often give teachers posters and other resources when they are finished using them for advertising. Often a district or school will offer materials for posting that pertain to all students such as assessment preparation posters. The sky's the limit for turning good ideas into valuable teaching tools. You can, we're sure, think of numerous ways to decorate your room, engage your students in learning, and provide "teachable moments" all at the same time.

***Patti** provides writing posters that serve a functional purpose on one bulletin board in her classroom. Some of the posters in her collection:*

- *outline the writing process*
- *list transitional devices*
- *suggest terms for sensory details*
- *ask questions for revision*
- *suggest steps for editing and proofreading*
- *provide questions for writing reflection*

She encourages students to refer to these posters as they compose and revise. The posters serve the added benefit of providing resources for students who have failed to bring their composition text or writing folder materials to class. Patti has acquired posters the same way she has acquired much of her classroom furniture: scavenging. Her best source for instructional posters is the exhibit hall at professional conferences and conventions such as NCTE and its affiliate meetings.

In addition to functional posters, Patti likes to use colorful, aesthetically pleasing posters to add ambiance to her classroom. Over the years she has accumulated a considerable collection that fits the bill. A tip: have posters laminated to facilitate their use over many years. Patti also likes to cover her bulletin boards with colorful fabric that adds to her classroom's mood and is more durable than sheet paper. A variety of colors and patterns of inexpensive fabric can be found in the bargain bin at fabric and craft stores. Along that same line, discontinued wallpaper rolls can sometimes be found at a very inexpensive cost.

Bulletin boards, however, can be the secondary teacher's nemesis. You plan and design a great board for the beginning of the year; you promise yourself the board will change every six weeks. You soon forget that promise amid numerous, more immediate demands. For many teachers, the board they remove near the end of school is the one they put up at the beginning. Elementary school colleagues, who are well known for their incredible bulletin board turnover time, just can't imagine why others consider them such a difficult and daunting task.

***Kay** owes her "bulletin board philosophy" to a former science teacher. When he observed her working hard to keep her three bulletin boards current and interesting, he intoned, "Why are you spending time designing bulletin boards that students will seldom notice when you could devote that time to preparing other instructional materials?"*

He suggested Kay do as he had done for many years: have students keep the classroom bulletin boards continually changing. So she decided to make bulletin boards a part of students' work awarding credit for their efforts. Kay's science colleague discussed the process with her, shared an evaluation sheet that he used in biology and made suggestions for a similar approach for her classes. She now assigns each student or pair of students the responsibility of installing new bulletin boards each week. The boards have become teaching tools "made by students for students." Of course, Kay still manages the occasional bulletin board herself, particularly at the beginning of the school year.

There are many possibilities when you concoct your own approach to student-generated bulletin boards. Teachers can assign subjects, have students choose subjects from a teacher-provided list, or allow them to submit ideas for their own boards. Boards closely tying into curriculum instructional units are generally the most successful. In fact, teachers can incorporate bulletin board displays into instructional plans, perhaps as project options or even as visual aids accompanying student presentations. Reserve the right to give students guidance on subject choice to avoid difficulties or inappropriate ideas. Students who design the boards learn much from their research; likewise, students who view the boards in the classroom learn good lessons too. Bulletin boards often seem more meaningful to students when classmates create them rather than when the teacher does all the work. Furthermore, quality is often enhanced due to the competitive nature of students.

Even though preparing a bulletin board may seem like an obvious task not requiring extensive explanation, **don't assume** that students will know how to choose effective subject matter, design meaningful displays and implement their plans. Provide students with clear guidelines and specific instructions about how to proceed.

Kay *describes criteria for successful boards and warns students away from the obvious pitfalls. She oversees the projects to be sure that students don't take on more depth than they can handle on a single board. They are required to present their plan on a 3" by 5" card that Kay must approve at least a week before they plan to begin actual work. She checks the plans for appropriateness, focus, and feasibility and intervenes when a student's plan exceeds the assignment and/or space limitations. When this problem occurs, Kay helps narrow their focus. On their evaluation sheet, she asks students to assess their own work and suggest an appropriate grade; she also assesses their work and averages her score with theirs for a final grade. They're usually honest in their assessments, and they generally* *follow the stated guidelines. In the end, students seem pleased to have this input into their grades.*

The key to successful bulletin boards is to provide guidelines and continuing help. Reinforce the responsibilities and expectations, which can be taught with this assignment: punctuality, careful planning, and the general responsibility of completing the assigned task. (A sample bulletin board evaluation sheet is included in the appendix for this book)

Displaying **student work**, whether it is writing, art, posters, projects, or other creative endeavors, is a valuable instructional and attitudinal practice. When students know their work is going to be displayed, they generally will make a more thoughtful endeavor; but perhaps even more important, seeing their work displayed demonstrates the value placed on their efforts.

New types of tape and other sticky substances, which will adhere to cement block walls and won't damage classroom walls have made displaying posters and student work easier. Student-made posters, which rotate daily or weekly can also be displayed on easels placed around the room for a gallery effect. Students can "spotlight" their favorite authors, best-loved poems, or a student-display of literary terms with illustrative examples in an English class. Students in science could spotlight their favorite scientist; those in social studies could feature historical figures. Even math and technology have their notable super stars. Students' writing in all subject areas can also be displayed to spotlight their efforts.

One example of an opportunity to display **student work** is a Writer's Corner: a corner, wall, or bulletin board dedicated to the sole purpose of "publishing" student writing. A classroom for any subject matter could benefit by designating a specific space to regularly display student work, including writing in or about that content area.

*Writings in **Kay's** classes find their way into her writing space in different ways. When she reads quality writing she thinks others would enjoy, Kay asks the student writer's permission to display the piece. If he objects or is not ready to be "published," she respects his wishes and tells him she'll ask again another time. If a student wishes to post a piece in the space, Kay asks her to be sure the writing reflects good taste and will not offend or hurt anyone's feelings. She reserves the right to remove pieces from the writer's space; she always offers the writer an explanation. Kay has seldom had to remove any work. However, she does not allow unsigned pieces. When they appear, they are removed until the writer of the piece is identified. Writer's Corner is always a popular place especially when new writing is posted. Kay occasionally posts a piece she* *has composed to see her students' reactions. It's important for students to know that teachers do more than just assign and grade writing. Teachers are writers, too.*

Teachers' physical spaces are their domains; their classroom, in effect, is their "office." They share these domains with students. Occasionally, a teacher must share her room with other teachers and students. When these situations arise, teachers should talk to their colleague about the room. Just as knowing your expectations is important for your students, it's important that anyone who shares your space knows your expectations. Share classroom rules pertinent to the physical space with him and ask that he hold his students accountable for adhering to those rules. Find space for him to keep needed materials and offer to share equipment. Clarify with the visiting teacher what aspects of the room (your desk, filing cabinet, etc.) are off-limits. If you do not want the teacher and his students to use supplies from your desk or other storage spaces, make that clear and preferably keep them out of sight. Ask if he and his students rearrange the room, they put it back as they found it. Through these means, everyone using the classroom profits.

Space surrounding the teacher's desk and tables is professional/personal space which we feel teachers should ask students to respect. If students wish to use something from this space, we require them to practice common courtesy by asking permission. We recommend generosity with supplies, equipment, personal books, and other items, but we also think students should be required to follow the rules. When they don't, we ask them how they would react if someone looked into their backpacks or helped themselves to something from their lockers without their permission; they quickly understand.

Creating a physical space takes time. Radically changing it takes planning. However, how a teacher handles the physical space in her classroom can say a great deal about what is going on there. When it's a pleasant, interesting, organized place to work and learn, both teachers and students benefit.

TIME MANAGEMENT FOR TEACHERS

Perhaps the greatest challenge for teachers is finding time to do everything that effective teaching requires. Increasingly, teachers are held accountable for preparing students for state assessments in addition to their already-full instructional task list. Beyond actual instruction, teachers wrestle with the ongoing need to grade assignments, quizzes and tests;

keep accurate attendance and grade records; design and produce quality assignments, quizzes and tests; and keep parents and administrators informed of individual needs and performance. The list goes on and on.

Instructionally, skills once thought the responsibility primarily of English teachers (reading, writing, speaking, listening, viewing) have become a shared responsibility across content areas. For example, the necessity for and value of developing critical and analytical reading skills has spread across subject areas. Once the majority of writing instruction occurred in English classes, but more recently teachers of all subjects have recognized the value of writing across the curriculum. Teachers in multiple content areas who now process writing assignments know the time that entails.

This demanding state of affairs makes organization vital. Teachers adept at time management who employ conscious strategies to help them balance the work load will not only rise to the numerous demands placed on them, but will also find their teaching lives less stressful and more fulfilling.

Seating Charts

As previously discussed, one helpful organizational structure is the use of ***seating charts.*** These can be determined alphabetically; on a first come, first served basis; or using numerous other systems. Yet, once seats are determined, it is useful for students to understand they are to sit in their seats consistently. Although students can certainly make requests for seating changes, we feel that it is important for the teacher alone to retain the right to make final decisions about who sits where. This simple structure makes various daily activities a teacher faces much more efficient. (*Read more about seating charts in the sections of this book titled "Organization" and "From the First Day."*)

Information Card

Requiring students to complete an *information card* on the first day of class or any time a new student enters a class will prove useful and timesaving throughout the school year. These cards will provide teachers with necessary information at their fingertips when they need to contact parents, send deficiency notices, etc. Furthermore, these cards can easily be turned into a convenient database making the information even easier to access. Increasingly, classrooms are equipped with computers that provide teachers with a database that readily provides certain kinds of information.

If that is your situation, review what information you can access from your computer. You may still want to solicit additional data that will prove useful throughout the school year. (*Read more about information cards in the section of this book titled "From the First Day."*)

Student Aides

If a school allows students to work as *teacher aides*, take advantage of this opportunity. A well-trained aide can save teachers from having to spend valuable time in repetitive, mechanical tasks such as alphabetizing, addressing envelopes, filing, putting up bulletin boards, maybe even word processing and copying. Before allowing teacher aides to do any tasks that involve student work such as averaging grades or grading papers, consider the possible ramifications. Privacy issues need to be kept in mind. Teachers will also need to assess an aide's accuracy and consistency before assigning certain tasks. It is helpful to train aides in your procedures, so that eventually they will be able to implement them without extensive instructions each time they approach a task. (Read more about Student Aides in the section of this book titled "Teacher Behaviors That Impact Classroom Management.")

Record Keeping

Although some teachers consider it tedious, precise and accurate *record keeping* is essential. Accurate record keeping will endear a teacher to administrators, serve as valuable documentation, and help absolve a teacher of liability in the unlikely event of a catastrophe. A former student teacher, who took a teaching job in another state, related the following in a letter to **Patti:**

> *"One of my eleventh grade boys was killed in early January, while cutting my class. He was with a group two blocks from school. A few days later, the local police subpoenaed all of my records including grade book, attendance forms, writing portfolio, etc. and requested a signed detailed deposition from me about the young man and his friends. Another reason to follow attendance rules and paperwork, eh? Boy, was I glad that I am so particular about such matters. You always taught me to document everything in my little notebook! Thank goodness I had turned him in for cutting that day and many more. All of this is being used in a trial, but there's more. The FBI subpoenaed records from me too."*

Most teachers are not likely to encounter such severe situations, but even in less extreme circumstances, teachers will be well served if they can provide carefully maintained records. We have developed a few practices that we faithfully follow thereby minimizing the time we spend record keeping, yet ensuring our records are accurate and complete. We provide those practices as classroom-tested tips:

- **Mark attendance and turn it in regularly**. Word will spread and students will refrain from cutting your class, since they know detection is likely. Check classroom attendance against school records even when there has been a substitute. If you check a sub's records and discover someone has cut, you'll be surprised at the reaction when it is turned in after the fact. Patti overheard one of her students who got caught this way remark to his classmates, "She even knows what we're doing when she's not here!"
- **Don't call roll out loud**. This takes away from valuable instructional time. In addition, it creates time for students to become distracted from the learning focus. Instead, mark attendance while students are working on an assignment or reading. For example, a teacher could do this while students are writing in learning logs or engaging in a warm-up activity. Using a seating chart makes this a quick task. Of course, it will probably be necessary to call roll out loud on the first, maybe even the second, day of class.
- **Establish a procedure for students to follow when securing signatures on absence slips, permission forms, admit slips, etc**. For instance, Patti only signs such items when taking roll. In order to have them when she is ready, she teaches students to give them to her as they enter class. If a student doesn't give one to her, she requires that student to return at a later time (after class, at lunch, after school, the next day). She doesn't allow students to interrupt another class's instruction to secure a signature that should have been remembered during their own class periods. She also does not sign field trip permission forms at the last minute on the day of the event. These procedures provide students with opportunities to develop their responsibility.
- **Designate a desk or filing cabinet drawer for management**. Among other management materials, keep a folder for each class period. Drop all absence notes, tardy slips, admit slips, copies of notes to or from parents, and anything else pertaining

to each period in its folder. There is no need to organize the contents of this folder. Spend time looking for a specific item only if the need arises. This method provides documentation without spending time recording information.

- **Document all parent contacts**. This can be as easy as recording the date of the contact in the grade book along with a symbol to indicate if it was a phone call, progress report, letter, or conference. Alternatively, save room on the back of the information card students provide early in the school year (see previous) to make note of parent contacts. This information can be updated as needed and remains with the information card for easy access when communicating with parents. Another strategy is to maintain a "Parent Contact Notebook" where you log each contact.

Although some of these practices may seem stringent, the teacher's consistency and a little student training will make all parties accustomed to the efficiency such procedures provide. Simple policies such as these help teachers ensure that essential housekeeping chores and record keeping tasks occur with minimal disruption to instruction. Furthermore, such procedures enable each student to receive the consideration she needs without distracting from the learning activity of others.

Checklists

Don't overlook the value of simple checklists. The process of creating and using checklists, basic as it seems, has become standard procedure in many professions. For example, the use of checklists in the medical profession is credited with reducing mistakes thereby leading to decreased infection rates.. Pilots utilize checklists to make flying safer for themselves and their passengers. Teachers will find multiple benefits in incorporating this practical exercise into their standard routine.

If, as a homeroom teacher, you have a series of tasks on the first day of school, you can be sure to cover everything by creating a checklist for yourself. Use a checklist to help you remember everything you wish to tell parents at open house or in a conference rather than depending on your memory in these potentially stressful situations. Planning extra curricular activities such as field trips, hosting multi-school events, or organizing programs like induction ceremonies becomes less onerous when using a checklist to ensure no details are forgotten.

Teachers have much more to do than there are hours in the day. By constructing checklists, they can make numerous tasks more efficient and reduce the possibility of overlooking important aspects of or steps in their process. Once created, checklists can often function as templates for tasks that are repeated. They can also be saved from one year to the next making future planning less burdensome. Checklists cannot only help a teacher maximize her efficiency, but they can also contribute to decreasing the stress of a typical school day. You can find model checklists for field trip planning and substitute preparation in the Appendix.

Managing Student Papers

Middle and high school teachers see numerous students every day. Although elementary teachers see fewer students, they are responsible for teaching multiple subjects thus often generating multiple papers per student. When teachers collect homework, quizzes, tests and assignments, they can find themselves sorting through stacks of student work on a regular basis. There is only one teacher, but many students and often a tremendous amount of student work to process. Not only is this task a challenge, but it can also consume a teacher's valuable, yet limited, time. Furthermore, dealing with so much student paperwork can run the risk of misplacing an individual student's paper from time to time.

Each teacher will have to devise his own method for dealing with the volume of student papers that teachers must process. Patti has developed a system for handling student papers that helps her manage her numerous stacks of student work as well as results in few claims of lost papers. The cornerstone of her routine is consistency. She has taught students to use practices that complement her routine, and she disciplines herself to regularly adhere to her system. This attention to regularity not only assures that she rarely misplaces student papers, but also makes her task of dealing with numerous student papers on a daily basis less frustrating.

> *Sometimes I collect student papers at the beginning or end of the period; other times I have students place them in a designated "finished" stack as they complete their work. Whatever method I use, all of the student papers from one class that were handed in on time stay together –an important component of my procedure. I immediately clip them together and place them in my "To Grade" folder where they stay until I am ready to deal with them.*
>
> *The top paper indicates the class period and assignment from the information I have taught students to include in their headings. I deal with only one set of papers at a time. I won't get out another set until I have either finished with the set with which I am working or re-clipped the papers together and returned them to their*

appropriate folder. Once a set of papers has been graded, I put it in my "Record" folder. When they are recorded and ready to return, I put them in a tray that I keep for their class's "ready to return" work.

As students hand in a late or make-up assignment, I use a colored marker to label the paper "Late" or "Make-up" along with the date I received it and promptly place it in my "Late" or "Make-up" folder. Late and make-up work follows the same procedure as on-time work, but does not get graded until the on-time work has been marked. Students who hand in work later than the rest of the class may have to wait to receive their graded work - another one of those natural consequences.

Lost Student Papers

It won't take long for a student to announce, "You lost my paper!" This is always a touchy situation. Sometimes students will use this ploy to "cover" for an assignment they didn't hand in, but be very cautious about making that accusation. When teachers are consistently organized about how they handle students' papers, they can manage these situations with confidence. Despite a teacher's organizational efficiency, sometimes a paper sticks to the back of another one or gets mixed up with another period's work. If that is the case, the problem is easily resolved; unfortunately, it's not always that simple.

Early during one school year, ***Kay*** *had a student who was very upset when papers were returned and hers appeared to be missing. The student swore she had turned her paper in with everyone else's. Kay allowed her a sufficient amount of time to redo her work, the only fair option in a situation such as this. She apologized to the student and spent much time searching for the missing paper. The next time papers were returned, a similar occurrence took place. The same student's paper was supposedly missing. Kay immediately became suspicious and asked the student how this could have happened again. The student was given time again to resubmit her work. From this time on, Kay began to take the few minutes necessary after collecting class papers to check each student's name against the names in her grade book or to count papers to be certain all students had submitted work on time. When the student was informed immediately that her paper was not in the stack, there was a swift end to the mysteriously vanishing papers. She had no excuse to offer. A few minutes work* *solved the dilemma of the missing papers. Instant attention at that moment in this case worked wonders.*

In the rare instance, when a student claims that **Patti** has lost her paper, she has a fairly set procedure for addressing the student's concern.

The first thing I do is ask the student to go through all of her papers and tell her I will do the same. This often results in the student locating the "missing" paper. I faithfully go through all of my student papers to be certain that I have not somehow misplaced the paper. If possible, I do so in the presence of my students, so they can observe my commitment to resolving the issue as well as my systematic approach to handling their papers.

If the paper is not located, I chat with the student. My comments go something like this, "I work very hard at staying organized so that I won't lose anyone's paper. If you handed in your paper when the rest of the class did, I can't imagine how it could have gotten separated from the others." If the assignment in question is a late or a make-up assignment, I add, "Papers handed in separately from the rest of the class run a much greater risk of getting misplaced or lost because they are not with the rest of your classmate's papers."

While explaining this, a student who is trying to "pull a fast one" will usually drop the issue somewhere along the line. If she doesn't, I use my best professional judgment to determine if I think she is legitimate or not. I frequently offer an opportunity to compensate for the assignment with another, yet different, assignment. Often the prospect of doing another assignment will cause the missing paper to suddenly appear.

It is in these situations that a teacher's organization and consistency pay off. A conscientious teacher will not need to mediate the lost paper claim very often. If it does arise, it is helpful when the full class has observed her particular attention to handling their papers day after day. In fact, sometimes a classmate will clue the teacher in if a student is trying to evade her responsibilities. The teacher's manner and attitude in addressing a student's claim are also critical to a positive outcome. When a teacher becomes defensive, critical of the student, or resentful about the student's assertion, the possibility of a productive resolution is considerably reduced. We've always found that it's best to operate as though every claim is legitimate and exercise exceeding courtesy in working through the issue.

Consistently using a systematic method for handling student papers:

- Helps a teacher economize the amount of time spent in shuffling student papers.
- Demonstrates the teacher's organization to students.
- Diminishes the possibility that a student paper will get lost.
- Gives the teacher confidence when a student accuses her of losing a paper.
- Makes it possible for the teacher to retrace the path an individual student's paper will have taken once handed in.

Organizational Strategies

Detailed organizational procedures not only enhance student learning but also help relieve teacher stress. We have discovered various ***classroom organizational tools and techniques*** that contribute to efficient functioning. We provide these as suggestions.

- Sets of stacking ***trays*** can facilitate organizational strategy. Use one set, with a tray labeled for each class period, for active items. Keep things that need to be given to individual students such as make-up quizzes and tests, make-up assignments, and work needing completion in these trays. Use the other set, also labeled by class period, for graded work that is ready to return to students. Only the teacher should have access to these trays.
- Designate a specific section in the classroom, perhaps on the ***chalkboard,*** for upcoming quiz and test dates as well as due dates and other deadlines that students need to remember. Posting this information places responsibility on students for keeping informed.
- Consistency in ***heading papers*** with necessary information speeds organizing and grading. As teachers know, every minute counts and lost seconds add up to lost hours. Establish a consistent format for all papers and hold students to it. Patti's format requires student name, date of paper origin, and class period in the upper right corner as well as an identifying title on the top line. She keeps this format on the chalkboard as a reminder. Such consistency will enable a teacher to "plow" through papers more quickly and efficiently as well as facilitate identifying late or make-up papers. This leaves more time for instructional focus.
- Thoughtful ***assignment formatting*** can facilitate grading therefore making it less time-consuming. For instance, using a format that clearly numbers each item individually will make it

obvious at a glance, if a student has responded to all items, and if not, which are unanswered. Direct students to use headings and subheadings and to underline key elements when writing assignments on their own paper. All of these seemingly minor techniques will facilitate working through what seems like a ton of student papers.

- A teacher can minimize the time spent in mechanical activities such as copying, collating, and stapling by reusing ***handouts***. Patti produces sets of fifty numbered copies and requires students to write on their own paper. When they finish an assignment, she collects the handouts and her aide organizes them numerically. This procedure prevents papers and tests from "traveling," as well as conserves her time in the future. Consequently, she is no longer at the mercy of a malfunctioning copy machine or a paper shortage, and contributes to the preservation of several trees.
- Create ***templates*** for forms that are used repeatedly. These may include such items as learning log grade sheets, grade review sheets, writing rubrics, reading logs, or project progress reports. Each time one is used, fill in the pertinent titles, dates, and specifications. Keep them on a computer and print them out as needed or photocopy the templates. Both of us remember the days of ditto machines complete with purple ink on our faces in the grocery after school. Computer word processing and plain paper copiers have made life so much easier for teachers!
- When ***constructing quizzes and tests***, develop multiple forms as you go. For example, when writing true/false items, write a converse variation of each item to use on an alternate version of a quiz or test. This procedure is much easier with computers. After making multiple forms of the same test, teachers can truly appreciate the value of numbering tests, requiring students to write answers on their own paper, and making sure that all tests are returned so that they can be reused. Furthermore, be good to yourself by developing formats that are quick and easy to grade. For instance, if using fill-in-the-blank items, require students to write the answer *only* next to the number of the test item on their answer paper.
- We recognize the value of **essay** and **on-demand questions** that require students to use written expression to demonstrate understanding of concepts. Although taking more time to grade, this kind of testing requires students to use thinking

skills that are not exercised with objective tests. Teachers can employ strategies that help to streamline the grading of such test items.

- Add two or three such questions to an otherwise objective test.
- Offer three or four questions from which students can choose one or two.
- Construct test questions that clearly delineate the required components expected in an effective response. For example, teachers could direct students to "state a position and give three pieces of supporting evidence." In this way, teachers can readily determine when the requirements have been met.
- Require students to highlight, underline or number evidence of their understanding of a concept or principle in their written response.

- Textbook publishers routinely provide **test generators** that accompany their texts. Often these test generators provide a function that easily creates multiple versions of a test. Explore this possibility with the text used in your classes.
- Consider using ***commercial tests*** or parts of them. Just be sure to have taught *everything* that is included on the part that is used. Another time-saver is ***electronic grading machines*** that utilize standardized answer forms. With some imagination, you can adapt those answer forms to more than the obvious true/false and multiple-choice formats. Have students answer objective sections of tests on an electronic grading form and write responses to open response and essay items on separate paper. Once both parts are graded, an aide can collate them so the teacher can calculate each student's final test grade.
- ***Returning graded papers*** can consume valuable instructional time. Patti minimizes this loss by letting her aides arrange each set of graded papers by seating groups (rows/tables/clusters.) When returning papers, she hands each seating group's (row/table/cluster) papers to one person who takes hers and passes the papers on; each student extracts his from the stack. When a student is absent, his papers are collected by his seating mates, clipped together and held by the teacher for his return. Students are willing to help out an absent classmate knowing the favor could likely be returned one day. This assistance provides an opportunity for students to exercise cooperation and good will.

- Read about timesaving strategies for managing daily assignments and grading papers in the "Grades and Grading" section of this book.

Our best advice: continually seek ways to streamline all of the work that you, as a dedicated teacher, must do. Some of your paper load can be minimized with clever strategies. Think smart. Don't merely proceed with your first impulse or the way you have always seen things done. Take advantage of consistency, routines and systems to maximize your efficiency. Make student accountability work to your advantage. All of our suggestions have come from actively seeking methods to make our functioning most efficient. This effort has not only lowered our stress level, but has also allowed us to do more for our students.

FROM THE FIRST DAY AND BEYOND

First impressions are powerful. From the first day, teachers begin to establish their classroom atmosphere and expectations. The impressions teachers make on the first day and during the first week of school produce long-range effects that can help or hinder them throughout the rest of the school year. Teachers *determine* whether their first impression of students becomes their ally or a deterrent to their goals. Consequently, we urge teachers not to leave their first impressions to happenstance.

The first impression for which we strive is marked by demeanor that is businesslike, organized and definite, yet pleasant. And, yes, it is quite possible to convey an organized and businesslike impression, yet remain pleasant. We remember as beginning teachers hearing the adage, "Don't smile until Thanksgiving." Our classroom organization, management, and framework accomplish for us what not smiling apparently seemed to accomplish for others before us.

Teachers' manner and behavior from the first day establish a tone that can and probably will endure in their classrooms throughout the year. If a teacher's first impression projects an atmosphere that is haphazard, disorganized, and uncommitted to learning, that impression can persist causing students to approach the class with a similar haphazard, disorganized, and uncommitted attitude. Students often mirror the teacher's manner and behavior. Consequently, teachers' prospects for inspiring and influencing conscientious student performance are enhanced if teachers model the behaviors they want to see in students, consistently from the first day. *Without consistency, teachers unconsciously shift classroom climate from day to day keeping students on their guard which inhibits a constructive learning environment.*

The attitude we want students to assume from the outset is that our classrooms are all about learning; therefore, we start teaching the very first day. The practice of seating everyone, taking roll and then postponing instruction or giving busy work by using excuses such as, "This is only the first day." or "There will be schedule changes to come." conveys a message that learning is not important. We want just the opposite to be impressed upon our students.

Consider the desired impression and allow time to plan for it. If teachers lack the luxury of time because they were hired at the last minute or they are stepping in to assume a long-term substitute assignment, we recommend conveying an impression that the classroom is businesslike and organized. Experienced teachers recognize that they can often "loosen up" in terms of management; but it's very hard, if not impossible, to "tighten up" classroom management after the fact.

Case in point: Of **Patti's** many student teachers, she remembers one who learned this lesson the hard way:

From the outset she questioned my classroom framework with its specific policies and procedures to which I held students accountable. Despite numerous discussions, she insisted that she "didn't want to stifle the students."

When it became her time to teach, she was casual and informal. It wasn't long before students started to take advantage of this classroom demeanor. There were claims that she had lost their assignments, not told them about a requirement, or that they had been summoned by someone requiring them to leave the classroom. She didn't have a system in place to quell such distractions from learning, thus she became quickly overwhelmed.

One particularly bright, but troubled, student openly rebelled driving my student teacher to tears. I've wondered if this student was reflecting her discomfort with the lack of security that structure would have provided. Needless to say, my student teacher had a very real-world introduction to the realities of teaching.

Later she was hired at a local high school, and I have heard that her students chafe under her tight rein. In an overreaction to her introductory experience, she apparently went to the opposite extreme in her management approach.

There is a happy medium, but it's not totally accomplished the first day, first week, or even sometimes the first grading period. In our experience, different classes take varying amounts of time to arrive at the point where we can "loosen up." We know we can "loosen the reins" when our students demonstrate they can and will observe school and classroom policies and procedures without continual monitoring and intervention. With some classes this occurs within two weeks, others may take until Thanksgiving. Consider teachers' energy and efforts those first few weeks an investment in the balance of the year. Once classes can function somewhat independently, teachers will expend less energy and effort on management and can focus more on instruction.

How do teachers achieve student independence in adhering to classroom policies and procedures?

Procedural Orientation

Management consultant Dr. Harry Wong states, "Effective teachers introduce rules, procedures, and routines on the very first day of school and continue to teach them the first week of school . . . The number one problem in the classroom is not discipline; it is the lack of procedures and routines." *The First Days of School*, Wong, 1998, P. 141, 167

We wholeheartedly agree. Here are some suggestions for consideration when planning an opening day. Teachers will want to work out plan details according to their individual styles.

Seat students according to a **seating chart**, which you might consider preparing in advance from class lists. Seating charts provide numerous advantages, especially when a teacher is facing a group of unfamiliar students. One of those values is the message they convey to students from the initial class meeting: this teacher is organized and has clear expectations. Seating charts also make it possible to more efficiently manage the opening of school housekeeping chores that are typically required. *Refer to the section of this book on "Organization" for more about seating charts.*

As we have mentioned before, consider asking students to complete an **information card** both legibly and completely. This will include basic information of legal name, name they prefer to be called, mailing address *including zip code*, and home phone. The primary function of such cards is to be able to easily make parent contacts and to provide a place to document those contacts. Teachers may want to add elements such as both parents' full names and indicate with whom the student lives, parents' place of employment and the work phone number(s).

Gathering a bit of personal information on these cards helps teachers know students better. Ask students to list any information they would like teachers to know. Give them some examples: shyness, hearing or vision needs, other pertinent medical concerns. Assure students the information they offer is for the teacher only. *Read more about information cards in the "Time Management" section of this book.*

Present **classroom rules**; consider helping students understand the need for them and their value. Arbitrary rules may not work effectively. Students may be more receptive and responsive to teachers' rules, if they understand the rationale. *See the section "Groundwork and Guidelines" for more details about rules and the rationale for them.*

Once basic classroom rules have been established, the next orientation step is helping students begin to learn the classroom's **routines and procedures**. It's not generally effective to tell students once and then expect them to follow all of your procedures flawlessly from then on. Ideally teachers want students to not only understand the routines and procedures but to observe them on a day-to-day basis. We think an effective way to achieve this is to approach teaching your routines and procedures as you would any lesson. Furthermore, support students in their learning process by repeating, reviewing, reminding and reinforcing your routines and procedures until students become so accustomed to them that they follow them independently.

Patti *uses what she calls a* ***Class Information Sheet*** *to teach and reinforce her classroom procedures. She describes this sheet as her classroom's "procedure manual" and compares it to such manuals students may have in a job. She and students talk about procedure manuals in the military (Our school has an R.O.T.C. unit.), auto repair, computer programming, etc. to establish a rationale for this document as well as for the value of adherence to the procedures it outlines. Patti shares her "procedure manuals" (faculty handbook and writing portfolio handbook), and describes her accountability for the procedures therein.*

Her students' Class Information Sheet is detailed, since it outlines all procedures students will need to understand throughout the year - make-up tests, grade processing, assignment format, etc. Providing this information in writing gives students a reference tool and begins the shift of accountability to them. For older, college-bound students this tool provides a model of the syllabi they are likely to receive on the first day of their college classes with the expectation that they will read and adhere to it. Patti teaches these procedures during the first week of class. She encourages students to use a highlighter, margin notes, and underlining to help them sort through the information , a reading lesson in itself. A quiz over this information sheet is assigned.

Patti knows that her students will have a greater probability for success if they observe these procedures. She also knows that it becomes less likely for a student to "fall through the cracks," if the procedures are followed. Finally, she knows that her effectiveness as a teacher will be enhanced and stress level diminished, if she makes this investment.

Once students begin using the procedures, they not only become second nature but most students recognize, often from first hand experience, how various procedures benefit them. It is not unusual for a student to express something like this, "At the beginning of the year I thought you were hard (or mean or strict), but now I'm really glad that I'm in your class." Perhaps not yet conscious of it, what Patti's students are trying to express is that they feel comfortable and confident in their potential for success in her class. Creating thoughtful and effective classroom policies and procedures, helping her students learn those routines, and consistently adhering to them helps her students – regardless of ability level – maximize their potential for success as well as allows Patti to increase her instructional effectiveness.

Instructional Orientation

In addition to establishing classroom environment and expectations during the first days and weeks of the school year, we include instruction in academic needs and tasks, for which early mastery will be necessary for students' comfort, confidence and success all year long.

We present Kay's beginning-of-the-year instructional orientation strategies as a model. Patti uses many similar methods. Teachers should find an idea or two that would work for them.

Some time ago, ***Kay*** *noticed that many of her students were not proficient in some of the relatively simple tasks that teachers often assume they know – note taking procedures, oral report skills, and proper use of special features in textbooks, such as footnotes, captions, illustrations, charts, glossaries, indices, and tables of contents. Many teachers assume that when their students reach middle or high school, they are familiar with these classroom tasks. But Kay has found that students often lack confidence in these important areas. Therefore, at the beginning of each school year, she makes time to teach and explore the tasks necessary to meet the academic needs of her students.*

Many students take few, if any, **reading notes** *from their textbooks and other materials. Kay has discovered that they either have not been required to do this task or simply do not know how to do it efficiently.*

Consequently, she provides a review of note taking procedures taking care to apprise students of the fact that note taking styles can be individualized to suit the subject, the particular learning styles of the students, and the requirements of the teacher. This process can occur in any class, although it needs to be adapted to the subject text.

Students are often anxious about making ***oral presentations****. Kay offers help by modeling several styles and listing guidelines to assist students with good oral presentation techniques and skills. She assists them with strategies for dealing with the anxieties caused by speaking in front of groups. Student presentations and oral work are always improved with this brief work that troubleshoots students' needs.*

Even though students use textbooks throughout their school careers, many of them still do not make effective use of textbook "tools" to stimulate and improve learning and information gathering. As textbooks become more complex and versatile, actively teaching strategies for their effective use becomes even more important. At the beginning of the year, we find that careful overview of the textbook with students is invaluable. Many young readers overlook important parts of their textbooks, and seldom seek to use these valuable resources effectively. When we instruct students in the use of these textbook "tools," we notice marked improvement in attitudes toward reading, in reader comprehension and in a genuine interest in the text's materials. One activity that students of all ability levels enjoy and benefit from is "scavenger hunts" that provide hands-on reinforcement of textbook content and features. Often textbook publishers will provide such "scavenger hunt" tools.

Brief "seminars" in academic tasks and "tools," just like the work we do to manage our classrooms for teaching, offer students rules and guidelines for optimum learning, rewarding both students and teachers with enhanced competence, comfort, and success as well as proficiency in using materials.

Leaving the first day as well as the first week of school to chance is a decision that will impact teachers, students and their classroom experience for the balance of the school year. During the first week, teachers have the opportunity to set the tone of their classrooms and instruction that will predominate throughout the rest of their experience with that group of students. We feel the first day and weeks of school should be a teacher's most carefully planned times. Although it is unlikely that actual classroom experience will go precisely as planned, the planning will enhance the possibility that how the classroom proceeds will be positive and constructive.

VI ~ Instructional Management

LESSON PLANNING

Lesson planning is one of the most important things teachers do. In addition to facilitating the learning process, effective planning demonstrates to our students the reasons why we are assigning learning tasks. Like so much else in the constellation of teacher planning, an effectively designed and implemented lesson plan can forestall student misbehavior. On the other hand, students know when we haven't planned and can be counted on to take full advantage of that lack of preparation. Well-organized lesson plans are a vital key to teacher and student success. Without them our job would be harder, our classrooms would be disorganized and both we and our students would be unfulfilled.

Planning effective lessons requires an instructional rationale. If a teacher isn't clear about the instructional purpose of his lessons, the tasks may seem like "busy work" which students won't take seriously. Teachers might consider sharing the instructional rationale for their lessons with students.

Plan to engage students in active learning. *If the teacher is doing the bulk of the work, the teacher is the one garnering the benefit of that learning activity.* When planning, periodically step back and consider if you have a tendency to preempt learning opportunities in which your students could actively engage. For instance, a teacher who consistently lectures robs students of opportunities to discover information on their own; as well, the teacher spends considerable time preparing those lectures. Why not plan activities where students engage in research, collaborative discussion, and independent learning to uncover for themselves the information that would have been presented in a lecture? Reflect on how lecturers unearth information. Then plan similar activities to engage students with the information as well as teach them research and discovery skills. This active learning approach incorporates learning **rigor** that is frequently cited as a measure of instructional quality.

Interruptions – good, bad or ugly – can occur. Think of lesson plans as working tools that are fluid and ever evolving. When a good teachable moment arises, don't pass up the opportunity in order to strictly adhere to a lesson plan. Don't be afraid to take advantage of spontaneous teaching opportunities. **Kay's** experience is a particularly apt example of the value of keeping lesson plans fluid:

Sometimes at the beginning of a class period, I offer short enriching reading assignments such as editorials, poems, etc. while I complete housekeeping chores. One morning in my humanities class, I distributed copies of a controversial newspaper editorial about an incident at a local museum. When class began, I realized that a heated discussion had grown from the editorial and students were engaged in enthusiastic debate. Rather than stifle their enthusiasm, I entered the discussion and, before the period ended, students were planning e-mails, faxes, and letters to the editor in response to the initial editorial. The outcome of grasping this "teachable moment" led to four student editorials printed in the local newspaper over the next few days. The value and success of this serendipitous moment should be obvious. I used the original lesson plan the following day with students <u>more</u> enthusiastic about their learning.

Kay's experience illustrates responding to a good, valuable interruption of a lesson plan. Then there are the "bad" interruptions. For instance, fire drills, inclement weather, unexpected visitors, and unannounced assemblies can demolish a carefully planned lesson. Don't get upset. Because such interruptions are inevitable, do not allow them to create stress. Just remember: lesson plans are fluid and they will be there waiting. Stay flexible because one consistency among schools is unanticipated interruptions.

"Ugly" interruptions can also compromise a lesson plan. Students can become recalcitrant, resistant, and uncooperative. Effectively planning meaningful lessons and communicating instructional rationales can usually offset such behavior. Once in a great while when a class becomes particularly obstinate, we address the situation head-on and talk candidly with students about the source of their resistance. **Patti** encountered such a group of honors sophomores:

During the first few weeks of the school year, I could sense that my honors students were growing increasingly disgruntled but couldn't pinpoint the source of their frustration. One day as I was introducing the lesson, the students seemed to erupt. Clearly we needed to talk. I made a very conscious effort to depersonalize their criticisms and to communicate without being defensive.

My open attitude encouraged students to voice their grievances: the material was too difficult, grades were too low, and progress reports were to go home soon. With a little urging, students confessed they previously could avoid reading an entire book by relying on study questions and commercial notes.

Thinking quickly, I offered them apparent ways to raise their grades that were readily achievable such as literature vocabulary lists with quizzes and chapter quizzes. In return, I asked them to read complete works and engage in learning and employing active reading strategies. The point: I helped my students achieve what they were seeking and was able to secure their commitment to meaningful learning activity in return. In essence, we became partners. During the end-of-the-year awards ceremony, this class spontaneously gave me a standing ovation – a clear sign that our partnership had been successful for all of us.

Strategies for Lesson Planning

Every teacher will have a somewhat different approach to lesson planning based on his subject matter and individual preferences, but there are some key elements that we feel should be part of every teacher's lesson planning process regardless of his personal style.

- It's hard to start planning a lesson from scratch. When planning a lesson for the first time, amass all the **material** you have available on that topic. Don't overlook the resource materials that probably accompany your textbook. Ask other teachers if they have materials on the subject matter they'd be willing to share. Peruse the Internet for existing lesson plans on the topic. In particular, we recommend teaching resources from the *New York Times, Newsweek, Time, The Wall Street Journal, National Geographic* or other newspapers and magazines. These outlets and others often have resources available at many teacher conferences and conventions. We think you'll be amazed at the volume of teacher resources available online. Once you have a collection of resources, browse through the materials. More than likely, ideas will spring from that information.
- Don't feel compelled to incorporate all of the materials you unearth into your lesson. If it turns out to be an effective lesson, you'll want to replicate it in the future, which will provide opportunities to try some of the unused materials. If the lesson was less than successful, perhaps incorporating some of the unused materials in a revision of the plan will make it more effective when you try a revamped version at a later time.
- What do you want your students to learn from your lesson? It's important that you are clear about the specific **learning outcome(s)** that you desire. You also want to determine any required state or national **standards** that your lesson will address. Then outline the steps that you will guide students through that will lead them to those specific outcomes. Sketch out the learning activities you'll use to help students increase their

knowledge and make discoveries on their own. Sometimes an effective technique is to plan backwards by starting with your assessment tool and outlining your plan for how students will acquire the knowledge and skills to perform successfully.

• Next think about your students themselves. What will they already know about the subject of your lesson? Should you incorporate some initial diagnostic activities to assess their **prior knowledge**? What **background information** will they need to successfully engage in the lesson's activities? Will you simply impart that background, or will you create strategies for students to discover the background information independently?

• Once you have a **sequence** of learning activities, go to your resources and see if any of them could be useful at some point in the lesson process. Often existing materials can be adapted rather than trying to create everything from scratch. Identify the materials early in your planning process that you will need to create in order to implement your lesson. It's a good idea not to wait until you need a resource to look for it or to throw it together at the last minute. When you're a new teacher, this is a particular challenge; but if you plan conscientiously, you'll build a backlog of effective lesson plans and materials for future use.

• How will you **introduce** the lesson? A compelling "lead" is just as important in a lesson plan as it is in a magazine article, and it serves the same purpose: to hook students' interest and stimulate them to engage in the lesson. Creating activities that help students recognize the connection between the lesson and their own lives and/or the real world is always a worthwhile way to begin a lesson plan.

• Determine how you will **assess** students' mastery of the lesson. Objective test? Essay test? Scoring Guide? Rubric? Performance Assessment? Be sure to inform your students of how they will be assessed and the criteria for mastery at the beginning of your lesson. This clarification will help students determine how they want to proceed in order to prepare for success on your assessment.

There are probably as many lesson plan formats as there are teachers. Often schools mandate a particular lesson format. You'll probably try several formats until you settle in with one that's comfortable for you. We've found that in planning lessons for a mandated lesson plan format, we usually end up with two documents: the official lesson plan in the prescribed format and our working lesson plan that we often tweak, adjust, and supplement as we teach the lesson, especially for the first time.

Executing a lesson plan is not the final step. **Take time to reflect on how the lesson plan worked and make notes for future reference.**

Making this investment will save time and effort the next time around, and you'll be glad in a year that you took the time to reflect. Essentially, your lesson plans are never complete; new additions and deletions keep them lively and usable for many years. Continuously be on the lookout for new activities and strategies that can refine lesson plans. Be mindful of your evolving style as a teacher and the changing needs of students. Teachers change too.

> ***Patti*** *likes to say that her preference is to teach a particular lesson plan three times: the first time to create and test it, the second time to refine it, and the third time to get it just right. Then she says she's ready to move on to new creative challenges. Some teachers use particular lesson plans for a longer duration than Patti does, which is an effective time management strategy. Just beware of falling into the trap of using the same, old, tired lesson for years on end. The stimulation of trying new approaches, incorporating updated materials, and employing different techniques keeps you and your lessons fresh.*

A few lesson planning tips:

- Consider writing each day's learning goal on the board or projecting it with a PowerPoint slide for the beginning of each class.
- Save your plan book to use as a starting point for the following year's planning.
- Explore electronic and/or online lesson planning tools that may accompany your text.
- Prepare a personal planning book that you own in addition to your school's required book. The school's lesson plan book may have a specified format and could be collected at year's end. You may want to use your personal plan book for future reference and planning.

Thinking Skills

Now a word about the nature of instruction. We have referred to "higher order thinking skills" throughout this book. We feel strongly that it is essential to help our students, regardless of their age or academic inclination, to develop effective thinking skills. Such skills will help them in further education, with job success, and as fully participating citizens in their challenging and ever more complex communities, states, nations, and world. With that broad goal in mind, we build our lessons and assignments around learning tasks that ask students to employ concrete thinking skills. These skills can be incorporated into assignments, writing tasks, on-demand writing prompts, learning log prompts, student reflection activities, project guidelines – almost any worthwhile classroom activity. We further feel that it is our responsibility to help students understand what these processes entail and how to engage in them – not just assign students to, say, "contrast" two items.

When instruction and classroom activity center around knowledge level (e.g. "identify" or "recall") pursuits, students can quickly become bored and restless; and bored students can easily become disruptive. On the other hand, when students are cognitively engaged, they are less likely to become disinterested and troublesome. When teachers ask students to think and then guide them through processes that enable them to do so, the possibility that they will become engaged with their learning is greatly increased. And students engaged with their learning forget to misbehave. So, from a strictly management standpoint, engaging students in thinking tasks makes a teacher's life easier and students' learning more rigorous. Of course, there are numerous other, even more valuable, reasons to approach instruction in this manner.

Expecting students to participate in thoughtful learning pursuits isn't as simplistic as instructing them to "think" and expecting wondrous activity to occur. Indeed, for both students and teachers to be successful, teachers must set up learning situations that teach students *how* to perform a particular thought practice and then guide them through the related processes. When students organize, compose, construct, design, assess, predict, and use many other higher order thinking processes, it's hard for them to avoid becoming engaged with their learning. And engagement is a critical factor in student success as well as effective classroom management.

Of course, if teachers ask students to perform thinking tasks that are out of their reach, student reaction will likely be similar to that of continually asking them to perform repetitive lower level thinking activities. To be most successful, teachers must thoughtfully construct meaningful learning tasks that guide students incrementally through thinking activities enabling them, therefore, to continue to be successful.

What does this kind of instruction look like? It can be rather uncomplicated, actually. Instead of instructing students to compare two items or ideas and turning them loose, a teacher could more effectively provide students with a graphic organizer that juxtaposes the two items to be compared and provides a framework in which students can list similarities. Once similarities are identified, students can move to the next step, which might be to write a paragraph summarizing those similarities. If a teacher wants her students to analyze, she could provide them with a graphic organizer that guides them to divide the subject of their analysis into parts. Once parts are determined, then students can be led to examine each part and make notes. Finally, students can draw conclusions and write a simple analysis using the parts and their individual examinations as the basis for, say, an analysis paragraph.

It has been our experience that all students, from those that are academically struggling to the most academically advanced, can and will engage in thinking-based learning when meaningful lessons are thoughtfully constructed and insightfully taught. It has also been our experience that all students can and will engage in rigorous learning activity when it has been perceptively designed and skillfully implemented.

Over Planning

Our last bit of advice related to lesson planning is straightforward: over plan. **Kay** remembers a student intern who was practice teaching a lesson in her classroom:

I had reviewed the plan with the intern and urged her to have some "backup" for what I perceived as a sketchy plan with "no comfort zone" built in for the teacher. I urged the intern to have more material than she could use for that lesson. But when the time came to work the plan, the intern's lesson lasted twenty minutes; the students were not in a mood for discussion and they were obviously uninterested in the lesson. She was desperate to find a way to carry on for another thirty-five minutes until the end of the class, and her students immediately picked up on her problem. In this situation, the intern learned the valuable lesson of over planning. She lost control of her class, the idle students became restless, and disaster set in.

Always have more material than you could ever use or need. Even the most experienced teachers know that sometimes a lesson they expect to fill a class period ends up drawing to a close in twenty minutes. Perhaps a teacher plans for students to discuss the topic at hand for a third of the period, but they say everything they want to say in ten minutes. Or maybe some of her students, but perhaps not all, complete an activity in fifteen minutes that a teacher had planned for the class to work on for half the period. When the inevitable happens, teachers don't want students to sit idle for the balance of the period. That's a recipe for disaster. It's much more desirable to have more planned than a teacher can possibly get to and carry some of the lesson over to another day. A few of our suggestions to avert such management disruptions include:

- As teachers accumulate techniques and materials, keep an eye out for strategies and resources that can be quickly drawn upon when a lesson doesn't take as much time as expected.
- Keep a ready file with easily implemented activities close at hand in your classroom.
- When planning lessons, include activities and materials that can be held in reserve yet immediately drawn upon when a plan doesn't go quite as anticipated.
- Stock an accessible collection of activities in which students can engage without teacher intervention such as challenging word games, enrichment reading or creative writing activities.
- Maintain an ongoing classroom opportunity that can step in when a lesson culminates sooner than expected or when some students finish a lesson sooner than others. For instance, Patti's students have a book going in her classroom at all times. When any student finishes his work early, he can get his book from the classroom library and read. (Read more about this independent reading strategy in the "Reading Management" section of this book.)

The art of teaching is nowhere better applied than in creatively designing and implementing lesson plans. A lesson plan is a record of our evolving ideas and approaches for transferring learning to students. Working with lesson plans and continually changing them provide a creative outlet, which keeps the art of teaching alive. Mandated methods of planning in some districts may seem to jeopardize the art of teaching, but the clever and resourceful teacher will find a way to combine her artistry with necessary requirements. Lesson planning has kept us excited about teaching for many, many years and has prevented us from becoming bored and from boring our students.

TEXTBOOKS AND OTHER MATERIALS

Quality materials not only enhance instruction but also make teachers' lives less stressful. To expect classes to complete most texts cover-to-cover is generally unrealistic, especially if supplementary materials are included in the curriculum. Hopefully, teachers work in situations allowing them professional autonomy to choose what materials to use and what content from texts and resources to integrate into their instruction.

A *quality* text provides teachers with content, instructional strategies and materials they would seek or produce themselves, if given the time. Furthermore, *quality* texts are designed around best practices based on research and might be more current in that regard than school curricula. Significant practitioners, theorists and researchers often review better texts to make sure they're pedagogically sound. In some cases, leading names in a field actually participate in the creation of a text. Be sure to look at the contributors for your textbook(s.) If they are people you're studying in graduate classes or reading in professional journals, you may find that using your text is the best and easiest way to employ current best practices in your lessons. On the other hand, some textbooks are gimmicky and constructed to make sales rather than enhance instruction. When textbooks are adopted, be sure to scrutinize the options and look for the signs of quality.

Time is a scarce commodity for teachers. Good ideas may not be implemented from lack of time to develop them and the requisite materials for use in the classroom. Consequently, using content, instructional strategies and materials included with a quality text can help a teacher be successful. For instance, a quality literature text can provide contemporary, adolescent, and multicultural literature with which a teacher may be unfamiliar but feels is important. Good texts can help inexperienced or overtaxed teachers do a better job. For example, a teacher who has three preparations, two of which she is teaching for the first time, can be more effective and less stressed by using a text and accompanying support materials. Inexperienced teachers, especially, can benefit from using manufactured products, such as ancillary materials that accompany textbooks. By doing so, they can discover:

- what material is effective and what is not.
- what kinds of lessons and activities they want to use in their classrooms.
- that reviewing manufactured materials helps stimulate creative ideas.
- that using commercial materials, especially when planning a lesson for the first time, helps them do a better job of teaching.
- that using manufactured materials can benefit them in terms of time management.

Although master teachers or potential masters will not become solely dependent on texts or commercial resources, they recognize the value of materials other than those they generate. Effectively integrating materials from multiple sources is part of what makes them masters at their craft.

Both Kay and Patti relish designing their own teaching materials. They consider these efforts part of the art of teaching, and sharing these materials with younger teachers has given them great pleasure. But even after decades in the classroom, they find that many commercial materials offer excellent suggestions and give them additional ideas to incorporate into those lessons they have developed. They have discovered that multi-media materials and websites connected with quality textbooks are rich resources. They often find that high quality commercial materials provide them with added time to be more creative. Even toward the end of their long careers, when they thought they were beyond being impressed with textbooks and support materials, they have found themselves excited about many of the ideas in the new integrated language arts text their school adopted.

Today teachers receive multifaceted programs, not only texts. These programs have numerous support materials: resource books, technology components, videos, transparencies, audio – even web sites. Such resources can be invaluable instructional tools but require time for orientation. In fact, teachers can become overwhelmed by the abundance of support materials. Remember: you don't have to use everything or use it all at once. A reasonable approach would be to begin by becoming familiar with a new text and its teacher's edition; then focus on exploring support materials later. Even veteran teachers may be daunted when faced with breaking in a new text. For instance, they will need to make new margin notes and personal highlighting in the new teacher's edition. Some publishers offer in-service to familiarize teachers with their program components. Inquire about that possibility and take advantage of such opportunities. Publishers' consultants know the materials inside out; so why not allow their familiarity to ease your strain when faced with a brand new text and its resources? We admit from experience that several months, even a year, into using a new program we have discovered accompanying resources, sometimes incidentally, that would have been useful from the outset.

Subject areas such as science, history and technology are continually evolving. Consequently, keeping pace with new and changing ideas is essential for conscientious teachers. When adopting these texts, investigate whether or not the publisher provides annual supplements to keep pace with the times. If your particular text does not, we recommend incorporating contemporary sources such as newspapers, magazines, Websites, etc.

Teachers do not need to decide whether they will be textbook or non-textbook teachers. They can strike a balance between text, commercial materials, and teacher-developed resources - all tailored to students. Some tips for effectively utilizing texts and commercial materials in lesson planning and instruction include:

- Take advantage of a quality text by *making use of it.*
- Do not sacrifice creativity by becoming solely dependent on a text or commercial materials. Rather, allow a good text or quality materials to stimulate and support teaching creativity.
- Do not assume that good teaching is starting at the beginning of a text and laboriously working through to the end. Pick and choose what best coincides with the curriculum, standards expectations and assessment, students' needs and interests, and teacher preferences.
- Teach material in a sequence or chronology that suits curriculum and goals. This may not be the sequence in which material is presented in a text.
- Do not feel the need to use everything in a text or within the accompanying program. Be discriminating.
- Do not feel it necessary to use materials just as they are; tailor them to students' needs, state or district standards, and teaching style. Some publishers recognize the value of this customization and provide manipulatable teacher resource technology.
- Make *sure* that *everything* covered on a commercial test has been taught during instruction before using that commercial test. To assure that a commercial test reflects actual instruction, a teacher may need to eliminate some of the test items or revise her lesson plans.
- Employ real world materials in instruction: newspaper and magazine articles, brochures, pamphlets, etc.

We recommend that teachers participate in the selection of new textbooks, if possible. Inquire about the adoption cycle and procedure in your school, district, or state. Learn to judge quality material; don't assume that because something has been published, that its quality does not need to be examined closely. Scrutinize texts for current pedagogy and best practices. Learn to evaluate texts and commercial materials in terms of state/district/school standards and assessment requirements.

A mix of excellent textbooks and personal creativity helps teachers connect to their curriculum and their students' changing interests and needs. Do not be timid about using your own ideas and the materials you develop. Just because you have an excellent textbook and a rich supply of supplementary materials, do not stifle your creativity. Study your curriculum guidelines and formulate ideas to fit the needs and interests of your students.

> ***Kay*** *always tests her ideas in the classroom; and with any idea, no matter its source, she discards it if it doesn't work. When possible, she reworks the idea according to student needs. She finds that successful lessons can emerge from the restyling of an initial failed attempt. When reusing a created lesson, she updates the material. Kay has found that change makes her a more engaged teacher and keeps her classroom relevant.*

When teaching something for the first time, beginning to plan with more than a blank legal pad or computer screen makes teaching life easier and the results much better.

> ***Patti's*** *preferred method for planning a unit the first time is to assemble all of the original, commercial and borrowed material that she can locate and review it all. As she is reviewing, an organizational structure begins to formulate and she starts to get ideas about how she wants to proceed. Ultimately her units consist of a combination of her text, commercial materials customized for her classroom and materials that she creates on her own.*

In addition to commercial materials, another resource for planning is your colleagues. Don't be afraid to ask them to share and be willing to return the favor. Such reciprocity benefits everyone – the teacher, her colleagues and the students. When borrowing, observe a few common sense courtesies that will sustain a positive arrangement with colleagues:

- Be sure to return what is borrowed promptly in the condition in which it was received.

> ***Patti*** *recalls loaning her* Our Town *files to a colleague. When they were returned, the folders were in disarray and many items were in the wrong folders. I had to spend time sorting it all out. As you can imagine, I was reluctant to loan anything else to this teacher.*
>
> *Similarly, I often loan videos from my personal collection to colleagues. I have taped annotations with information such as length, date, and summary on the*

jackets or jewel cases. When a colleague returns a video without its original jacket or jewel case, it seems frivolous to make an issue out of a video container; but I certainly am reluctant to loan my videos to these offenders in the future.

- Be sure to return materials checked out from the school media center promptly. We recall tracking down filmstrip sets or videos that had been in a teacher's room for months. Spending a planning period searching does not engender collegial good will.
- Be sure to give credit to the source when using a lesson or concept that was created by or originated with someone else. This is particularly vital when using another teacher's materials. Teachers cannot expect students to refrain from plagiarizing, if we don't model good practice ourselves.
- Be sure when lending material to a fellow teacher, you remind them to update and reformat the resource to make it their own.

***Kay** recalls loaning files, project guidelines, and other resources to fellow teachers and seeing them later in the hands of students bearing her name on student handouts.*

Students would surely be more respectful of their teachers' materials and lesson ideas if the borrowing teacher would give credit for the lending teacher's original idea, but adapt the resource to make it his own.

Today the wealth of materials available to teachers is stunning. The diversity of contemporary materials helps teachers tailor instruction to more closely meet individual student needs. Technology products open a world of background and resource materials unavailable just a few years ago. It is easy to become overwhelmed; but instead, let the wealth of resources inform your planning and instruction. Keep your mind open to new classroom strategies as more sophisticated materials make previously unheard of instructional techniques accessible.

MANAGING HOMEWORK

To homework or not to homework?
That is the question.

How valuable is homework? Is it still relevant in the contemporary school environment? Has the Internet made homework less effective? Have copying and cheating on homework become widespread? Are students too busy for homework to be a meaningful learning tool? Are families feeling the pressure of homework that interferes with family time? These are all questions for teachers to address when making decisions about homework policies. We recommend keeping some guidelines in mind when planning homework:

- Do not give homework for the sake of giving homework.
- Have a rationale for homework assignments and share it with students.
- Design purposeful homework assignments; avoid busywork.
- Apportion lengthy assignments over a number of days.
- Do not use homework as punishment (e.g. "If you do not behave, I'll give the class six pages of homework.")
- Consider student access or lack thereof to resources (workspace, lighting, distractions, computer, etc.) when planning homework assignments.
- Have realistic expectations of students and their capacity for completing homework. For instance, many older students hold jobs that make completion of extensive homework difficult. Others may extensively engage in valuable, yet time-consuming, extra curricular activities such as performing with the local ballet company, practicing with the school band, rehearsing with the drama department, or playing on the basketball team.
- Anticipate the potential for plagiarism the Internet presents. Plan homework activities that require original student input.
- Be aware that students may copy each other's homework. Furthermore, keep in mind that technology makes "sharing" even more tempting.

Many schools have clearly articulated homework policies that outline acceptable types of homework, quantity, and/or assessment requirements. Sometimes such policies are determined by the district office, local school administrators, school management committees or by content departments. If your personal homework philosophy does not agree with a mandated policy, seek opportunities to share your concerns and provide suggestions for policy revision. For instance, if a mandated policy does not include a provision prohibiting homework as punishment, initiating discussion could ultimately lead to the addition of such a provision. In the meantime, adhere to policy, even if you are not in agreement with it or some aspect of it.

Teachers have many options when assigning homework tasks. Using variety in types of homework assignments avoids monotony, discourages copying, and reinforces the connection between homework and instruction. Some options available to teachers include:

- Practicing skills
- Completing assignments not finished in class
- Preparing for tests
- Reading
- Preparing for new study: launching an upcoming assignment, prereading, or prewriting
- Researching
- Continuing an ongoing project
- Providing enrichment or extensions of study

Various groups involved in the educational process have perceptions about the nature of homework. Parents, administrators, students, and teachers all have a vested interest in homework decisions. The teacher's job is to keep homework effective as a classroom instructional tool. Furthermore, teachers must consider expectations of various stakeholders, then develop homework policies, procedures, and assignments that will accommodate those expectations as well as meet instructional goals. Parents' expectations about the nature of homework may not coincide with a teacher's. For example, parents may not consider reading assignments that do not produce a written product to be homework. Informing parents of your homework policy, the types of work you may assign and any significant changes in homework quantity (e.g. a six weeks' independent reading project or a research paper) may forestall conflicts.

How much homework is too much? How much is too little to be meaningful? Perceptions may vary. Some considerations when determining homework quantity include:

- District or school homework policy
- Student age
- Student achievement
- Student motivation
- Conditions such as attention deficit disorder (ADD, ADHD), learning disabilities (LD), obsessive compulsive disorder (OCD), physical limitations such as vision impairment or reduced mobility
- After-school employment

- Consistent, structured after-school activities (e.g. orchestra rehearsal, soccer, debate practice)
- At-home responsibilities such as babysitting

Be realistic about the demands you place on students for homework. Unrealistic homework expectations cannot be relied upon to further instructional objectives and generally lead to frustration for all parties. We don't feel obligated to assign homework every night, on weekends or over holidays. Keep in mind how *you* feel about grading papers and planning lessons at home and be informed by this attitude as you determine appropriate quantities of homework. Piling on a heap of homework doesn't necessarily correlate with extensive learning. Sometimes less is more.

Be prepared for homework policy breakdown. We both have experienced situations when most of a class has not completed homework, when a class balks at a homework assignment, or when individual students consistently refuse to do homework or persistently submit it late. Professional judgment that balances the need for consistency with reasonable flexibility may be the most productive approach. Examine the circumstances of the breakdown and make a judgment call that reasonably addresses the difficulty.

> For instance, two-thirds of a class does not hand in a homework assignment. A teacher could give a zero to each of the students who did not hand in the assignment and move on. Or a teacher could discover, for example, that a fellow student had been injured in an auto accident the night before and students were distracted from their homework. Under those circumstances, a flexible teacher could give bonus points to those who handed the assignment in on time and give a one-day extension with no bonus opportunity for those who did not. Various situations will arise when the teacher will have to make individual judgments realistically, yet fairly.

What does a teacher do when the majority of a class consistently refuses to complete homework? That's when it's time for the teacher to examine her homework policy. **Patti** experienced this situation after transferring to a new school.

> *Before school began, I asked teachers how student performance compared to that of those I had been teaching at another district school. They indicated it would probably be somewhat better. Yet by the end of the first six-week grading period, students in some of my classes were going to receive*

> *failing grades. Analysis of the situation revealed that failure to hand in homework was one recurring factor in students' poor performance. I further analyzed my observations and insights gained about the students during the weeks we had been together: many came from economically struggling homes, worked numerous hours at part time jobs during the school week, and were academically unmotivated.*
>
> *It became clear that my homework expectations were not consistent with students' academic ambitions and habits. Consequently, I proposed a bargain: I would provide class time for working on assignments and students' only homework would be completion of assignments not finished during class. In return, I expected them to arrive for class prepared with required materials and engage in fifty solid minutes of quality effort each day. If they did so, I agreed not to make homework assignments. Students' attitude, behavior and performance as well as their grades improved significantly.*

Just as in lesson planning, when homework doesn't succeed, don't panic. Remember that it is a learning tool you may have to fine tune from time to time and from class to class.

How on earth do teachers deal with all of those homework papers?! A new middle or high school teacher may think, "If I assign homework in every class, every day of the school week, I could have 750 papers to grade each week on top of everything else I must do! What do I do?!" Review the various types of homework a teacher might assign. Not all lend themselves to strict item-by-item assessment.

- For instance, if students are working on an ongoing project outside the classroom, a teacher may ask them to produce a weekly progress report. The value of this report is in the information the teacher gains about students' progress and in helping keep students on task. Therefore, credit for the report could be given, but each item need not be "graded." Credit could be given as a recorded check mark to indicate satisfactory completion of the requirement, a certain number of points for a satisfactory report, or credit toward the final grade on the completed project.
- When students have practiced skills for homework, value is not in individual answers but in the act of practicing the skill. Consequently, teachers could spot check for skill mastery and give credit for assignment completion as they scan students'

papers. In addition, the exercise could be used for class review and discussion of some items.
- Extra credit could be offered for enrichment and extension activities, which by nature usually do not require intensive checking of individual items.

In summary, strategies that can aid **homework assessment** include:

- Clarify and communicate a rationale for every homework activity before assigning it.
- Keep assessment in mind when designing homework activities.
- Vary the type of homework activities, and therefore, the method of assessment.

The local district or school may prescribe the percentage that homework will represent in students' final grades. If not, teachers have the discretion to make that determination. We believe homework should be an opportunity for students to improve their skills and for teachers to monitor individual growth and mastery. From our experience, we recommend that teachers do not make homework such a large percentage of the final grade that failure to complete it could, by itself, result in student failure.

Teachers can contribute to student homework success. Do not assume students know how to do and use homework effectively and meaningfully. Time spent instructing a class about homework strategies is time well spent. Teachers hear the excuse, "I didn't understand" when students do not complete homework; take that as a signal - instruction in homework skills may be needed. Study skills such as focusing on one section of an assignment at a time, reading footnotes and captions as well as text, and following directions explicitly are just a few of the subtle, yet powerful, skills students may not employ. Taking class time to teach such homework strategies will reward both student and teacher. We provide a few suggestions to prepare students for homework before they leave the classroom:

- Incorporate time for homework preparation into lesson plans.
- Allow time before the end of class to clarify homework assignment directions.
- Build in class time for students to ask questions about the upcoming homework assignment so they know how to approach it.
- Teach students to read all parts of a homework assignment to make sure they understand how to do each part.

Homework doesn't have to be drudgery. In fact, homework can be a valuable component in the teaching and learning process. The key to keeping homework viable is teacher planning and implementation. We view homework as a significant component in lesson design and give it the same quality of consideration given to classroom activities in our lesson planning.

MANAGING GROUPS & GROUPING

Some teachers say they don't like grouping because students waste time, don't stay on task and tend to socialize. On the contrary, with planning and structure student group activity can be highly productive and motivational. The ability to work effectively in groups is valued, if not required, in the contemporary workplace. Today's employers expect students to arrive with collaborative proficiency already mastered. Essential skills that students develop from group activity include the ability to share, cooperate, negotiate, delegate, manage, mediate, and prioritize. In addition, students learn social dynamics firsthand from collaborative endeavors.

Beyond these important values, classroom group activity offers an array of instructional benefits. Reticent students may feel more comfortable sharing in a small group. Students reluctant to pursue an assignment may feel more confident about the challenge, if they are working with a partner or in a group. In a small group students have the opportunity to observe one another's study skills, thought processes, organizational techniques, and other learning strategies. Besides, students generally like to work with partners or in groups.

As with so much else in classroom management, a teacher's rationale for grouping influences the style and format of classroom groups. Reading or writing work, discussion, or project groups could be formulated and implemented differently based on their purpose. A range of outcomes can be achieved with various kinds of grouping. For instance, when students are grouped to work on an assignment, the format of the group may be different than when students are grouped for discussion. Furthermore, different kinds of assignments may necessitate different kinds of grouping. Finally, long-term group projects or performance activities may require yet another type of grouping.

- One of the simplest ways to group students is to permit them to work with a partner during class on an assignment. Among numerous advantages, **pairing** encourages students when they might be intimidated by an assignment. Instructing students they will have to work alone if they deviate from their task is usually sufficient motivation for them to stay focused. Pairs might be effective when students are overwhelmed by larger groupings and could even be used as a transition to differently-sized groups. Pairing might also be used successfully for peer reviewing and peer editing, although both activities can be accomplished in larger groups as well.

- **Informal grouping**, which is spontaneous and loosely-structured, works well for tasks that need quick action. Activities such as prioritizing ideas before beginning a writing task, sharing points of view, identifying issues, and brainstorming lend themselves to informal grouping. With this type of grouping, for example, a journalism teacher might give simple instructions such as, "Move your desks together in groups of three or four and spend a few moments brainstorming possible alternative leads for this editorial." Reporting in such informal groups may be oral. *Not all students will profit from this type of spontaneous endeavor; therefore a teacher should be aware of her students and exercise professional judgment by establishing time parameters before leaping into informal grouping for the first time.* Even with short, informal sessions it is important for the teacher to circulate and participate in the groups' work.
- **In-class study groups** reinforce academic confidence. Sharing information and assignment attack strategies can model valuable study skills for reluctant students. After working in study groups, students are often better prepared for tests and other tasks than by studying alone. All students can benefit from the collective efforts of group members. For instance, information that one student has recognized as important may have been overlooked by other group members. In-class study groups reinforce to individuals the value of collaborative effort. Additionally, skills developed in such study groups may carry over into post-secondary education. Students usually form these groups on the suggestion of the teacher. As with all collaborative work, both formal and informal and with in-class study groups in particular, teacher tasks include monitoring and providing feedback. A teacher's participation and interest keep students on task and allow opportunities to oversee and direct each group's work and anticipate problems students might later encounter.

- Although teacher-structured and teacher-guided, **formal grouping** provides students with the opportunity to experience the benefits of collaboration and enhanced learning. In this mode of grouping, the teacher determines the size and composition of each group as well as defines the tasks. When the teacher determines group composition, a heterogeneous mix can be assured. Furthermore, formal grouping helps students unaccustomed to group activity to learn and apply appropriate skills. Students often stay with a formal group over a period of time for multiple activities. This practice allows for trust to develop, learning styles to become familiar, and individual accountability for group success to be instilled. Reporting is usually in a written format with clearly defined guidelines that enhance accountability.

When formal grouping is employed, anticipate the need to *train students in effective group practices*. Instructions to students might include:

- Move quickly and efficiently into the assigned group.
- Begin work promptly.
- Talk only to members of the group.
- Follow task directions closely.
- Stay focused on the topic or task.
- Designate individual roles (facilitator, recorder, etc.)
- Ensure that everyone participates and no one overly dominates.
- Alert the teacher if the group needs assistance.
- Return furniture back to its original position before leaving the classroom.

The task or assignment and its purpose will determine housekeeping issues such as:

- Whether the group will have a designated facilitator and/or recorder
- Whether each student will write and hand in a report
- Whether the group will hand in one group report

Consider how groups are formed and facilitated. The purpose for which the group is convened usually indicates how to determine group size, composition, and duration. Generally smaller groups of three to five work most effectively. When groups are larger, reticent students are often overlooked and groups may become unwieldy. *When students have little group experience, teachers might initially pair them, later increase membership to three, and eventually move students to groups of four or five.*

How can teachers tell if their groups are working effectively? Requiring regularly submitted written proposals, task assignment lists, progress reports, and work logs informs the teacher of group progress, success or breakdown. When students are informed of specific assessment criteria at the onset of group work, potential breakdowns may be avoided. In addition, specific assessment criteria will help focus groups' work. Group activities can be worthwhile and productive but they are not opportunities for teachers to take time-out. *Everyone* in a classroom must be engaged for group work to be successful.

What can be done when group breakdown seems to be occurring? For example, several students complain that not everyone in the group is participating. The teacher might offer suggestions for students themselves to troubleshoot this occurrence: evaluate and reassign individual tasks within the group, discuss individual time constraints, negotiate alternative work strategies. Giving students autonomy to solve some of their own group problems develops valuable collaborative skills and problem solving techniques. If the student-initiated attempts are unsuccessful after genuine effort, the teacher may need to intervene by sitting down with the group and confronting the problems. The teacher may offer an alternative task that proves less desirable than continuing as a group, letting the students make the final decision themselves. For instance, the prospect of completing the assigned task as individuals might be a solution. With that alternative, many students might recognize the increased individual workload and choose to find ways to operate within the original group structure thus sharing the work. If any students continue to be recalcitrant, their grades can reflect their nonparticipation without affecting the group's final grade.

Merely instructing students to get in a group and do an assignment will probably result in few positive outcomes. *Teaching students to be effective and productive group members provides the greatest possibility for positive learning outcomes.* Consider trying the following strategies:

- Have students model good and poor group participation.
- Have students role play various group scenarios and how to address them.
- Have students produce a teaching video, which illustrates effective group functioning and how to achieve it.
- Have students develop group tools and reporting instruments.

- Have students create the class rubric for particular group activities.
- Have students review posted group guidelines before they move into groups.

We both incorporate group activity as an integral component of our instruction. Not only have all students in our various classes from accelerated to challenged learners functioned effectively as group participants, but they often find group activity more appealing than working in isolation. A well-planned and effectively executed group activity can provide an optimum learning opportunity for students while helping a teacher manage his paper load. What more could you ask from an instructional strategy?

- Group activity provides valuable life lessons.
- Group activity teaches collaboration essential in the world of work.
- Group activity provides students with the opportunity to make discoveries.
- Group activity allows students to pool their knowledge and skills.
- Group activity provides support for reluctant students.
- Group activity provides modeling behavior for numerous learning processes.
- Group activity generally appeals to students.
- Group activity can lighten a teacher's load.

SHOWING & VIEWING

Technology has changed the ways we teach and students learn. It has also necessitated that classroom teachers become wizards at using and maintaining equipment of various kinds. We still remember the 16-millimeter projector and our lack of proficiency at using it. As young teachers, we could never seem to get the films correctly threaded onto the projectors. We'd send students to ask the librarian (We didn't have "media specialists" in those days.) to come and assist with the difficult task. In our earlier teaching years, most machines were hauled to a teacher's room on a one-day basis. The librarian was in charge of the equipment and films had to be ordered from the district film depository or the public library weeks ahead of when they were to be shown in the classroom. The titles, needless to say, were limited. Those were still the days of filmstrip projectors and record players – the dynamic duo of high tech in the classroom of the

1960's through the early 1980's. We also used clunky overhead projectors and a dinosaur called the opaque projector.

Today the name of the game is multimedia instruction. In most schools, CD players are readily available and easy to use; and LCD projectors are rapidly becoming classroom fixtures. The computer and the Internet are the "new stars" in the classrooms of the new century. But that's another book! Students expect the same technology at school that they access elsewhere, and woe to the teacher who isn't competent using it or doesn't make it a part of the teaching/learning experience.

When she started using videos and VCR's, ***Kay*** *wasn't completely competent. One of her most embarrassing moments in the classroom occurred when she couldn't get the VCR and the TV monitor to work. She thought she had tried everything, and became more and more flustered with each passing moment. She could feel her great lesson slowly falling apart. Finally, she relented and sent a student for the AV librarian. The librarian was a helpful person, but had little tolerance for incompetence with machines. Kay was sure there was a major problem with these machines. Only the AV librarian could save the day! When she arrived, Kay pointed to the monitor. There was desperation in her voice as she said, "I've tried everything, and it just won't work." The librarian walked to the back of the machine. As she picked up the monitor cord that needed to be plugged into the VCR cart, Kay held her breath. "Oh no," she thought. The librarian moved slowly to where Kay was standing, and quietly hissed, "Next time, remember to check that everything is properly plugged in!" That said, she exited the room, and the lesson began. Never again, did Kay fail to "plug it in." To this day, the plugs are the first things she checks.*

Operation of today's machines is relatively simple. Be sure to show one or two of your students any quirks in your equipment set-up, so they can assist you or a substitute in using equipment. However, we advise that you consider the potential difficulties when leaving electronic equipment accessible when you have a substitute.

Perhaps because of their ease of use, DVD's in the classroom, just like television sets at home, have often been used as babysitting devices. Put the kids in front of the TV, mom, and go on about your work. Put a DVD in the player, teacher, and keep students entertained in a manner with which they are familiar.

However, there's much more to the appropriate use of video in the classroom than merely shoving the DVD in the machine and turning off the lights. A video, to be considered appropriate, should impact or enrich the teacher's instructional units. Showing a video out of context more than once, can earn you the title "DVD Teacher" or your class can become "DVD 101." Students will seem pleased, but colleagues may be livid. So, what can you do to assure the appropriate use of videos in your classroom? In the long run, *you* must judge how appropriately you use this technology; but here are some guidelines that we have found helpful.

- **Choose possible videos for viewing as you plan your lessons for a unit.** Write them into your lesson plans at an appropriate place where student viewing will make the most impact on your instruction and/or your students' learning. Showing videos out of context may be evidence of a teacher's weak planning and coordination. A carefully scheduled video can provide a very effective conclusion to a unit of study, or an introduction or connection to the next phase of a curriculum module.
- **If you must rent or borrow a DVD, plan ahead for possible interference**. Any interruption during viewing can compromise your schedule and your lesson plans. Some rental stores offer special deals for teachers who are showing a particular video in the classroom. If you plan to use the same video each time you teach a specific unit, however, request your media center or Department Chair to purchase it for your classroom use.
- **Always check district and school policies concerning the use of videos, books, and classroom speakers.** Most schools provide usage guidelines in writing in teacher handbooks. Instances abound of teachers who were reprimanded or fired for using controversial materials without observing stated guidelines.
- **If a video might be considered controversial or carries a restricted rating, send a note of explanation to parents** and have them sign permission for their students to watch that video. In the note, explain how the film connects to your curriculum; inform them of language, violence, etc. that may be offensive to some students and their parents. Tell them that in your professional judgment, the film has many redeeming points and share a few of those values. (See the Appendix of this book for a sample note to parents.)
- **Plan to provide alternatives for any students whose parents may wish them to by-pass a video.** This procedure will often "get the teacher off the hook" if complaints arise. Although you may disagree with parents' objections, it is within their right to do so. Teachers must be prepared with alternatives if

they don't want to forego using a video at all. Be sure that there is no subtle or overt penalty for students who choose the alternative rather than viewing a video.

- **Be sure the physical classroom set-up is conducive to viewing**. Allow students seating alternatives during viewing experiences. Make special arrangements for students who may have trouble seeing or hearing. Ask them beforehand if they will need to sit closer to the screen. Some students are self-conscious about physical impairments and may not mention their difficulties unless the teacher privately intervenes.
- **When showing a video, monitor attentiveness.** When the lights go down, some students invariably opt for a nap, an opportunity to complete work for another class, etc. This behavior is less prevalent when the teacher monitors viewing and uses a viewing assignment to direct learning. Reinforce student accountability with a prepared lesson or viewing sheet, which connects closely with the film or video being shown. Some teachers give daily class credit for "staying on task" during the viewing of a video. It goes without saying, that if viewing is directly tied to the course of study, students will be more likely to be attentive.
- **Clearly convey expectations as well as consequences that relate to student viewing.** Teach and then expect appropriate viewing behavior. **Don't assume** students know it's not appropriate to discuss a film while viewing. After all, that is what often happens when viewing television at home for entertainment.

> ***Patti** points out to her students that viewing video in the classroom operates the same as reading: "You can't read if you're sleeping or working on an assignment for another class; and you can't view if your head is down on your desk or if you're finishing an assignment."*

- **Students must recognize the task of viewing a video to be an integral part of the lesson** and not some "extra entertainment" with no learning value. When teachers use videos as babysitting tools, they compromise them as learning and teaching tools for themselves and their colleagues. The teacher who is using a video as part of an instructional unit may have to remind students that viewing films are "learning experiences" which can, fortunately, also be entertaining and fun.

Make thoughtful and wise use of technology in the classroom. For example, showing a scene from several filmed versions of a Shakespearean play can provide students with options for their own classroom performance of that same scene. Students viewing a film adapted from the **novel** they've just completed can enrich their understanding of the book and provide grist for discussion of literary elements and the various ways a novel can be interpreted. A travelogue of a location being studied in **social studies** can make the history and the place itself more real for students. Using segments of a video series, such as Ken Burns' *Civil War* and others of his works that are now commercially available, can provide countless opportunities to enhance classroom instruction. Using video can help students conceptualize **scientific mysteries** such as internal human anatomy, dinosaurs, weather phenomena, etc. A background video can help students understand the Middle Ages, therefore deepening their understanding of Chaucer. A background video that demonstrates the development of the internal combustion engine could help **auto mechanics** students better grasp concepts behind the mechanical procedures they are being taught. Informational videos can provide valuable illumination that can contribute to students' understanding of a complex topic. Numerous videos are available that can help students connect the learning in their classroom to the real world beyond the schools' walls. One of Patti's favorites is "October Sky" (1999) in which youngsters use **math** to get themselves out of trouble.

Viewing a video adaptation prior to a reading assignment can assist student reading comprehension. Skillfully presented by the teacher, viewing before reading can be a valuable aid for challenged readers. Surprisingly, Patti has found that struggling readers do not refrain from reading even though they have seen a video adaptation first. On the contrary, striving readers seem to read with more confidence when they have mental images from a video for support.

It would be wise for media librarians or department heads to canvas departments within a school asking individual teachers to list the videos and films which they show as a part of their curriculum. Teachers can add the grades and levels at which they show these videos to their lists, in order to avoid overlap. If there is overlap, teachers can compromise or negotiate about the use and the necessity of using particular videos in their instructional programs. Nothing spoils a teacher's "video lesson" so quickly as hearing students remark (as Patti experienced), "Oh, we saw that last week in Mr. ____________'s science class." Patti still wonders what the film adaptation of Harper Lee's *To Kill a Mockingbird* has to do with science!

Kay and Patti both recall the days when the extent of audiovisual resources in the classroom was filmstrip and 16mm film. In the early years of her career, ***Patti****'s English Department rented 16mm films from commercial distributors once each semester and devised an elaborate plan so that each English teacher could show the film during the rental period. Ship of Fools (Porter), The Reivers (Faulkner), and Far From the Madding Crowd (Hardy) were just a few of the films for which the English Department developed instructional materials. Because it was an uncommon occurrence, students eagerly anticipated each upcoming film lesson.*

Patti *also remembers her frustration at not having a mode for incorporating appropriate television programming into her lesson planning. In particular, she recalls wanting so very much to be able to use the PBS production of The Six Wives of Henry VIII in her senior British literature classes in the 1970's. Another time she wanted to use a Phil Donahue (remember him?) interview with a doctor pioneering artificial insemination in conjunction with her class's study of Brave New World. The* only *possibility at that time was to gather all of her students in the media center to view the daytime broadcast in real time. It was certainly satisfying when media technology caught up with our instructional aspirations.*

How times have changed! Computers and DVD players along with LCD projectors are rapidly becoming standard equipment in many classrooms. In addition to feature length literary adaptations available on video, teachers have access to a wealth of video resources they can easily incorporate into their lesson planning. In addition to the rich resources provided by public television, commercial networks and cable channels offer an extensive variety of documentary, magazine, feature and news programming. The proliferation of specialized cable channels such as The History Channel and National Geographic Channel has tremendously increased sources that provide background, historical and scientific information presented in a format that is appealing and understandable for students and that can enhance an instructional plan.

Of course, when recording from television, there are concerns regarding commercials and copyright. A valuable planning tool for teachers is **Cable in the Classroom**, a public-service initiative of the cable television industry. This website catalogs programming and resources that would be of interest to teachers and students. In fact, cable networks make educational programs that are commercial-free and copyright cleared for a year or more available for taping for classroom use. Cable networks also provide online content, including interactive learning experiences and activities. Cable in the Classroom is a teacher's clearinghouse for accessing these resources. Cable in the Classroom also provides information regarding copyright restrictions for classroom use as well as access to an archive of educational resources. Teachers can access this useful site by going to www.ciconline.org.

We were advocates for incorporating visual and audio technology into instruction long before technology became a way of life. We've personally experienced many occasions when using a video or audio instructional component has motivated students, captured the interest of previously indifferent students, and excited apathetic students. That said, we also feel strongly that using video and audio in the classroom requires a concrete instructional plan that integrates media for a meaningful instructional purpose. Otherwise, the benefits of media in the classroom are diminished.

MANAGING TECHNOLOGY

Technology in the classroom has revolutionized education. Moreover, we are told even more sophisticated technology is still to come. For veteran teachers who have had to grow into the technological age, this phenomenon may be a challenge. Although a new teacher may be computer savvy, the prospect of managing one or more computers in the classroom or a whole class of students with laptop computers can seem daunting.

There are a multitude of instructional techniques for incorporating technology into instruction. In fact, whole books have been written about using technology in the classroom. Our purpose is to suggest ways for managing that technology.

How you will be asked to manage technology will depend on how fully technology has proliferated throughout your district or local school. Almost all schools have a lab or a bank of computers somewhere in the building set up for teachers and students to use. Almost every school office relies on computer connections to link them to a central office or board of education. In most urban and many rural areas, teachers may have personal computers on their desks and enough units in their classrooms so that every two or three students, at a minimum, can share access. Many schools have one or more computer labs that may be dedicated to teaching computer literacy classes, business course word processing, journalism, and computer programming. Special labs or groups of computers may be set aside to run specific software. Some labs are available for teachers who want to bring entire classes for computer related work, such as word processing writings for a class literary magazine. In many schools, large numbers of computers are placed in the media center to access CD-ROMs, electronic encyclopedias, and the Internet. Some schools have even mandated that teachers use electronic grade books. Increasingly, schools provide teachers, and in some cases students, with personal laptop computers for instructional use. How you manage technology will depend on your individual school's hardware and software and how it is used. One thing is certain, regardless of the technological status in your school, it will continue to increase.

Because technology use is of major importance in education today, to address all the concerns that it presents is the job of another book dedicated to the subject. But there are predictable situations that may impact teachers whose majority experience predates computers, new teachers or those returning to the classroom since computers have become so prevalent.

E-Mail

- Many schools are using e-mail to replace a daily or weekly bulletin. Be sure to read it regularly, just as you would a paper document.
- Some principals and counselors are communicating with teachers on a daily basis using e-mail. Check for these e-mail messages regularly.
- Some parents urge teachers to contact them at their workplace by e-mail. This process replaces the missed phone calls or the messages their children conveniently delete from an answering device.
- Some teachers may suggest that students contact them by e-mail concerning homework needs or questions about ongoing assignments. If you want to communicate with students in this way, use a school e-mail address rather than a personal or home address.
- Teachers may also collect assignments electronically and offer feedback on students' home computers. Again, if you choose to use technology in this manner, use a school e-mail address to do so.

Although an efficient means of communication, e-mail can quickly consume a large chunk of teachers' valuable time. The one thing of which no teacher ever has enough is time. Before releasing your e-mail access to students and parents, thoughtfully consider the possible ramifications. The demanding tasks of basic planning, teaching, grading, recording, and reporting require more time than most teachers have. Add the new task of monitoring and replying to e-mails from parents and students, and a teacher can easily find himself feeling as though teaching consumes his life 24-7.

As a society we have recognized (at least informally) how easily e-mail messages and responses can become overwhelming to the point of interfering with our required tasks. Unfortunately, unless a school district or a school itself places e-mail limits, or at least establishes e-mail guidelines for students and parents, an individual teacher can easily become inundated and distracted from her important instructional duties.

What's a teacher to do? We recommend that teachers become **proactive.** Don't **assume** that parents and students understand the already time-consuming nature of your teaching responsibilities (Which they, by the way, expect you to maintain at peak performance level.)

- **Communicate with parents at the opening of the school year.** Share your daily schedule with parents including all of your classes, additional duties and extracurricular responsibilities. Tell them that your only opportunity to respond to e-mail queries or return phone messages is at times other than during those daily, regularly-scheduled tasks. Caution them that you may not be able to respond to e-mail messages instantaneously and offer alternative possibilities for making contact with you. (Refer to the Appendix of this book for a sample letter.)
- In your **opening of school message(s) to parents, at open house and parent conferences,** explain diplomatically that your time for responding to e-mails is limited and restricted to times when you are not performing instructional duties. Set aside a time each day to check and respond to e-mail. Share with parents that beyond that designated time, you are limited in your ability to respond to e-mail.
- **Provide student and parent e-mail access to your *school* e-mail address *only*.** Communications to your school address may become demanding, but just imagine being bombarded with student and parent messages at a personal e-mail address. Distributing your personal e-mail address to students and parents could have repercussions for you (and anyone else who uses that address) for years to come.

    In order to remain a healthy and productive educator, you need some time totally free from school responsibilities. Once students and parents gain access to your personal e-mail address (home phone or cell phone numbers also), it will be virtually impossible to keep your personal and professional lives separate.

- **Remember that e-mail communications can last forever and make the rounds almost infinitely.** Once you hit "send," you have lost control of who sees your message as well as how many times it's forwarded and to whom. To protect yourself, be sure that any e-mail messages you send to parents and/or students can bear intensive scrutiny before you hit "send."
- **Always be conscious of the tone an e-mail message may convey.** Many have learned from painful experience that the intended tone of an e-mail message may not be the one a recipient reads into your words. Remain continually aware of how tone may come across in e-mail messages, especially ones to parents. Choose your words carefully and frame your message in a manner that would be difficult for anyone - but especially a parent - to misinterpret.
- **Always proofread e-mails you send to parents and students.** Don't forget that as well as the content of the message, an e-mail's presentation is a reflection of you. In personal e-mail exchanges with friends, you might want to relax and choose to disregard usage, sentence structure, and mechanics. E-mail communications with students and parents should never be considered informal. Judgments will be made about you from your spelling, grammatical usage, sentence construction and word choice. *Ensure that those judgments will put you in a positive light.*
- **Keep a copy of all e-mail messages to and from students and parents.** If in the unlikely event that a conflict arises over an e-mail communication, you want to be sure to have your own record of the pertinent messages – both ones you received as well as sent.
- **Copy a counselor or administrator on e-mail exchanges with parents.** Alert them in advance that you would like to do so whenever you respond to a parent using e-mail. This is a safeguard in multiple ways. First, the parent knows someone else is privy to the communication. Next, that staff member can monitor your communications and alert you to any possibilities for misinterpretation. Finally, as administrators experience how demanding the use of e-mail for parent contacts can become, they may be amendable to creating school guidelines that make parental use of e-mail communication with individual teachers more manageable.

It goes without saying that e-mail is certainly playing an increased role in classroom communication. Therefore, teachers must be conscientious about accessing e-mail and returning messages in a timely fashion if their districts or schools communicate in that mode. On the other hand, e-mail demands can quickly become overwhelming. Teachers need to be aware of that possibility and be proactive in e-mail management to assure that e-mail does not interfere with their quality of instruction or their personal lives.

Social Networking Technology

The latest technological development to influence teachers, classrooms and instruction is social networking. This phenomenon is new enough that school uses and classroom applications are still being explored. Many school districts block school use of Facebook, My Space, and/or You Tube. Increasingly, though, schools are beginning to examine how these social media might be effectively integrated into school communication and instruction. We've heard of school districts that are cautiously removing blocks for teachers and, in some cases, students for instructional use.

An immediate application of social networking could be for the communication of classroom information. Teachers could post assignments, projects, deadlines, procedures, field trip opportunities and requirements, etc. for students and parents to access. We don't recommend considering social media as the exclusive means to convey this kind of information, but they certainly can be utilized as a follow-up or even reminder tool. Any means by which a teacher can effectively inform students and parents as a group without sending individual messages has tremendous potential. In fact, social networking could very possibly be a tool that reduces the potential avalanche of individual e-mail messages that teachers may face.

Another valuable use of social networking for teachers is to expand the community of professionals with which a teacher can interact. Teachers can post questions regarding a particular curriculum feature, seek recommendations of materials, share successful lessons, solicit suggestions regarding classroom management strategies, or any number of other useful applications. Teachers with a particular interest can interact with others who share that interest. Social networking opens the potential for teachers to connect with specialists, even ones in very narrow fields. No longer is a teacher limited to those in her immediate environment for support, guidance, assistance, or sharing. This means of interaction with other professionals or specialists poses exciting possibilities that definitely warrant teacher investigation.

Instructional uses of social media need to be thoroughly considered *before* implementation into your curriculum. The first consideration is student access. If students don't all have access to a particular social media, then curriculum use must be, at the very least, optional. Nevertheless, we can see exciting potential for expanding instructional experiences beyond the classroom or even the school. A class could post instructionally related inquiries or communications seeking response from others with the same interest. For instance, a class that has read a particular novel could post interpretations or reviews to which others familiar with the novel could comment.

One caution when integrating social media communication into student experiences: anyone with access can post and respond. There are no guidelines restricting respondents to those who have expertise, knowledge, or even suitable experience to give them the authority to comment on a particular subject. For example, posting comments or inquiries regarding a particular class novel could generate feedback from anyone, whether they have read the novel or not. Such comments may or may not be valid. Anyone with access can post any information regardless of its accuracy or relevance. A teacher deciding to introduce this kind of technological option should teach her students about such limitations posed by these new media. Furthermore, remember that those who post don't care about your students as you do. Any of them could make sarcastic comments or even poke fun at something your students have posted. You need to keep this possibility in mind when opening the gate for this kind of interaction.

Another consideration that we recommend teachers contemplate is student, parent and administrator access to teachers' Facebook, My Space, or Twitter accounts. Think about your perception of your account(s) and how you want them integrated into your daily life. Do you want students or parents accessing and reading comments posted by you or your family and friends? Are you comfortable with students responding to posts on your Wall? Have you or your friends posted photos to your account that parents or administrators might find compromising? We've heard of instances where administrators and even parents have objected to something, not related to or intended for school consumption, posted on a teacher's Facebook page. Remember that even if you don't use a social media account for school concerns, people connected to school could find your account. Teachers are advised to keep in mind that they are "public" figures, and the "public" aspect of their persona is readily apparent with social media. In this day and age where virtually anyone can access information about anyone else, teachers must recognize how information on their social media pages might be construed by those connected to them as teachers – students, parents, and administrators. The wise teacher exercises thoughtful discretion in light of these circumstances.

Familiarize yourself with the privacy options offered by various social media. As a teacher with an account, you want to seriously consider your privacy settings whether or not you wish to incorporate social media into your instruction. Utilize your privacy settings to limit the information any student or parent might access in your personal account. Besides keeping your private life private, these safeguards limit the possibility that students will read something personal on your Wall and inappropriately interject it into your professional life. Furthermore, use privacy settings to safeguard against a parent objecting to something posted on your Wall and generating issues and/or complaints about you to the administration.

We recommend an article on Facebook, *Back to School: Tips for Teachers,* written by Jesse Dwyer Friday and posted on Facebook on Sept. 13, 2009. Ms. Dwyer suggests creating friend *lists.* One of your friend lists could be "Students," and you can adjust your privacy settings to control what members of that list see. We think that is a sensible approach that will enable teachers to exchange information and ideas with students while guarding their personal privacy.

In our twenty-first century environment, we have come to understand that technology is a continually evolving phenomenon. In order to remain relevant in their classrooms, teachers must stay informed as new modes of communication emerge. However, those same teachers must also approach the implementation of these emerging technologies with caution keeping the welfare of their students and their own professional well being uppermost in their consideration.

Power Point and Other Projections

Another relatively new instructional phenomenon is the ability to easily incorporate projections into your instruction. This ability adds exciting new possibilities to the nature of teaching. When teachers can locate material and visuals online, they now have the capacity to project that material for an entire class to share. We remember the days of using a giant dinosaur called an opaque projector in a primitive attempt to project material for an entire class to view. How far we've come!

Many of the same safeguards that apply to decisions surrounding selection of videos apply when choosing items, including those available online, to project.

- Observe district and school policies concerning projections and/or other visuals incorporated into instructional content.
- Consider projection materials as you plan your lessons for a unit.
- Continually remain aware of appropriateness for your students and classroom use in the material you project.
- Project material that is relevant to, enhances, and/or enriches your instruction.
- If a projection might be considered controversial, think twice before using it.
- Be sure the physical classroom set-up is conducive to viewing.
- Assure that all students can satisfactorily see and read any projections.

Like any medium, ineffective and/or overuse of projections can result in student disinterest. Rather than randomly inserting impulsive projections during a class, we encourage teachers to make thoughtful, meaningful use of projection technology to complement their instruction.

Many contemporary students will use projections such as PowerPoint when preparing presentations and projects. You can help them refine their use of projections by guiding them to consider their audience and purpose when deciding what to project and how to incorporate projections into their work. If presenters are inclined to project large amounts of text that students in the back of the classroom cannot read, they are not considering their audience in presentation planning. When students present slide after slide of text, audiences may become disinterested and presenters will not be able to accomplish the purpose for their presentations. Likewise, if students flash picture after picture on the screen, they may not have thoughtfully considered how to meaningfully integrate visuals into their presentations. As teachers, we can help students become effective users of projection technology in the same manner that we can help them maximize the value of their textbooks and create effective oral presentations.

Technology as a Reference Tool

The computer provides a very exciting reference tool. Many teachers remember the research excavations they put themselves and their students through with sometimes futile trips to the library. Now the Internet, which has become one of the most essential research tools in school libraries and media centers, can provide instant access to what often seems like an unlimited bank of information. This exciting use, however, is fraught with dangers and difficulties from plagiarism to the accessing of sites that offer information of a less than suitable quality. In fact, one of the biggest challenges we have found when students undertake Internet research is actually the availability of *too much* information. Therefore we have developed some strategies that at least begin to address the ever-changing vista of computers and instruction.

- **Don't assume** that every student is proficient in all aspects of computer searches. While students may be adept at performing searches for casual interests, they may not employ effective search strategies to help them ferret out the most useful information for assignments and projects. **Be prepared to teach students effective search strategies for your subject matter and class.**
- **Teach students strategies for evaluating web sites for authenticity, reliability, and objectivity**. In this Internet-dominated era when anyone can spout information (whether accurate or not) on a blog, it becomes essential that we teach students how to critically evaluate statements and information they wish to incorporate into assignments, papers, and projects for the classroom.
- **Teach students how to cite electronic resources from CD-Rom encyclopedias to Internet sites**. Mini-lessons in appropriate citation methods and teacher modeling of their own use and citation of these resources offer students the opportunities to learn effective ways to avoid the pitfall of plagiarism. MLA (Modern Language Association) and other handbooks, along with some textbooks and web sites, provide explanations and examples of electronic citation methods.
- **Seek out your librarian or media specialist** and ask for her input regarding instructional suggestions that help avoid the pitfalls of student Internet use for class work.
- **Provide students with appropriate guidelines for searching the Internet and limit free surfing time.** One strategy to limit free surfing time is to assign classroom tasks that will require using all their Internet time in order to satisfactorily complete the assignment.
- **Constantly monitor students in your charge when they are independently using the Internet.** Be sure students know what the consequences are for accessing inappropriate material. Don't hesitate to apply these consequences.
- If your school does not have an **Internet use policy**, look for opportunities to suggest that it would be universally valuable

to draft a school wide policy that states guidelines and consequences for violating those guidelines.

If teachers are to successfully incorporate technology into their classrooms, they, as well as their students, must learn to use it effectively. Keep in mind that proficiency with word processing, computer searches, and/or social networking sites doesn't automatically translate into productive use of technology resources for instruction. In order for some veterans, new or returning teachers to use technology effectively for instructional purposes, training might be in order. Many districts provide training for individuals and entire faculties through staff development. Local universities and other technology training centers offer refresher courses and training in special software and its uses. Textbook publishers may offer school or district training for the technology resources that accompany their books. Be sure to inquire about this possibility; it's often available for no charge. Although this training may take time after school or in the summer, it will surely pay dividends in making teachers feel secure in their knowledge and use of these constantly evolving tools.

Requiring Technology Use in the Classroom

Do not assume that all of your students have ready access to technology. Teachers who intend to make student technology use mandatory need to be sure that all students have adequate access to the necessary equipment. Many, if not most, students probably have computers at home; but for those (however few) who do not, convenient accessibility to school technology is vital. Check to make sure that school labs and media centers are open before and after school to serve the needs of students who do not have home access to technology. Public libraries and after school centers often provide technology that students can access. Before you *require* technology use for anything for which a student is to be graded, ascertain that every one of your students will be able to successfully complete the requirement. If students are expected to use technology for their class assignments, they must have simple access to it and assistance in its proper use.

Machines and their Maintenance

One of the biggest headaches that comes with using technology is maintaining the machines – computers, printers, scanners, projectors and other high tech tools. Fortunate schools have on-site personnel whose job is to maintain school technology in good working order. However, even these technicians will often be unable to fix certain problems and breakdowns. Think about the disruption and inconvenience caused when no one in the building can get the teacher photocopier up and running and the external service person can't get there for three days. Approach computer use with this same awareness.

Sometimes a classroom teacher is given the job of school technology coordinator, working on a planning period or after school to help keep technology in sound working order. Teacher patience is absolutely necessary when seeking assistance with school technology. Be unfailingly reasonable and courteous with those colleagues given the job of maintenance and troubleshooting. Otherwise you might find yourself at the bottom of their priority list.

In addition, remember that students often know much more than their teachers about both using and maintaining computers. Consider allowing them to show their expertise in the classroom and learn the many tips they have to offer. A reciprocal teaching-learning situation is refreshing and very useful for those moments when a quick assist is in order.

Many schools or districts offer staff development to teachers to learn to deal with everyday problems such as printer paper jams, Internet disconnects, or any of the myriad problems that affect even the best-maintained equipment on any given day. Be sure to sign up for technology staff development.

It's always a good idea to have a contingency plan in your back pocket when engaging students with technology. . In the event that the required technology malfunctions or becomes unavailable, you don't want instruction to come to a standstill. The last thing you need is a room full of students with nothing to do because the technology equipment is unexpectedly out of commission. With a back-up plan in place, you can quickly regroup and carry on in order to maintain order and productivity.

Technology has transformed the classroom and all aspects of teaching more than we could have imagined. It is with us to stay and seems to evolve monthly into something new that we must learn to master. But as with all things, its uses and sometimes its abuses can add stress and problems to our teaching lives. However, technology adds great potential as a timesaver in teachers' overloaded lives as well as provides exciting instructional possibilities. We feel the best approach is to be thoughtfully proactive and make sure that you're up-to-date with the technology that will be available to you and your students.

READING MANAGEMENT

Reading is at the heart of what teachers do. Teachers in every subject area ask students to use reading in order to learn content material. As English teachers ourselves, we think it's safe to say that a motivating ambition of our colleagues is to develop students who will be able to read proficiently in their pursuits beyond school and to nurture students who will engage in reading for their own enrichment, enlightenment, and enjoyment.

In the lower grades, teachers help students learn and develop active reading strategies. Then teachers give them plenty of guidance and opportunity to apply and practice those strategies to develop their own reading proficiency. Sometimes, even in the upper grades, we must aid our students in remediating their reading skills. The teaching of reading involves a complex and sophisticated constellation of skills and strategies. Often secondary teachers are not trained to teach reading, per se, but sometimes find themselves needing to do so either by assignment or to meet the needs of their students. Useful materials to assist teachers in this situation are plentiful. Our focus in this book is on management strategies that will facilitate teachers' efforts to foster their students' reading activities and enrichment.

Both of us successfully use reading workshop-type activities and independent reading to introduce our students to a variety of literature as well as provide them with the opportunity to make some of their own reading choices. We feel that teachers in all content areas can provide the same benefits to their students by offering reading related to their subject. Having the opportunity to make **choices** about their reading is a major influence on student enthusiasm for reading.

We heartily recommend that all teachers consider some variation of this approach. We particularly urge teachers in content areas other than English to consider incorporating their own version of a reading workshop or independent reading plan. Such reading can enrich students' exploration of their subject matter far beyond the technical or informational aspects of their textbooks. Furthermore, this kind of reading can often provide a real world connection that can give your subject added significance for many students. Supplemental reading also provides a means for students to investigate applications of the concepts in your content area. Furthermore, teachers can experience the management benefits provided by ancillary reading plans.

Why not begin right now considering possible titles with which to build your classroom library? Some of Michael Crichton's titles come to mind for science classes. One of Patti's favorites for a social studies library is “The Devil in the White City” by Erik Larson. Not familiar with it? Check it out. It’s historical nonfiction that reads like an intriguing novel. Don’t think a classroom library will work in a math class? Just “Google” “math fiction books.” When she last checked, Patti found a site that recommended 365 fiction titles related to math. We hope your quest for titles, which your students will not only benefit from but also enjoy, will hook you as it has us.

Supplemental enrichment reading in your class is not restricted to long works. Short stories provide some of the same benefits as longer works. Using “The Cold, Cold Box” by Howard Fast in a science class or “Harrison Bergeron” by Kurt Vonnegut in a civics class provides the perfect set-up for students to debate issues related to the class’s subject matter. Essays on concepts and issues related to your content area also provide instructional opportunities. Teachers might further consider biography and history readings regarding particular aspects of areas such as science or government. Some publications offer essays, and/or nonfiction writings collected in annual anthologies such as "Best Science Writing 2008," "Best Journalistic Writing 2009,"or "Best Travel Writing 2007" - definitely worth a look for geography teachers. Don’t overlook contemporary sources. Newspaper and magazine articles can often provide the most current information and thinking on topics related to your subject matter; plus they provide valuable real world connections. Internet searches make locating these supplemental reading resources easier than ever.

Kay’s Story

Reading Groups

Kay uses a reading group approach with her older, advanced students. Her operative strategy is to introduce students to contemporary writers. The goal is to have students read contemporary literature and then share their ideas and interests with peers. To achieve this goal, Kay emulates popular public reading groups. She selects several books, usually four to six works available in multiple copies, and allows the students to peruse the selections. Once a student chooses a book, he teams up with students who want to read the same book to form a reading group. Members meet and discuss their expectations for the group; then they set a reading timetable. The groups may meet periodically during class to discuss literary elements, such as characters or themes. Alternatively, Kay suggests that students finish their selection and then meet to discuss the book in a style more like that of public reading groups. These reading groups are truly collaborative exercises. Students are given the task of selecting discussion points and one student may volunteer to direct the students in discussion and assist the group in reaching their goals. Interesting final projects can be generated from the reading group approach. Teachers may grade or evaluate the outcomes of these projects however they wish.

Sometimes a panel discussion is held, allowing each student in the reading group to speak about his reaction to the book, share favorite passages, or answer questions from an audience of classmates. The teacher or a student from the group may monitor the discussion to assure that it proceeds smoothly and allows each student to participate.

Kay has had students design reader's guides, much like those that publishers offer to public reading groups. These guides often combine information about the author, brief discussion of the book, and a list of other works by the same author. The heart of the reader's guides, however, is the list of questions, which aid a reading group's discussion of the book. Professional models available in books, through bookstores, and on the Internet can give students additional ideas for developing reader's guides. When guides are completed, individual students use them to lead the panel discussions. Kay picks the most useful reader's guides and makes them available to other students who may want to read the books.

Additional activities of the teacher's choosing may be used to evaluate students' reading and to offer future choices for other readers. Also the group might work collaboratively designing a single reader's guide. The above ideas work particularly well with fiction, but could also be used with other genres, such as works of non-fiction. Kay finds that students enjoy the reading of contemporary works in reading group set-ups, and relish the camaraderie the reading group experience offers. Graduates have returned with stories about the public reading groups they have joined after leaving high school.

Independent Reading

Kay works independent reading projects into her classroom by connecting them to the assigned traditional reading, which students do throughout the year. The key to keeping students happy with an independent reading project is giving them an appropriate amount of time to read independently and complete any work associated with the project.

When Kay's students are reading Chaucer's *Canterbury Tales* in senior English, for example, she has them independently reading short stories. Chaucer's *Canterbury Tales* are models for those works, which later became short stories, so the connection seems apt. She draws up lists of contemporary short story writers. Students read a single volume by one writer. Projects range from oral book talks to comparative essays based on the short story writers' works. Students research their chosen writers and prepare author/story posters displayed in the classroom urging fellow students to sample additional authors and their short stories. Kay conducts additional independent reading projects in poetry, biography/autobiography, the novel and non-fiction. Time is the single most important factor to consider when students undertake any kind of independent study. Having some choice about what they read makes student investment in independent reading a real bonanza for all parties. Kay continues to champion independent reading when she hears comments such as: "I never would have discovered this writer on my own;" "poetry is so wonderful, I didn't know there were poems like these;" "I read this book to the very last page, and I've seldom done that before." Results such as these merit the time and energy spent in engaging students in independent reading. Several suggestions for teachers who wish to undertake independent reading with students are:

- Be organized
- Assign projects within an appropriate time frame
- Authorize book selection (from a prescribed wide-ranging list, if possible) but be flexible
- Select a method of evaluation that is appropriate for the level of your students; be creative
- Monitor student progress; however, beware of being too structured (independent reading must be independent – brief conferences will keep students reading and on task)
- Have at least some familiarity with books chosen by students. Internet searches can ease teachers' research of unfamiliar titles

Style an independent reading experience with your students from which both parties can profit. Develop one that suits you and your students. Remain open to changing it periodically.

Patti's Story

Reading Workshops

Patti has found various forms of reading workshops invaluable in working with students who are not used to reading, who don't read, or who think they dislike reading. She has found the reading workshop to be almost a magic wand for encouraging such students to discover books they will read because they find them interesting and enjoyable, not just because they've been assigned in a class.

She often organizes her reading workshops around a theme which students have been exploring in shorter fiction, nonfiction and informational reading. She provides multiple copies of four to six thematically related titles and allows each student to choose which to read. Much of the reading occurs during class on reading days or when students have completed other work. She has developed a collection of "generic" materials that allow students who are reading different books to engage in the same activities. These include:

- reader response activities
- literary elements activities
- learning log prompts
- oral, performance and visual projects
- sentence starters
- mapping activities
- quotation activities

Teachers can also find numerous resources for a variety of books simply by "Googling" each title. The Internet has made an array of title-specific materials to assist instruction easily accessible. Consequently, reading workshop instructional approaches are more feasible than ever before.

Patti also uses groups to encourage students to discuss their reading with classmates. Sometimes all students reading the same book are grouped together while at other times groups are composed of students reading different books. When students are inexperienced or reticent about discussing their reading, she provides them with discussion prompts to get them started. Students also engage in letter writing about their books to students in other classes. Sometimes they are instructed to write about a specific aspect of their book such as the characters or the setting. Once they develop fluency with and confidence in forming and sharing ideas about their reading, they are given opportunities to structure their own letters. Technology provides opportunities for students to explore ideas about their reading with students and others far beyond their own school. Just "Google" a title to discover not only resources but often discussion forums specific to that work.

Each reading workshop culminates with an activity-oriented pursuit. One of Patti's favorites is for groups comprised of students who have read the same book to create, perform and record commercials "selling" their book to classmates or other classes. A valuable resource in planning her reading workshops has been Joan Kaywell's series, *Adolescent Literature as a Complement to the Classics* published by Christopher Gordon. It suggests numerous thematically related titles as well as plentiful reading workshop activities.

Independent Reading

One of the smartest management moves Patti ever made was to institute independent reading in all of her classes. At the time she decided to give this strategy a try, her classes consisted of students who were not strong academically and who were reluctant readers at best. She began by constructing a classroom library with two to five copies of titles from the English Department's supplemental book room. When she realized how valuable this independent reading was, she actively expanded her classroom library by scouring used book stores, library used book sales, flea markets and yard sales. Ultimately her classroom library has become a diverse collection of literary classics, traditional titles, adolescent novels, and contemporary writing. Aware of the diversity among her students, she has made sure to include titles that would appeal to males as well as titles that would appeal to females. She has also sought titles that would appeal to African American, Asian, and Native American students as well as other cultures. She makes sure that her selections span a very wide readability range. Often events suggest titles that she quickly acquires for students who might be ripe with interest. For instance, when the film *Titanic* caught everyone's attention, she quickly added copies of Walter Lord's *A Night to Remember* to her collection. It's important for her to have some familiarity with recommended or provided books, but Internet searches have made this considerably easier than in the past.

Patti introduces the independent reading component of her classroom organization early in the school year. She gives students written guidelines that include how they will receive credit for their reading (See the Appendix.). Then she gives brief book talks about several titles. She also points out authors who might appeal to certain students. S.E. Hinton, Robert Lipsyte, and Walter Dean Myers are sure to be favorites, especially for boys. Finally she gives students the opportunity to choose their books. Her rule of thumb: if after reading twenty-five pages, a student doesn't like the book, he is encouraged to try another. Her goal is for all students to read a book because it appeals to them, not because it is an assignment. This is essential to the success of her classes' independent reading program.

Periodically Patti schedules reading days when she, along with her students, spend the class period enjoying their books. Students also know when they finish their class work and are caught up, they can get their book and read for bonus points. This takes a bit of guidance, but as soon as students get hooked on their books, it serves to keep them on task with their class work as well as avoid pesky idleness. This plan works so well that even when Patti has a substitute, students follow the procedure, much to the astonishment of some substitutes.

Students who have never read a complete book are amazed when they find a book they don't want to put down. Those who have never read much find themselves talking about their books in the hallway. Students who never thought they were readers are thrilled to discover a sequel to the only book they have ever read. One student was determined to read Richard Wright's *Black Boy*. It took him all year to read that one book, but because he was so moved and inspired by it, he never gave it up. When film or television versions have serendipitously occurred such as *Homecoming, Having Our Say,* or *Mary Reilly,* students surprised themselves when they preferred the book.

Patti's teacher's heart is warmed by overhearing boys in the hallway talking about Nate in *The Learning Tree* almost as though he were a real person. Or to hear chuckles as students react to something in their books while they are reading. When students reading *Goodnight, Mr. Tom* begin sniffling, Patti shares with them that she knows just where they are in the book because she sniffled there too. One of the many pleasures offered by the reading workshop is the opportunity for Patti and her students to relate to one another as mutual readers, not as teacher and students. Perhaps Patti's favorite reading workshop anecdote is a fitting conclusion to her story.

One morning it was announced over the intercom that students were to remain in their first period class so a school wide locker cleanout could commence. Five or six students at a time were to be dismissed to clean out their lockers. Consider that the hallway was lined with lockers and imagine the din. This went on for a good forty-five minutes. As the first group left to clean their lockers, one of my students asked if he could get his book. Of course. Then another and another and another student got their books. Despite all of the commotion outside the classroom door, my nonacademic students were sitting in the classroom leisurely reading their books - by choice.

When the principal strode by monitoring the hallway activity, he stuck his head in my doorway to see how we were doing. His jaw dropped when he saw students that he knew from past disciplinary encounters or that he viewed as potential troublemakers, yes, reading. He was stunned. All he could get out was a weak, "How did you do this?" I asked one of my students to share something about the book he was reading with our principal, which he did. My students and I shared our own chuckle as the principal backed away almost visibly shaking his head in wonder. I could sense the new esteem my students felt for themselves. It was then that I knew I would always provide independent reading opportunities in my classes.

WRITING MANAGEMENT

Although we could write a book just about teaching writing, that is not our purpose. Instead, our focus is on what is perhaps the English teacher's greatest management challenge: dealing with writing assignments. Recent educational trends have moved toward extensive use of writing in *all content areas*. Any teacher who values what and why his students think, will recognize the benefits of incorporating writing into his instruction regardless of his subject matter. Although this has not always been welcomed with enthusiasm by teachers who have observed the management challenges faced by English teachers, many teachers in various subject areas have discovered just how valuable student writing can be for learning, critical thinking, analysis, clarification and many more higher order skills that are valuable for students in all of their content classes. When teachers of any subject ask students to write as part of the learning activity in their classroom, they can significantly contribute to student success by assuming some responsibility for helping students develop, hone and refine their writing skills, especially those particular to their subject matter.

Assigning every student a five hundred-word report or essay to write by Friday is not writing *instruction*. Contemporary teachers recognize the benefits of teaching students to employ the writing process. Furthermore, writing projects have demonstrated the value of writing groups, peer response, teacher-student conferencing, and writing portfolios. Yet these effective strategies are more complex to implement than is an assignment with every student writing in the same format, on the same topic, at the same time and handing it in by a deadline. We have discovered and developed some management strategies that facilitate implementation of current best practices for nurturing writing development. Many of these strategies can realistically be incorporated into any subject matter by teachers who recognize the value of writing across the curriculum.

Using Writing for Punishment

Student attitudes about writing greatly impact their writing success. Students may come to class with already-embedded negative attitudes about writing:

- They hate it.
- They fear freezing up when asked to write.
- They can never think of anything to write about.
- They worry about all the red marks the teacher will put on their papers.
- They don't feel they can be successful as a writer . . .. and many more.

Teachers can actively work to help students overcome their mental blocks against writing by providing writing situations in which they can be successful. Even more critical, teachers and administrators must be very cautious not to promote negativity toward writing.

Using writing for punishment encourages students to perceive writing negatively. What would be the effect if language arts teachers assigned math problems for punishment? Math teachers wouldn't be very happy, would they? Perhaps a school uses writing for punishment in its after-school or in-school detention program or various teachers employ writing for punishment purposes in their individual classes. What can writing teachers do? It can be difficult to become a lone crusader, but form a coalition of writing teachers and wage a campaign to heighten school awareness of the importance of attitude in writing success and the detrimental effect of using writing for punishment. Research and professional articles are readily available to support this cause; one source is the National Council of Teachers of English web site (www.ncte.org.). Not only would success in this endeavor make your life as a writing teacher easier, but it would also enhance your students' possibilities for writing success.

Process Writing

Our personal student memories of writing instruction consist mostly of *assignments* over which our English teachers "bled" with red pens, not actual *instruction.* As novice English teachers we had no more idea about how to teach writing than we did about how to teach calculus. Consequently, we both examined our personal writing procedures and applied those observations to our methods for instructing our students. Little did we know at the time, but we had inadvertently hit upon concepts underlying an enlightenment in writing instruction that occurred with the emergence of the writing process and new direction coming from national, state, and local writing projects.

With less confident and less skilled writers, Patti methodically guides students through writing process activities at each stage of the writing process:

- prewriting activities
- drafting activities
- revising activities
- editing and proofreading activities
- reflecting activities.

These activities are often presented on worksheets because such students are so accustomed to worksheets in other classes that they are less intimidated by the notion of a writing assignment if they encounter it in segments in a familiar format. Worksheets have a bad name in some places, but our philosophy is "There are worksheets, and then there are *worksheets*." When students are guided through a process for developing a skill such as writing, they gain experience to draw upon when they next employ that skill. This can be successfully accomplished using worksheets.

Students receive credit for their work at each stage of the writing process, so their entire grade doesn't depend on one finished *product,* but rather reflects their efforts to engage in a meaningful *process*. After all, it's while students are engaged in a process that learning actually occurs; so we believe it's appropriate for teachers to assess and for students to receive credit for those endeavors. This technique also reassures insecure writers that completing a writing assignment is not an insurmountable task but rather one they have the possibility of accomplishing if they just work through incremental steps. Students are required to hand in their work for each stage of the writing process along the way for teacher review and feedback and then accompanying their finished piece. An additional benefit of this procedure is that it makes plagiarism much more difficult.

Both Kay and Patti use variations of this method with honors and advanced classes. Guiding these students through a writing process is a valuable learning strategy, but implementation usually does not need to be quite as micromanaged. Helping more confident and proficient writers refine their skills and strategies in employing an effective writing process is a worthwhile endeavor, especially early in the school year.

Prewriting

Announcing in class that students will be expected to write a piece starting that very day is not an effective method for stimulating thoughtful student writing. Part of students' success comes from writing about topics in which they have interest and for which they care. It is easy to recognize when a student has completed a writing requirement in which he was not particularly engaged. Teachers can help students discover what they are interested in writing about and what their thoughts are about a given topic. Issues within your subject matter often stimulate student interest. Consider these issues, particularly ones for which students can recognize a contemporary real world connection, as rich sources for student writing possibilities. Enthusiastic discussions that arise within your class can signal student passion for an aspect of your content. Be sure to capitalize on such fervor by suggesting that students may wish to explore the subject of that discussion as a writing topic. Patti uses learning logs (See "Learning Logs and Writers' Notebooks.") to continually nudge students to explore their opinions and ideas on any number of issues and to discover topics of importance to them. Equally important, learning logs provide a place where students can explore their thoughts and ideas about a particular topic before they begin drafting. When prewriting has been effectively implemented, students know what they want to say when they begin drafting a piece of writing.

Stay alert to hallway conversations or student interactions before or after class. Often their discussions reveal subjects of importance to them; all they need is an astute teacher to suggest that might be something about which they could write.

> ***Patti*** *once overheard a student expressively exclaim, "I just hate it when . . . . .!" All Patti said was, "Why don't you write about your feelings on that issue?" and the student discovered a meaningful topic for exploration in a personal essay.*
>
> *In another instance, Patti overheard a student who worked at a local department store humorously regaling her girlfriends with stories about exasperating customers. She pointed out to the student those anecdotes would make great material for a personal narrative. It never occurred to the student that such experiences could be used for a writing assignment; but with a simple suggestion from her teacher, she created a piece that was a delight to read.*

Choice is critical for student writing success. If the teacher always dictates what they will write about, students may only feel invested once in a while. When students choose what to write about, their chances for discovering meaningful topics with which they want to engage and invest greatly increase. Even within structured assignments such as literary analysis essays or technical writing, building in opportunities for student choice at some point during the writing process will enhance student commitment to the writing experience.

Revision & Editing

Teachers often express that the teaching of revision and editing is perhaps the most challenging aspect of teaching writing, and we agree. Teaching about and requiring students to complete exercises in grammar, usage, and mechanics rules do not automatically transfer to actual revision and editing in their writing. Merely directing students to revise and edit their writing before handing it in won't do the trick either. As teachers, we must expect to teach our students *how* to revise and edit. It's a tall order.

Teaching specific usage and mechanics skills then directing student editing of those skills often intimidates content teachers and discourages them from incorporating writing into their classes. We maintain that teachers in the content areas can engage students in a host of writing activity that contributes to development of quality student writing before students ever get to the revising and editing stage of the writing process. Teachers of science, math, social studies and other content areas can make significant contributions to the development of quality writing by helping students to:

- discover meaningful topics for writing,
- engage in constructive prewriting activities,
- organize their drafts,
- develop and support the ideas expressed in their drafts,
- thoughtfully review their drafts,
- consider their word choices,
- revise how they express and support their ideas.

Take note that these activities provide students with considerable guided writing process experience but none require extensive grammar or usage expertise.

Our philosophy is that content teachers can best help student writers by focusing primarily on ideas and the effective expression, organization and development of them. English teachers can then concentrate on the technical aspects of writing, including that which occurs in other content classes. In the most productive writing situations, content teachers and English teachers find ways to collaborate so that students benefit from the content expertise of subject teachers and the technical skill of English teachers. When content teachers know they will not be exclusively responsible for the grammar, usage and mechanics fine points in student writing, they may be more interested in incorporating writing as a tool for learning and demonstrating learning in their classes.

For English teachers, we can suggest some techniques for managing the challenging task of teaching students how to revise and edit. Avoid trying to teach every single skill with every writing assignment. Choose one or two essential writing and editing skills on which to focus with each assignment. Conduct mini-lessons focusing on target skills in close proximity with student revision and editing of their own work. For instance, if a teacher has chosen support and development of main ideas as a target writing skill, she can engage students in an elaboration mini-lesson immediately before their initial revision of their draft. If she has identified subject and verb agreement as a target skill, she can teach a subject and verb agreement mini-lesson immediately preceding student editing of their own work.

How teachers respond to student work has a tremendous impact on student writing success. Marking every error in red on a finished product reaps limited returns. Imagine how discouraging it can be to a student, who has labored over a piece of writing, to have it returned covered with marks showing what he did wrong. Would that encourage *you* to approach subsequent writing assignments with enthusiasm? Positive reinforcement of strong aspects of student writing encourages students to continually repeat those characteristics. Pointing out errors in the application of one or two target skills gives students something upon which to focus in remediation without overwhelming them. Consider the fairness to students of penalizing them for writing errors with skills that have not been taught or addressed in the class before or during the writing process. These penalties often contribute to the death of budding writers. Some concrete strategies for encouraging students to engage in revision include:

- **Model revision for students using transparencies or technology that makes such modeling possible**. If a teacher doesn't model what she wants her students to learn, they are probably learning something else or nothing at all.
- **Analyze models of writing, including the work of students, that parallel the current assignment.** This can be done as a whole class activity or students can engage in this analysis in groups. A teacher-provided analysis guide will focus students.
- **Provide students with revision and editing directions**. Direction guides could include items such as, "Underline each main idea and number its supporting statements. Add supporting material when your analysis indicates the need." or "Underline every abstract descriptive word such as 'good,'

'nice,' 'bad.' Replace each with a more concrete descriptive word."

- **Make revision tools available to students at all times**. These tools can include lists of **transitional devices** and **sensory words**. Furthermore, lists of **concrete verbs** that can replace commonplace verbs such as "run," "walk," "go," etc. can be useful to students. In addition, lists of **concrete descriptive words** that can replace tired adjectives and nonspecific adverbs such as "good," "bad," "nice," "slowly," etc. will aid students in their revision and editing.
- **Require students to print their word-processed drafts and mark revisions directly on that draft by hand.** If they only revise on the computer, the teacher is unable to observe and assess his students' individual, specific revision skills and needs. When they demonstrate revision directly on their drafts, students create a map of their revision process and skills. This visual allows teachers to determine what further instruction is needed as well as enables conferencing about very specific aspects of each student's revision.
- **Provide students with revision pens**. These can be colored fine-point markers with which they are required to make revisions and edits on their drafts. It is helpful if these pens are colors other than black or blue so that revisions contrast with student work. This not only motivates students to revise but also makes their revisions readily apparent to the teacher. Keep a box of such pens easily accessible to students and encourage them to use one any time they revise.
- **Once students have revised, edited and rewritten their piece, require them to underline the revisions and new text** with a revision pen. If students revise on a word processor, require them to print each version of their work and underline the revisions with a revision pen. This makes them more aware of their revision process and their work more readily apparent to the teacher.
- **Require students to hand in all versions of their work**: first draft as well as all revisions and edited versions. Students can be required to stack these in order with the draft on the bottom and the final piece on top. Again, this heightens their awareness of their revision process and helps the teacher recognize their efforts.
- **Ask students to reflect on their revision and editing activity *in writing* immediately after the process is concluded**.

Specific reflection questions could be provided such as: "Describe your personal revision process for this piece of writing," "What strategies worked well for you?", "What will you do differently next time you revise and edit?"

Peer Response

Often teachers are reluctant to ask their students to engage in peer response because they feel students don't effectively analyze each other's writing or they quickly fall into unrelated conversation. As with all other skills, teachers cannot assume students know how to respond to another's writing. Teachers can assure effective peer response activities when they teach students *how* to analyze and effectively respond to writing.

Giving students the knowledge and vocabulary to talk about writing can begin in earlier stages of writing instruction. Skill mini-lessons and revision instruction can contribute to building this fluency. Providing students with specific features to identify and specific questions to answer about a classmate's writing can also facilitate their response.

When initially teaching students to respond to writing, it is not necessary for them to actually *talk* to one another. Give each student another's piece as well as a sheet of questions to answer about that paper:

- Write questions that require more than just a "yes" or "no" response. For example, don't just ask, "Does the writer use descriptive details?" Expand the item by adding, "List several descriptive details used by the writer. If the writer did not use descriptive details, suggest where he/she could strengthen the piece by adding some."
- Always include some questions that elicit strengths and positive features of the piece.
- Require responders to identify themselves on the response sheet.

When they have finished responding to the peer's writing by answering the questions, instruct them to staple their responses to the back of the original piece of writing. Then observe the interest with which students read the comments made by their peer responders. If a student indicates that she doesn't understand something written on the response sheet, refer her to the responder for clarification. This may also generate a spontaneous discussion about their writing.

After engaging students in written response a few times, pair them to engage in oral response. Still give them specific questions to answer about each other's papers. Initially require them to record their partner's responses to the questions about their own piece for reference during revision and editing. This requires students to stay focused on the response task as well as reinforces writing features on which you want students to concentrate.

Some classes may become proficient enough to orally respond to one another's writing without the guidance of specific questions or the requirement of written responses. Nevertheless, consider goals for your students and the desired outcomes before abandoning specific questioning and written responses.

We can attest from our own experience to the success of employing this type of instructional process with *all* students - from the most academically challenged to the most academically proficient. The teacher's satisfaction and delight from investing in this method of writing instruction comes when he can observe his students relating to one another as writers and genuinely engaging each other about their writing.

Writing Reflection

Only the most sophisticated students will independently reflect on their writing experiences after completing them. Yet all developing writers can grow from such activity. Guide students in this valuable writing stage by requiring them to reflect each time they complete the full writing process. For students inexperienced in reflection, a set of guiding reflection questions will be helpful. For more experienced writers, some general guidelines are still recommended. For instance, a teacher could ask students to reflect on each stage of their writing process for a particular piece, or students could be asked to reflect on how effectively a piece "speaks" to its audience or accomplishes its purpose. To help students make effective use of reflection as well as ensure that they actually engage in it, we recommend requiring that students record their reflections in writing. We ask our students to staple their reflection to each piece before placing it in their writing folders.

Portfolios and Writing Folders

Your school, district, or state may have specific guidelines for writing portfolios in place. If not, we suggest implementing a system that helps students collect their writing. Writing is a developmental process. Documenting writing growth is valuable not only for the teacher but also for students. This documentation can be accomplished with the use of a writing portfolio. Students can observe their own writing development by returning to their portfolio periodically to review previous writing. Furthermore, a writing portfolio allows them to choose previous endeavors to further revise and refine from time to time.

A few management techniques can enhance the value of the portfolio. Provide students with a form for keeping a record of their portfolio's contents. This form might include the date the piece was added to the folder, the teacher for whom it was completed, and the assignment to which it was in response. Consider encouraging students to add completed writing assignments to their portfolio from classes other than their English class. Requiring students to staple their reflections onto each assignment at its completion provides them with useful insight when they refer to previous work. Although it requires some clerical effort, passing student writing folders on to the next year's English teachers will be valuable for the overall writing plan for a school.

Evaluating Student Writing

Of course the tallest order for a writing teacher may be responding to "all that student writing." Think about it. If you spend just five minutes reading and responding to each student's writing assignment and you have 120 students, you need 600 minutes or ten hours to respond to just that one writing assignment. Five minutes really isn't much time to read and provide *quality* response to a piece of writing, and we know that students should do more than one writing assignment a semester in order for their writing skills to develop. Those of us who teach writing know just how challenging this task can be. What's a writing teacher to do? We can suggest a few strategies to help manage the time spent responding to student writing while maintaining meaningful feedback to students.

- Use prepared rubrics and scoring guides for response. Tailoring a scoring guide for each particular assignment enables some of a teacher's response to take the form of a checklist of criteria identified at the outset of the assignment. But don't limit response just to checks. Leave room on the scoring guide for personalized comments. Patti likes to have sections labeled "strengths" and "needs" for this purpose. Be sure to include at least one positive comment for each student paper.
- When tailoring a scoring guide for a particular assignment, include items that focus on the target revision and editing skills for that assignment.

- Strengths and needs of student writing in a particular assignment often recur from one student to another. Prepare a list of standard comments from which to draw as you respond to those recurring strengths and needs in student papers. Furthermore, rubric criteria identified at the outset of an assignment can also be responded to in standardized comments from which to draw. When utilizing this strategy, though, always make a few individualized comments for each student's work.
- Write responses to individual student writing on sticky notes. When teachers refrain from writing directly on student papers, they acknowledge ownership and autonomy of the writers as well as show respect for their writing.

We discovered long ago that if we sat down with a stack of thirty writing assignments to plow through, we'd get testy around the tenth or twelfth paper and our critical response would become inconsistent as we became saturated with and tired of our task. To ensure that all students receive a similar quality of consideration, we now employ alternate procedures. For instance, once we have finished assignments in hand, we might divide each class's papers into groups of five. We can respond to five on a planning period, five to seven after school, and five to seven at home at night. In this manner we can complete a class of thirty to thirty-five papers within two days providing quality, consistent response to each piece of student writing. This procedure makes the task less daunting.

Although writing instruction is one of a teacher's most demanding responsibilities, it can also be the most satisfying. When students who enter a class resistant to writing respond to one another as writers, when a student becomes genuinely excited about a piece of writing, when students experience the satisfaction of authentic writing for real audiences, a teacher is rewarded for all of her dedicated effort.

LEARNING LOGS & WRITERS' NOTEBOOKS
Tools for Management and Instruction in All Subject Areas

Writing notebooks or some variation of them have been around a long time. With the advent of increased interest in writing instruction during the past two decades, however, tools for encouraging students to write for diverse purposes and in varying genres has inspired the use of notebooks and journals in school classrooms. The use of journals, learning logs, and writers' notebooks has been employed to meet the needs of specific areas of writing which had often been overlooked in an earlier era focused on essays, research papers, and literary analyses. Now with renewed interest in writing to learn (learning logs), authentic writing for real audiences (transactive writing of various sorts), and continued use of writing to demonstrate learning (open response questions, assessment essays, literary analyses, etc.), new uses for notebooking tasks in classrooms have sprung up.

Kay and Patti each incorporate an ongoing writing–to-learn endeavor as an integral part of their instruction. Learning logs and writers' notebooks provide invaluable instructional and learning opportunities for both teachers and students. Although both instruments utilize writing, their value is certainly not limited to English classes. Teachers of social studies, math, science and most any other subject can make productive use of such writing tools to support content instruction; to encourage writing in and about their content area; to motivate students to analyze, interpret and explore; as well as a host of other worthwhile teaching and learning functions. When incorporating one or both of these writing tools into a classroom, teachers will be delighted to discover their ancillary management benefits.

Patti's Story – Learning Logs

After participating in a summer writing project, I returned to my classroom eager to implement numerous strategies for writing instruction I had learned. One of the first I tried was journal writing. My students' journal writing that first year was only a step beyond diary-style entries; but it laid the foundation for what would eventually evolve into the most valuable management and instructional tool that I employ – learning logs.

The simplistic prompts I initially provided for students (e.g. What is your favorite day of the week? Why?) helped them overcome resistance to writing and develop their writing fluency; but they did little to address skill development and were sometimes vulnerable to potential allegations of privacy invasion. Furthermore, this approach only scratched the surface of the learning potential the journal format offered. A series of refinements over the years has resulted in a learning tool that gives students continuous skill-based writing practice enabling progressive skill development over time. In their eventual incarnation, my learning logs provide regular, consistent, and focused practice in writing, thinking, and reflecting. In addition, regular learning log writing builds time into each class period for the teacher to take roll, sign permission forms, regroup, tie up loose ends from the previous class, deal with individual students, or just collect her thoughts.

To illustrate the range of possibilities that learning logs provide, consider the variety of applications within my English classes. During literature study, classes use learning log responses for study of literary elements, reader response to literature, literary analysis, and literary interpretation. When concentrating on writing, log responses are employed for prewriting, exploring the writing process, understanding and developing writing skills, reflecting on writing, and exploring numerous potential writing portfolio subjects. Active preparation for the state assessment is accomplished with open response prompts that mirror test item format. Learning log practice in my classroom often parallels the state test by asking students to read and respond to a real-world newspaper or magazine article. Finally, students make use of their learning logs for reflection and self-evaluation.

In its eventual manifestation, the learning log has become a strategy that can enhance every facet of content and instruction, relate classroom focus to real-world issues and events, provide management assistance, and readily demonstrate attention to the state core content and assessment. In short, the learning log may be a near ideal, all-encompassing classroom instrument. Although it should not become the sole method of instruction, the learning log can be effective as a tool that consistently supports instruction and management in any content area as well as provides all students with an opportunity for success.

Audience and Purpose

When introducing learning logs to students, I devote time to helping them clarify their audience and purpose. I also communicate this audience and purpose to parents on the parent information sheet that I distribute at open house, on parent conference day, and in parent letters. It doesn't take much prodding to help students understand that *they* are the audience for their own learning logs. Logs provide a safe place where students can figure out what their ideas are and explore how to express them, experiment with writing techniques, and take writing risks. I emphasize that they will not be graded on what they write as long as it follows the directions and responds to the prompts.

I further communicate that one purpose of the learning log is to provide students with sustained practice for the spring state assessment tests that consist primarily of open response, on-demand writing. I also point out that the log provides the opportunity for students to prewrite for the required writing portfolio as well as reflect on their own writing process. Overarching all of these pursuits is the practice that students gain in critical thinking and writing skills.

Prompts

The core of learning log effectiveness is the writing prompts. Prompts can be written that:

- provide learning value in all content areas
- address all aspects of content and instruction
- guide students through a thought process
- stimulate students to engage beyond superficial observations
- require students to employ higher order thinking skills
- facilitate elaboration in students' writing
- provide alternatives for students who might be uncomfortable with personal revelations

Developing expertise in constructing effective prompts takes thoughtful practice. My initial foray into using journal writing in instruction involved general prompts that were most often unrelated to the day's instructional focus:

> If you were building a school, what would you include in it? Why?

Over time, I learned to develop prompts that are tied to themes, concepts, or units of instruction:

> All of the stories in this unit feature characters struggling with conflicts. A conflict can sometimes be helpful. Describe a real, imagined, or observed incident in which that was the case. Explain how it was helpful.

As my proficiency and sophistication in creating prompts evolved, I learned to craft prompts that served a multiplicity of learning functions:

> Data from *The Center for Information & Research on Civic Learning & Engagement* about voting patterns of 18-24 year-olds show the following:
>
> - In the 1992 presidential election, 48% of 18-24 year-olds-voted.
> - In each presidential election year since, between 32% and 47% of 18-24 year-olds voted.

> - In the 2008 presidential election, when much media coverage was given to youth voter turnout, approximately 51% of the same age group voted.
>
> Are you and your friends looking forward to casting your first vote when you're eighteen? Draw a conclusion about how your attitude does or does not represent the viewpoint of your age group nationwide. Explain your conclusion and support it with evidence. (Note: This prompt was used at election time.)

Notice the variety of concepts and skills the above prompt spans:

- It is multidisciplinary. The prompt isn't limited to writing in an English class, but could effectively be incorporated into various social studies classes: civics, political science, government, history, or current events. It also asks students to examine statistical data which involves math as well as social studies skills.
- The origin of the data is cited providing an opportunity to reinforce the importance of crediting sources.
- Students are asked their feelings and attitudes within a context. Consider how the prompt and the responses it generates would be different if the voting data was not included.
- It asks students to connect their personal viewpoints and perspectives to the larger world beyond themselves and the school. Furthermore, it connects with current real-world activity and concerns by scheduling its use in conjunction with actual elections.
- Rather than asking questions that would result in "yes" or "no" responses, students are asked to use higher order thinking skills such as drawing conclusions and explaining. It further requires students to support their conclusions with evidence.

When our state developed a core content for instruction as part of its education reform package, learning log prompts like those above were easily adapted to that skill-based core content as well as to the open response and on-demand writing assessment formats used annually to measure teacher accountability as well as student progress:

> Data from *The Center for Information & Research on Civic Learning & Engagement* about voting patterns of 18-24 year-olds show the following:

- In the 1992 presidential election, 48% of 18-24 year-olds-voted.
- In each presidential election year since, between 32% and 47% of 18-24 year-olds voted.
- In the 2008 presidential election, when much media coverage was given to youth voter turnout, approximately 51% of the same age group voted.

Analyze the voting interest among acquaintances in your age group and use that along with the above data to **generalize** about your generation's voting attitudes. Present your observations and **conclusions** in the draft of a possible article for the school newspaper. Skills: analyze a situation, generalize, draw conclusions

Periodically I give a "free writing" prompt. Students enjoy and request these opportunities to determine their writing topics. Their requests indicate they have become comfortable with expressing themselves in writing and view writing as a viable means for exploring their thoughts, feelings, fears, frustrations, joys and opinions.

Once they have become familiar with the nature of learning log prompts, I invite students to submit prompts on topics of interest to them. When we use a student-generated prompt in class, that student receives bonus points. I've been pleased with the nature and sophistication of prompts submitted by my students.

Besides stimulating academic responses, prompts can also *inspire* student writers:

> *Not all of my classes did learning logs during various points in their evolution. An honors student from a class that did not do them commented one day, "Every day I read the writing directions (prompts) you have on the board and think about them. They're really interesting. I'd like to write about some of them."*

Needless to say, I eventually integrated use of learning logs into those classes. *Refer to the Appendix of this book for a variety of sample writing prompts in various subject areas that could be used as learning log prompts.*

Safeguards

A report or two about challenges to student journal writing as an invasion of privacy suggested that perhaps from time to time a student may feel uncomfortable writing about something personal, yet feels she is obliged to do so because it is a school assignment. With that in mind, I devised a simple strategy that provides alternatives. When writing a prompt that solicits description of and expression about a personal experience that parallels or illustrates something we are studying, I often add the phrase, "that you have experienced or *observed*." This allows students to write about themselves and their own experience or to describe an instance they have witnessed. I further suggest numerous options such as, "that you have observed first hand, on television, in a film, or read about in a book." This technique provides numerous "safe" alternatives for students and has the added benefit of offering additional sources, if a student has not had a related experience or can't think of one about which to write. I have never been challenged on invasion of privacy grounds; but I am confident that if I ever am, my learning logs and prompts will withstand scrutiny.

Student Orientation

Each of my students is required to provide a large spiral notebook that he will use exclusively for his Learning Log. To facilitate evaluation, I instruct students to copy all aspects of the prompt that I provide on the board or project on a screen in each learning log entry before they begin writing their responses. This practice also encourages students to think about the prompt before jumping into their writing. Likewise, I hold students accountable for maintaining a consistent, prescribed format for their learning logs, so that it is possible to assess an entire class's logs in a reasonable amount of time.

Early in the year I present lessons that teach prompt analysis as well as definitions of key words ("analyze," "evaluate," "infer," "discuss," "support," "explain," "evidence," etc.) Subsequently, some prompts are clearly self-explanatory while others benefit from brief explanation or instruction.

Assessment

Learning Logs are assessed once each grading period and carry the grade weight of a test. The learning log provides students who don't test well an opportunity to earn an equivalent grade over which they have some control: students determine how conscientiously they follow the log directions, how much effort to put into their log entries, plus the extent and quality of their responses. Furthermore, they have the opportunity to earn bonus points on some entries by going significantly over the required word minimum that is stated with the prompt. The scoring criteria that I establish during the first week of school include, "your grade will be based on completeness, following of directions, and quality of effort."

I employ a grade sheet *(see appendix)* for which I developed a template. This scoring sheet allows me to scan entries for the stated criteria, without laboriously reading every word of every entry. Students can turn down the corner of two, or three, or up to five entries for which they'd like me to respond. I am careful to do just that . . . *respond* and not evaluate. In this manner, it is not uncommon for me to sustain a written dialogue with a student over many weeks. By focusing assessment on measurable qualities such as completeness and following directions, students generally feel liberated thus allowing them to concentrate on their ideas and the expression of them in writing without worrying about writing what the teacher wants to read or using every comma correctly. *Read more detail about Patti's Learning Log procedure in "Thoughts About Learning Log" in the Appendix for this book.*

Tips

Keep these guidelines in mind if considering use of a learning log of your own design, yet similar to that described above:

- Relate learning log prompts to the curriculum and classroom activity.
- Incorporate skill development into learning log prompts.
- Focus on critical thinking that employs students' ideas and opinions.
- Depersonalize certain learning log prompts by providing non-personal options.
- Look for ways to use learning logs to connect your course of study to the world beyond your classroom.

Writers' Notebooks

Overview

The writer's notebook (multiple names are used to describe this tool) gives students the opportunity to use a notebook in much the same way that professional writers have done for years. But the writer's notebook in the classroom serves multiple needs, allowing students to think, write, reflect, and then draw from that written storehouse of material to compose for many purposes and audiences throughout the year. This tool lends itself to many content areas such as history, science, journalism – actually most any subject.

Writers' Notebooks as Tools

The teacher may decide on multiple uses for writer's notebooks. Some teachers:

- insist that drafting be done in the notebook;
- urge students to pre-write for special assignments in the notebook – lists, diagrams, webs – providing raw material for later drafting;
- offer quotations or "teacher-wisdom" about writing or other subjects and ask students to react to these nuggets thereby providing inspiration for future written efforts;
- prompt students to jot down ideas for possible writings and collect materials from sources, such as newspapers and magazines, which might interest them and lead to writing ideas or story lines;
- suggest doodling, drawing, and other artistic efforts as springboards to written creativity.

The writer's notebook is also a management tool. Daily writing in the notebook provides students with a writing routine without the worry of writing everything for assessment or grading. The writer's notebook is a tool with which to begin class – students write for a brief period while the teacher accomplishes necessary chores, such as taking role or preparing the classroom for a special activity. At the end of class, the writer's notebook provides opportunities for students to reflect on the day's work, play with an idea generated during a writing session, or pre-write for an upcoming assignment. Teachers must decide just what they want the writer's notebook to be in *their* classrooms. When planning to use a writer's notebook, teachers must assess instructional needs, curriculum mandates, and the needs of individual student writers, then use the notebook to meet those goals.

Writer's Notebook Requirements

Students should view the writer's notebook as a "safe' opportunity to plan and play with writing. The notebook is theirs to share with their teacher, not to hand in for a grade. Assessing a writer's notebook in any way other than for effort will usually kill its spontaneity. Teachers must determine how "to handle" the writer's notebook and stick to whatever methods they have chosen. Students, like professional writers, should think of their notebooks as friends, companions, and working partners in their quests to become better thinkers and writers.

Kay's Story – Writer's Notebooks

My only requirement for writers' notebooks is that they be sturdy, hardbound books, like the black and white composition books sold at drugstores and office supply stores. These books hold up to the demands placed upon them; they are now available in colors, so students no longer need to think of them as dull. I try to deter them from using notebooks meant to be daily diaries as a way to make the distinction between personal diaries and the writer's notebook. The first week, I display samples and offer personal testimony about use, cost, availability and other considerations. I show them my writer's notebooks and books with sample notebook pages from writers that they will recognize. I reinforce that writers' notebooks will be "work horses," and they should be able to carry the load.

Several years ago, I found myself with a small group of twenty-plus challenged seniors. Many had learning disabilities, and very few had ever been successful in an English class. I was a recent convert to writers' notebooks and other innovations that I wanted to introduce to these students. I realized, however, that my greatest challenge with this group might be changing their minds about how they learned essential English skills. I also had to convince them that they would like using writers' notebooks, which I assumed would be a difficult task. If I could get notebooks into their hands, then convince them this new method might be an acceptable way of "doing English," I felt confident that I could hold them accountable for bringing the notebooks to class and writing in them. I decided that I would be a partner in this new endeavor.

Picture this group of seniors. Thy first week, they grudgingly accommodated me in my attempt to use teaching methods, like reader response and basic collaboration. But they struggled with the newness of it all. What could I do, I wondered, to gain their trust and change their ways? I wanted them to use writers' notebooks and adapt to other ideas foreign to them. I wanted them to realize that there was more to mastering English than worksheets, grammar exercises, and questions at the end of stories.

I finally decided to make an accountability deal with my students. I suggested that I would take the responsibility for purchasing the notebooks. I had located the marble composition books at an office supply store – a bundle of three for $1.89 – a great deal. And not only, I told them, would I make the trip to the store, but I would put up half the price for each student's notebook. I overheard their comments: "She's gonna buy our book? She'll really go get the things for us? I can get an A for fifty cents?" But that gesture, I think, convinced them that I was a true believer in this "new thing," as they called it. They would give me fifty cents and I would match their contribution. Bingo! The next day I had fifty- cent contributions from over half the class. The following day all of the students had handed me their quarters, dimes, and nickels. I was surprised, yet pleased.

Now all I had to do was convince them to bring these notebooks to class and use them. They did. More of that story later. You will probably not want to be a partner in the purchase of writer's notebooks for all your students, but the books are very affordable and easily obtained. This story is related only to point out that writers' notebooks work with all levels of students.

A writer's notebooks are highly personal tools and putting too many rules and restrictions on their use often makes students resent them. My only requirement is that students date all entries. I also suggest that they may want to briefly describe entries so that when they peruse their notebooks looking for ideas, they will be able to quickly find what they need. When I collect the notebooks, my job is a pleasant one – looking at ideas, marveling at creativity, viewing unusual pre-writing strategies, sharing drafts of works in progress, and often being surprised by the personal interests and needs of my student writers.

VII ~ Grades and Grading Management

MANAGING GRADES AND GRADING

Early in her career Patti was uncomfortable with grading because she disliked the notion of making value judgments about others. This was probably rooted in her own experience as a conscientious student who strove for high grades. As such, she recalls numerous instances of holding her breath when receiving her report card waiting to see what her grades were and then not having a clue as to how her teachers arrived at those grades.

Kay remembers when she started teaching in 1967 that she longed to try non-traditional methods of grading. Like Patti, she was wary of making value judgments about students. She tried pass/fail. Didn't work; too open-ended. She tinkered with students contracting for grades - much too subjective. None of the "pie-in-the-sky" ideas seemed to work for her or her students. For many reasons, the traditional forms of grading prevailed in her classroom. In reality, students want structure and guidelines. For all their dreams of freedom, they are still motivated by grades; they want to know exactly where they stand when grades are in question. In addition, parents want to know how their children measure up to the norm, fellow classmates, and their parental expectations.

As we gained experience teaching, we realized that:

- Grading does not have to consist of teachers' value judgments.
- Students don't have to wonder what their grades will be.
- Students don't have to speculate about how their teachers arrived at those grades.

Grades are measures of student achievement and performance for which *they themselves* are responsible.

What is the purpose of grades and grading? It's really quite simple: **to measure students' learning and to indicate the quality of learning performance.** As such, students need to understand that the teacher does not *give* them a grade, but they *earn* that grade. Teachers help students comprehend this reality with actions as well as words. Unfortunately, teachers can – sometimes unwittingly - undermine this message.

- If a teacher tells his students they will receive grades they have earned but proceeds to use grades as punishment, his words won't make much of an impression.
- If students realize grades are not equitably awarded, telling them they must earn their grades will fall on deaf ears.
- If grades are given to a student because she is nice, cooperative, or cute, a message is sent to the entire class – one that will haunt a teacher throughout the school year.
- If a student is given a grade that he didn't earn because a teacher feels sorry for him, that student isn't helped in the long run.

Both students and teachers benefit when students feel confident that what they do or do not do in terms of learning determines their grades – not whether or not the teacher likes them. Using this concept to develop procedures means allowing students a means by which to know at all times what their grades are and to know exactly how the teacher arrived at the grades that appear on their progress reports or report cards.

Record and calculate grades accurately, conscientiously, and meticulously. **Documentation** is always important for teachers, but it is especially important when dealing with student grades. Be able to substantiate every grade given with concrete documentation; if a teacher can't, he leaves himself vulnerable. Students and parents challenge grades more than ever in this day and age. It's becoming increasingly common for parents to go to the board of education or even the media over a grading dispute. Make sure that you can operate with the confidence that, if called upon, you could satisfactorily justify every grade given.

It is often up to teachers how to specifically structure the grades in their classes, perhaps with school or district guidelines. We'd like to recommend some criteria to consider.

Include numerous components in final grades. Letting a final grade hinge on one or two major assignments or tests is fraught with problems. First of all, it does not allow students many opportunities for success; one slip-up could result in a failing grade for the entire grading period. Authentic grades that accomplish the purpose defined above should reflect student performance *throughout* a grading period, not just at the time those one or two items are completed. Keep in mind that all students do not learn in the same manner; therefore, providing a diversity of opportunities for students to demonstrate their learning and learning performance is desirable. Not all students test well; consequently, it is advisable to provide additional opportunities for such students to accumulate good grades to offset possible low test scores, yet still demonstrate their learning.

In grading assignments and projects **measure students' overall activity and performance by grading more than just finished products.** Learning occurs while students are engaged in the *process* of doing an assignment or project, so why give grade credit for only the finished *product*? We've all had experiences where we worked really hard, learned a lot, but produced a finished "something" that just didn't reflect that effort. Think about trying to learn to sew or do woodworking. Perhaps you gave it all you had, really did learn from the process in which you engaged, and knew considerably more when you finished than at the outset; but your finished dress or curio cabinet just didn't turn out very well. Would a sole grade based entirely on that dress or curio cabinet truly reflect your performance and learning? Some might say so, but keep in mind that grades should be a *measurement*, not a reward or value judgment.

When students know that only a finished product will determine their grade, then realize in the midst of developing their product that it may not be perfect, why shouldn't they throw up their hands and give up? Actually, many students behave in just this manner; but their teachers may not realize the source of the frustration. Grading multiple aspects of an activity provides students with numerous opportunities for success and motivates them to persist. For example, in writing assignments we give grade credit for each stage of the writing process (prewriting, drafting, revising, etc.), not just the finished piece of writing. We actually require our students to hand in all of their writing process work with the finished piece. In this manner, it is obvious to them as well as to us they have engaged in a learning process and not just thrown something together or cribbed a finished product from the Internet. This same strategy can apply in math, science, social studies, art, and most any other subject due to the process nature of learning.

Tell students how they will be graded when making assignments. When they know at the outset what will be expected in order to earn certain grades, students have the opportunity to perform up to the teacher's expectations. If students must guess at how a teacher will evaluate their work, they are handicapped before they even begin. Guessing incorrectly, students may focus on aspects of an assignment or project the teacher doesn't consider in her evaluation. In such a situation, both student and teacher lose. The student is frustrated because he genuinely doesn't know how to go about working toward the teacher's uncommunicated criteria, and the teacher is frustrated because the student appears not to have performed up to her standards. In actuality, the student may have been able to do just what the teacher wanted him to do, if he had known what that was.

Assignments in some classes are particularly susceptible to this circumstance because much of the evaluated work is subjective: writing assignments, open response items, and essay questions. As English teachers, we have faced this challenge throughout our careers. It is possible to make grading student work that does not have one and only one correct answer somewhat objective as well as consistent by using **rubrics** and **scoring guides**. By establishing scoring criteria, communicating them at the origin of an assignment, and adhering to them when evaluating student work, teachers remove the mystery surrounding the grading of subjective work. This concept applies not just to writing assignments but also to any project or activity in any class that entails a certain degree of subjective assessment. Consider collaborating with students to develop rubrics for upcoming assignments. Invariably students establish more rigorous standards than the teacher may have done on her own.

Rubrics account for another learning aspect: none of us perfects a skill the first time out, or even the second or third time. The first time you play tennis after having received instruction from a pro, can you reasonably expect to play a flawless game? How would you feel if that game was evaluated and ranked with perfection as the standard? Would such an evaluation motivate or discourage you? The same phenomenon applies in the classroom. Expecting students to produce perfect comparative literature essays, research papers, case studies, proofs, lab reports, or short stories is unreasonable . . . especially if it is their first effort. Rubrics and scoring guides allow teachers to establish realistic standards for performance, adjust those performance standards to encourage and reflect skill development, and include some scoring criteria that all students can accomplish if making adequate effort.

Finding a way to grade and provide credit for **daily work** without becoming buried in stacks of assignments is a teacher's continual challenge. Taking it as it comes and letting whether or not it gets graded fall to chance can drive a teacher crazy and will deprive students of useful learning experiences and feedback. Teachers do themselves a favor by actively seeking methods for dealing with student work. We have both developed procedures that allow us to process those mounds of papers fairly efficiently.

Patti determines points received on daily assignments using the following rubric:

6 points – Bonus; on time, directions followed, above and beyond the requirement, exceptional effort

5 points – Complete, on time, and according to directions with mostly correct answers

4 points – Complete or nearly complete, on time, according to directions with mostly correct answers
3 points – Somewhat incomplete and/or somewhat late and/or somewhat not according to directions with some incorrect answers
2 points – Very incomplete and/or very late and/or not according to directions and/or many incorrect answers
1 point - Inadequate and/or unsatisfactory effort
0 points - No credit: too incomplete and/or too late and/or not according to directions

At the end of the grading period she tallies each student's points and converts that total to a percentage based on the number of possible points. Using this system frees her from meticulously reading each and every response to each and every assignment item. This method makes it possible to expedite the checking of daily class work.

Kay tries to keep grading simple. Each assignment carries a specific number of points. For example:

- A simple homework assignment might be worth 10-20 points.
- A short daily quiz might tally 20-30 points.
- A major writing assignment carries 75-100 points.
- A test may be worth 100 or more points.
- A special project requiring a major time commitment might add up to 200 or more points.

An assignment rubric lets students know the value of each assignment. At the end of a grading period, the points students have accumulated are totaled and averaged to determine the grade. The district's grading scale is adhered to, and if students keep an account of their points when work is returned, they can always know where they stand grade wise.

Through many years of development, we both eventually refined **systems** for handling grades and grading that work effectively for us, for our students, and for their parents.

Patti's System

Patti learned early that ensuring her students know their grades both throughout the grading period and before receiving their progress reports/report cards benefits them and serves her well. It only took one student flying off the handle upon seeing his progress report to convince her that she must come up with a way to prevent the progress report/report card grade from being a shock. Keeping in mind that adolescents have very short attention spans, she devised a system that:

- Helps students understand the various components of their grades and how each component affects their final grade.
- Enables students to remember the work they have and haven't completed throughout the grading period.
- Allows parents to know when sluggish performance puts their child's grade in jeopardy while there is still time to rectify the situation.
- Conveys to students and parents that accountability rests with students for whatever grades are earned.

Initially Patti gives each student a **folder** and requires him to keep all graded, returned work in it. Each class has a designated filing cabinet drawer, so these folders never leave the classroom. Each student keeps a **Personal Grade Record** (See appendix.) in that folder. As graded work is returned, students are required to record it on this Personal Grade Record. Patti devotes class time to this effort because it is a valuable part of the overall learning experience. In parent conferences, she shows the student's folder and Personal Grade Record to parents which makes it clear that the student should know what he is missing and needs to hand in.

Halfway through the grading period, Patti sends **notices to parents** (See Appendix.) of students who are missing work or in other ways putting their final grade in jeopardy. Increasingly, schools use electronic grade books that allow parents access to their student's grade information. Although this assigns some responsibility to parents for keeping informed, it's still a good idea to conscientiously alert parents when students are at risk of failing. The last thing a teacher wants to hear from a parent is, "If I had known he might not pass, I would have done something." When teachers have clearly alerted parents in time for corrective action to occur, their credibility with parents, students and administration is secure and accountability for student performance lies where it belongs – with students and parents.

Before progress reports/report cards are distributed, Patti requires each student to complete a **Grade Review Sheet** (See Appendix.). She created a template and fills in specific details as needed for each grading period. Then students fill in their grades, perform the indicated calculations, and hand it in for verification. An added value of the Grade Review Sheet is that it catches any possible calculation mistakes allowing Patti to make corrections before turning grades in.

Once verified, students will not receive points for this assignment until it is returned with a parent or guardian signature. She awards bonus points for prompt return as an incentive. The potential problem of forged parent signatures usually works itself out. If a grade is called into question, Patti shows the student folder with the signed Grade Review Sheet to the parent(s). She usually doesn't have to say anything if the signature has been forged, because it is clear to the parent that Patti has done her part and that the student has not told the whole story. Read more about Patti's Grade Review Sheet in "Teacher Behaviors That Impact Classroom Management."

After calculating their own grades, students are required to **reflect** on that grade and how it became what it is. This is accomplished with prompts such as these to which students are required to respond in their learning logs:

> **Analyze** your grade in this class for the grading period just ended. **Relate** each part of your grade to your overall grade for the grading period. Then **explain** what you will do during the upcoming grading period to earn the grade that you would like to make.
>
> Based on your grade and Grade Review Sheet for this grading period, **predict** what your final grade will be for the semester. Then **explain** why you think that will be your final grade. **Develop** and **support** your explanation with reasons as well as examples drawn from your work during the grading period just ended.
>
> Based on your experience and observation, **draw a conclusion** about the relationship between the first grading period's grades and student success for the entire semester. **Draft** a motivational statement for next year's school planner based on this conclusion.

More in-depth reflection is required at semester's end when students complete an assignment called "Semester Success" (See Appendix.) This assignment asks students to consider class expectations and their class performance in relation to factors that have influenced their final grades.

Notice that learning log prompts ask students to employ academic skills such as analyzing, relating, explaining, predicting, and drawing conclusions. As well, they are guided to engage in critical thinking: specificity and detailed description. Furthermore, students are prompted to utilize academic writing skills: develop and support, use reasons and examples, and draft for an audience in an authentic format. There is no reason why housekeeping chores can't give students academic practice. In fact, reflecting on their grade and performance is an authentic application of academic skills.

Kay's System

With advanced program seniors, Kay generally relies on her students to keep up with their own grades during six week and semester periods. She urges them to tally their grades every week and to make time for conferences, if they feel their grades are slipping. However, she watches students' grades carefully, checking her grade book every week as points mount up or fail to accumulate. She checks the book for make-up work not completed. When a situation warrants concern, such as a student missing many assignments or a grade plummeting more than one letter, she calls the student in for a conference and phones or e-mails the parents. When a falling or failing grade is eminent, both students and parents must know before the grade report is carried home.

Kay tries to make the burden of keeping up with grades the students' responsibility. Nevertheless, even seniors will often be reluctant to admit to falling or failing grades. The heartache of surprise for individual students, their parents and the teacher can be avoided by setting up a method for frequently checking grades before report time. After the first or second grading period, patterns of student progress or lack of it are usually well defined. However, there are always exceptions. Conferences, letters, phone calls and e-mails can alleviate or eliminate difficult grade situations for every concerned party.

"Doing Grades"

At the end of a grading period teachers may feel as though they are meeting themselves coming and going. They're trying to finish up grading and recording in time to average grades and get them submitted by a deadline. Throughout this chore, teachers will typically be required to meet and teach all of their classes. We always breathe a sigh of relief once we get our grades turned in and "just teaching" seems much easier for a few days. Learn to **anticipate** those "crunch times" and take action to make them a little less hectic. Some organizational procedures we've found helpful at grade time include the following:

- Consider cutting off *your* grading a few days before the official deadline to allow more time to accomplish your multiple grade-related tasks.
- Make your deadline for make-up and late work a few days before the end of a grading period to allow yourself time to process these papers.
- Avoid making big projects or writing assignments due at the end of a grading period; instead schedule them more towards the middle.
- Plan due dates for grading-intensive assignments or tests with designated time in your schedule to grade each class's work. This may mean collecting the assignment from each class period on a different day of the week or giving a major test at least a week before the grading period ends.
- Plan instruction so that students are engaged in individual tasks requiring a minimum of teacher intervention during the last few days of a grading period when you're trying to finish grading, recording, and averaging grades. This is a time when a relevant instructional video might appropriately be used.

More and more schools are utilizing electronic grade recording programs that can facilitate grade calculating and reporting, but computers don't yet assume the majority of actual grading tasks. Planning ahead to allow yourself reasonable time to process, grade, record or enter grades will make "doing grades" much less stressful for you and therefore less so for your students.

Although grading can be one of a teacher's more burdensome tasks, planning and resourcefulness can make the process productive for students, informative for parents, and efficient for teachers. Unsystematic handling of grades can lead to frustration, defensiveness, and heartache for a teacher. Establishing a system for handling grades should be a priority among the various procedures required of teachers.

EXTRA CREDIT MANAGEMENT

For most students "extra credit" and "bonus" are magic words. For teachers, bonuses and extra credit can be tools for positive reinforcement, grade improvement and enhancement, and/or academic discovery. It is in everyone's best interest if teachers structure extra credit activity so that students will learn something from their efforts rather than using it merely as an exercise to accumulate points or enhance a grade. Based on our experience, for extra credit and bonuses to be successful, they *must* be useful work that is oriented to the curriculum and extend students' learning.

Every teacher will encounter a student or parent who requests extra credit at the end of a grading period to bolster a student's sagging grade. Work done under those circumstances may not result in much learning, since its only purpose is to improve a grade. Moreover, what incentive do students have to work during class sessions throughout the grading period, if they know they can enhance their grade by doing extra credit just before the end of the term? To avoid difficult last-minute pleas from students and parents, **anticipate** such requests, determine an extra credit policy, **plan** extra credit procedures, and **communicate** such policies to all concerned parties early in the school year.

For Positive Reinforcement

Opportunities to earn bonus points can be built into regular class activities to **positively reinforce** constructive learning behavior. This particularly motivates at-risk or lazy students to do daily class work and to apply themselves seriously to that learning work.

For instance, students in Patti's classes can earn over 100% on their learning logs and individual assignments by "going significantly beyond the minimum requirement". "Significantly beyond" can mean writing particularly thoughtful and well-developed responses, or it can mean sticking with an unusually long and involved assignment to completion. These points are awarded at the teacher's discretion as assignments are graded; but they aren't awarded indiscriminately, which would diminish their value. The points definitely have to be earned, so that students know *they* have *earned* them with their efforts. Such rewards encourage and motivate students to exert maximum effort in future assignments.

Sometimes small bonus opportunities can be offered for daily classroom work, quizzes, vocabulary lessons or tests. For example, on vocabulary tests, students can be awarded several bonus points for knowing additional word forms for a targeted vocabulary word (i.e. "erudition" for the target word "erudite"). The student's ability to correctly use two or more words from a target list in the same sentence might earn bonus points on a vocabulary sentence exercise. This strategy motivates students to go beyond the minimum learning requirements to extend their learning and rewards their efforts for doing so.

Students can also earn more than 100% on their learning performance grade (For more detail about learning performance grades, see the Behavior Management section of this book.) This **positive reinforcement** rewards students for attending class regularly and behaving like serious learners. Students earn bonus learning performance points for efforts such as making a particularly thoughtful or insightful contribution to class discussion, volunteering to read aloud, or volunteering to go first on a performance activity. This bonus technique is a powerful behavioral influence because it uses **positive reinforcement** to clearly reward *learning* behavior rather than rewarding behavior for behavior's sake.

Such opportunities can extend learning from original classroom work and reward enthusiastic learners. At the same time, such incentives can motivate reluctant or immature learners.

For Grade Improvement

Often students, despite hard work, don't have the grades to pass for a grading period. In some situations, it's reasonable to provide extra work that ties into or complements the lessons these students have found difficult. Legitimate reasons to offer such an opportunity might include:

- To compensate for missed participation opportunities due to extended illness
- To offer an additional alternative for students who may test poorly even when they "know the material"
- To provide an additional opportunity to learn content when a student has completed all required work but hasn't quite achieved mastery

In addition, extra options can provide students with added opportunities to learn or relearn material from challenging lessons. For example, if students fail a test based on a novel, they might read a related piece of literature and develop a written comparison to the original work. If they've had trouble with poetry, they might analyze the features they like best in poems they have chosen. **We recommend that extra assignments reinforce and connect to the original work, which was found difficult, as well as engage the student in learning.**

Definite guidelines are needed in cases where students seek extra credit to improve a grade. Consider the following requirements. To be eligible for extra credit work, students must:

- have completed *all* assigned class work and submitted it *on time*
- sign up for the extra credit and agree to *complete* it and submit it *on time*. Students who fail to meet this guideline become

ineligible for further extra credit during that semester. They *may* become eligible again in a new semester.

- follow the parameters of the assignment *thoughtfully* and *thoroughly* and complete a product which shows *effort* and *quality*

Often students may think that merely completing an extra credit assignment is enough in itself to improve a low or failing grade. It is important to communicate minimum requirements that must be met in order to achieve credit before students take on an extra credit assignment. Our belief is that extra credit assignments require *additional* work that demonstrates significant effort, engaged learning activity and a quality product. These kinds of assignments reinforce responsibility and teach values that can carry over to everyday classroom performance.

For Grade Enhancement

A potentially controversial use of extra credit is for grade enhancement. Enthusiastic learners may have a B+, but would like an A. In this case, a teacher who is willing to offer such opportunities must find a valuable lesson or mini-project, which helps learners make discoveries on their own. The most important aspect of extra credit projects for learning enhancement is to make them *worthwhile* learning tools. An example of **Kay**'s use of extra credit for grade enhancement:

A few years ago when teaching poetry, I mentioned the U.S. poet laureate. None of my students was aware of what a poet laureate did or which poets occupied the current or former position. I constructed an extra credit mini-project challenging students to find information about both U.S. and British poets laureate. They made posters, so classmates learned from each other's efforts.

The poet laureate extra credit opportunity generated so many posters that I shared them with English department colleagues for display in their classrooms thus providing my students with an authentic audience for their work. After several weeks of display, my students as well as others had learned about the role of poet laureate.

For Discovery/Academic Curiosity

In some classes, extra credit can reward the individual discovery process and promote academic curiosity. Much discovery, however, takes place outside the classroom as evidenced by **Kay**'s experience:

My humanities students were studying the history of photography, researching great masters, and learning to recognize the qualities of a good photograph. Halfway through the unit, I read in the newspaper about an exhibit of Vietnam War photographs taken by journalists who had lost their lives covering the war. The classroom connection was perfect, as photojournalism was an integral part of the study. I offered extra credit to anyone who wanted to drive to the state capitol, about 50 miles away, to view the photographic exhibit. To my surprise, many students attended the exhibit as a family outing giving the extra credit opportunity added value.

Activities outside of the classroom make popular extra credit exercises. However, the teacher who assigns them must also participate in the activity to effectively assess post-visit student work. Students can be required to submit evidence from a visit – a ticket stub, a program or handout, or a note from an event official as proof of attendance. Although the activity itself is the motivation for a visit, teachers can design related assignments to assess and enhance student learning. A follow-up report or presentation not only assesses what an individual student has learned from an activity but can also benefit those students who did not participate. Keep in mind, these projects (as with all extra credit) may mean extra work for the teacher, who must find, design, and assess this additional activity.

Be alert to equity matters when offering extra credit. When offering activities such as visits to community venues or trips out of town, be aware that not everyone will have transportation or be able to afford tickets. Be sure to provide some options that are accessible for all. Students can then select the opportunity which best suits their interests and their access.

Extra Credit Policies

Have an extra credit policy and make sure *everyone* knows it. Extra credit guidelines need to be clearly stated in writing the first time extra work is offered to students. Furthermore, inform administrators and parents of the extra credit policy early in the school term. Everyone concerned needs to have multiple opportunities to be informed of the policy early on.

Features that have worked effectively in our extra credit policies include:

- Extra credit work will only be available after *all* required work is satisfactorily completed.
- Extra credit work must be done at the time it is offered with no make-up opportunities.
- Extra credit work must reflect significant effort and result in a quality product. Rubrics can be designed for this purpose.

- Extra credit must be completed and submitted by the *teacher-designated* deadline.

The above policy features provide the following management advantages:

- Accommodate those inevitable students who can be counted on to finish their work before everyone else
- Provide engaging activity to prevent disruption by idle students
- Account for the fact that not all students work at the same rate
- Encourage good attendance with positive reinforcement
- Reward diligence on required work
- Require students to assume responsibility

Guidelines for teachers to consider when planning extra credit activities:

- Base extra credit on the current course of study.
- Provide meaningful learning experiences, not just "busy work." We do not recommend activities such as seek-and-finds or crossword puzzles unless they are *particularly* relevant to the current course of study.
- Design extra credit that requires students to use higher order thinking skills.
- Anticipate the need for and plan extra credit activities/assignments along with the required work when engaged in unit planning.

Keep in mind this teacher "trick" and see if it holds true in your experience. We can often count on several students to be willing to do almost anything for extra credit. Curiously, an activity that some students might procrastinate about as a required assignment, takes on added appeal for those same students when it's offered for extra credit. We've never figured out the psychology behind this behavior, but we've seen it played out over and over.

MANAGING MAKE-UP & LATE WORK

Most any teacher will tell you that **late** and **make-up work** are the banes of her existence. Any time a teacher must deal with work separately from that of the rest of the class, it requires more time to process. Furthermore, students are notorious for not taking the initiative to handle their own make-up work expediently, yet school administrators and parents expect teachers to make sure that students have every opportunity to acquire and complete make-up work. After struggling with this frustrating dilemma for several years, we both have developed procedures that at least have kept us from "losing our minds."

Kay's Procedures

Over years of teaching, Kay found that taking time before or after class to inform absent students about missing work was nearly impossible. Coming after school for this information was a hassle for both parties. She has found that a logging procedure has worked well for her over the years with older, more able students.

Students can be held accountable to each other by assigning them the task of keeping a **class log**. A log binder that is a list of each day's activities exists for each class. A daily sheet describes each class activity in detail, provides due dates for class work, and announces quizzes, tests, and other upcoming assignments. One student serves as "the logger" each week and "logs" on a daily basis. When students are absent or when they want to double check an assignment, they can easily consult the log, which is kept in the room at all times. This activity makes students accountable to each other for accuracy and responsibility.

Several times a week, Kay checks to make sure the log is in good shape. When it breaks down, absent students let her know. Usually the offender will sheepishly grab the log and make amends. Like all procedures in the classroom, the teacher must instruct students in how to prepare logs properly. As a bonus, teaching this procedure provides several great mini-lessons in careful listening, accurate recording, and concise writing. The class log is a useful tool with built-in opportunities for both teaching and learning. (Refer to the Appendix for this book to see a model of a Daily Log Sheet.)

Some teachers with younger or less able students prefer to keep the class log themselves to assure that all information will be timely and accurate. And in some classrooms the high absentee rate may cause a breakdown in smooth logging procedure. Kay admits that now and then unforeseen reasons cause her carefully planned procedure to need tweaking. She remembers one class where she had to assume log duties to make the system work properly.

In addition to keeping up with work, students must turn work in on time. This rule has great importance in the "real world" students will soon enter. Being punctual, meeting deadlines, paying bills on time – students must learn the value of timeliness. Holding them accountable for the timely submission of schoolwork is one way of reinforcing this most important lesson. If a teacher decides to accept late work from students, she should be sure to have a policy and *stick with it.* Once a teacher makes an exception for a student "just this once," all students will expect exceptions. Soon that teacher will be doing a great deal of extra work. Of course, exceptions may need to occur for long absences and other unforeseen difficulties.

Kay tells her classes that one indication of a conscientious student is handing in work on time. When they are unable to attend school, she encourages them to make arrangements to get work delivered, especially important projects, major assignments, or collaborative efforts. Many mornings she has opened her classroom door to parents on their way to work who have stopped off to deliver their ailing child's assignment. When the students return, she makes sure to praise them for their efficiency. Her standard make-up policy allows as many days as a student was absent to complete and hand in make-up assignments. However, some teacher discretion may need to override the policy from time to time.

Teachers may have a district or local school policy for make-up work after absences. Parents usually expect teachers to adhere to the established policy. If a teacher plans to institute a policy of his own, he should be sure to put it in writing and make sure all students know its parameters.

Patti's Procedures

During her beginning-of-the-year orientation, Patti tells students they are **accountable** for their make-up work: "When you have been absent, it is *your* responsibility to check the class notebook to see what you need to make up and what was handed in while you were absent."

The **class notebook** is the key to her make-up procedure. She uses a three-ring binder, which she personally updates each day. Although Kay assigns updating chores to students (with periodic teacher monitoring), Patti assumes that responsibility because she wants to be absolutely sure her students can confidently rely on the class notebook for *all* of the information they need to satisfactorily complete make-up work.

Patti may have a notebook for each class; but more often, she has a notebook for each teaching preparation and makes notations specific to individual class periods on notebook pages. The notebook pages are kept in chronological order to parallel daily class activity. The first notebook page lists "Assignments Handed In." Each time Patti collects an assignment, she records it on this page with the collection date. When she makes assignments, she puts a copy of each one in the notebook and writes any oral directions that were given in class directly on the assignment itself. Each time a quiz or test is given, she inserts a page announcing that information with instructions for make-up. Some pages can be standardized and photocopied with pertinent details added when a copy of that page is used. For instance, "Today a quiz was given over __________." or "Today we had a reading session. Make arrangements with the teacher to do make-up reading."

Since Patti provides this resource, she does not tell students what they need to make up; instead she refers them to the class notebook. It doesn't take long for absent students to pick up the class notebook as they reenter class and check what they need to do to make up missed work. Patti requires students to give her a **note** requesting anything needed from her to complete make-up work. This lowers her stress level and eliminates the need to remember what various students have told her they need. A note that reads "yesterday's work" is returned to the writer with a reminder that Patti requires *specific* information in order to provide the work.

Although Patti implements guidelines for handing in make-up and late work promptly, she establishes an absolute **final deadline** after which no work is accepted. It is chosen to allow time to process make-up and late papers before the crush of final recording and grade averaging for progress reports or report cards. Patti provides a detailed explanation of the deadline and how it works; after that, she frequently reminds students as the deadline approaches. As she reminds students of the impending deadline, she explicitly points out that it's a deadline for work that is already behind schedule and emphasizes that no work will be accepted after the deadline. One aspect of her reminders is the use of possible scenarios in which students might want to hand in assignments after the deadline. She tries to **anticipate** every possible situation and counteract its occurrence by addressing it *before* the fact. These situations include field trip absences, excused absences, in-school suspension, or not securing a copy of an assignment in time to do it by the deadline. After running through a litany of possibilities, she emphasizes that none of these would create an exception to the no-papers-after-the-deadline policy – and sticks to it. She wants to avoid students trying to hand in papers after the cutoff and claiming they didn't know about that deadline and the resulting **consequences**.

Students who have waited until the last possible day often demonstrate initiative and accountability by having a parent or classmate hand in an assignment for them. Although it is last minute and does involve make-up and late work, this initiative, nonetheless, indicates that students are learning to be at least somewhat **accountable.** Not only does Patti's procedure make her life less hectic and stressful, but it also provides valuable life lessons for students. Such benefits that extend beyond the classroom often result when a teacher thoughtfully develops and implements classroom procedures.

The first time Patti instituted the deadline, numerous students waited until the actual deadline day itself thus inundating her with late and make-up assignments. She immediately recognized the flaw in her policy and began rethinking the procedure to discourage this last-minute rush in the future. Part of the revision included deducting points from late and make-up assignments handed in on the actual deadline day if the assignment had been outstanding for an excessive amount of time. The **consequence** of procrastinating until the last minute was loss of some credit. By building in an incentive for completing make-up work and handing it in promptly, she offset the likelihood of another shower of varied assignments on the deadline day.

A simple, yet very helpful, tip for processing late and make-up work: When students hand in late or make-up work, immediately mark it with the date it was handed in. Patti prefers to do this in brightly colored ink. Make such notations consistently and let students observe you doing so. A week later or even at grade reporting time, when an errant student may try to claim an assignment was handed in on time in order to argue for a few extra points, it will serve a teacher (and her nerves) well to point to the date the paper was handed in clearly marked in green or purple or orange ink.

Develop a policy for make-up quizzes and tests before the need arises. Each time Patti administers a quiz or test, she lists the names of the absentees on a 3x5 card, clips it to the make-up quizzes/tests, and places them in an "active tray" for each class. In this manner, she can easily keep track of who needs to take these make-ups. Students are responsible for taking the initiative to do make-up, yet she monitors procrastinators not wanting them to fail because they haven't made up quizzes or a test. Patti reminds students prone to end up in that situation. She also uses peer pressure to nudge students into action by announcing that she can't return a class's graded quiz/test until everyone has made it up. This generally motivates most of the procrastinators.

Make-Up Work

The advent and proliferation of technology can help teachers manage make-up work. Increasingly, computer programs provided by schools, districts or even textbook publishers make it possible for teachers to post assignment directions, and in some cases, assignments themselves online. With such technology, students can access the information and/or assignment at will. This innovation is a great tool for teachers and students, but we don't recommend exclusively relying on technology to address make-up work needs. Computers crash and systems go down. All students do not have ready access to computers and the Internet. Our suggestion is to continue with a classroom policy and routine for getting information and materials to students and for collecting and processing that work. Consider technological access a support tool, but not the sole tool when addressing make-up work needs.

Late Work

Although we would like to make a blanket policy that no class work will be accepted late, in reality that generally is not a practical option. When students are conscientious and academically-motivated, they may, for the most part, complete and hand in class work on time. With younger, more immature, and/or less academically prone students, though, a no-exceptions policy could relegate them to failure early in a grading period. We, instead, advocate creating realistic classroom practices that enable even less academically-inclined students to complete work. For example:

- Provide class time and teacher assistance for working on assignments.
- Allow additional class time the following day, if warranted, for students to complete work with teacher support.
- Frequently review, remind and reinforce deadlines.
- Establish progress checks and updates for activities that extend over several days or require a certain degree of independent effort.

Often, students who would not complete work on time if left alone to do so, will perform satisfactorily with a degree of structure and support.

We believe teachers should recognize the needs of their students, create systems that will address those needs, provide students with multiple opportunities to be successful and positively reinforce productive performance. When those features are in place in a classroom, the number of students handing in late work is reduced.

Incentives for completing work and handing it in on time generally work more effectively to motivate students than do penalties for work handed in late. That said, we do not feel that late work should be without consequences. When work is handed in late, apply consequences; but do not make them so severe that they doom students to failure. Once a student realizes there is no possibility that he can be successful, he may quit trying and become a negative influence in a classroom. Losing a few points on a late assignment is a reminder that procrastination has disadvantages but does not relegate the student to potential failure that a "0" on that same late assignment might.

Make-up and late work can drive a teacher crazy if she hasn't created a routine for handling it and taught her students to follow that procedure. Increasingly schools are providing computers in teachers' classrooms that can ease grade calculating and reporting, but teachers still must grade and record/enter those grades. Anything teachers can do to facilitate that process will make them more efficient and less stressed. In our experience dealing with make-up work has never been easy, but it became considerably less frustrating once we established and maintained consistent systems within our classrooms for make-up work.

DEALING WITH CHEATING

We'd like to think all of our students are motivated by the joy of learning and appreciate the satisfaction of a task well done. In the real world, it sometimes just doesn't work that way. To begin with, we teach adolescents for whom immediate gratification rules and procrastination is a way of life. Furthermore, they do not have the life experience to appreciate the more subtle nature of intrinsic rewards. Add to that the acquisitive, materialistic, and competitive influences predominant in our society. With all these factors at play, we are bound to have some students who try to take the easy way out. Teachers may not know when their students have cheated on a test, copied a homework assignment, or plagiarized a writing assignment; but when teachers *do* recognize such behavior, students should experience **consequences** for their deception. **Teachers can manage their classroom to discourage cheating and make it difficult for students to engage in fraud.**

Schools and school districts often have a cheating policy. Familiarize yourself with it and incorporate it into opening-of-the-school-year class orientation. **Anticipate** potential situations by developing a personalized and clearly articulated policy that is communicated to students, parents, counselors, and administrators. We recommend a zero tolerance policy for cheating with unmistakably identified consequences for violation of that policy. You should be fully prepared to enforce your policy, if the need arises.

Quizzes and Tests

One of the most common forms of cheating is done on **quizzes** and **tests**. Diminish the possibility by **preparing multiple forms of each quiz or test**; then alternate forms among students or classes. Although a time-consuming effort, this thoroughness conveys to students from the very first quiz or test of the school year that this is a class in which cheating will not be easy. The preponderance of computers makes this task much easier than in the recent past. Some publishers provide test generators correlated with their texts that automatically scramble test items and quickly produce multiple versions of a test. Take advantage of this technology. **Develop a system for quiz/test administration in your class** that complicates possible efforts to copy or otherwise cheat when those are being administered. **Monitor your students while they are testing.** Rather than sitting at your desk and grading papers, walk among your students and use proximity to make cribbing or copying more difficult.

> ***Patti*** *consistently makes three versions of each quiz and test: morning, afternoon, and make-up. Students are required to write their answers on separate paper. She numbers each quiz/test and requires students to record that number on their response sheets. Once tests and response sheets have been handed in, she determines if any quiz/test has not been returned. Her system provides a means to determine which student(s) has not returned a quiz/test. Although initially time-consuming, this systematic approach allows her to reuse testing materials in the future, repaying her for some of that initial outlay of time. Furthermore, once students observe the system in play, they are usually discouraged from trying to "beat the system."*

Assignments

When students work on **assignments** outside the classroom, teachers have little means to monitor the originality of the work. Assignments with objective items – fill-in-the-blank, multiple choice, seek-and-find, matching, etc. - are so easy for students to copy that we feel they should be limited to in-class use and minimized even there. Useful for quick comprehension checks, students will only be utilizing their lower order thinking skills, when such recall exercises comprise the bulk of assignments. Open response items that require critical thinking provide much more valuable practice in higher order thinking skills and are difficult to copy without detection. **Patti**'s use of learning log prompts illustrates this point:

> *When reading and responding to entries in students' learning logs, I noticed considerable similarity in numerous entries of both a young man and a young woman. When I called the young man's*

mother, she was indignant that I should suggest her son had copied. She wanted to know why I didn't assume the young woman had done the copying. When I read a passage from her son's learning log that vividly described first person details of "his" labor and the subsequent delivery of "his" child, the mother's ire quickly shifted to where it belonged - her son.

Writing Assignments

Writing assignments pose a different kind of challenge – **plagiarism.** We hear about students purchasing essays and term papers over the Internet; we read student writing that is technically perfect but clearly not characteristic of other writing submitted by that student. How do teachers stay ahead of the "quick fixes" technology has made possible, not to mention old-fashioned copying out of a book or parent-composed papers turned in under a student's name?

First consider what might motivate a student to plagiarize. Sure, some students will wait until the last minute or will not be willing to make the effort that composing requires. However, many students are intimidated by the very idea of writing and have limited confidence in their ability to accomplish the task. Often students do not even know how to attack a writing task. The first thing that teachers can do to discourage plagiarism is assess students' writing development and begin **teaching them how to engage in the writing process as well as in practical writing strategies**. When students feel some degree of confidence in their ability to cope with a writing task, they will be less tempted to resort to plagiarism out of desperation.

The kind of writing that students are asked to do can determine the ease or difficulty of Internet plagiarism. Reports, term papers, topical essays, literary analyses, academic essays, short stories and poems abound on the Internet. When students are asked to write personal narratives, memoirs, and personal essays derived from their own experience, they are not only more motivated, but also will find it difficult to locate pieces to copy that reflect their actual experiences. Furthermore, assigning authentic pieces such as letters to an editor instead of essays, television news copy instead of generic reports, feature articles instead of biographies, film scripts instead of short stories, proposals instead of problem solution essays, etc. will have that same dual effect. Moreover, closely correlating writing assignments with the course of study will make the task more appealing as well as more difficult to plagiarize. For instance, talking back to Chaucer by establishing a voice for a character from *The Canterbury Tales* or composing a diary entry as the speaker in

"The Raven" provides an appealing activity that will be hard for a student to locate from an alternate source.

However, the Internet is not our only nemesis. Kay remembers colleagues' tales about "poetic" submissions such as the Twenty-third Psalm and a popular country western song that was currently playing on the radio. The students certainly were naïve to think that teachers wouldn't notice such copies. Watching their students' expressions as teachers revealed the original sources certainly added levity (for teachers) to the serious problem of plagiarism. Nevertheless, teachers must be vigilant with so many resources now at students' disposal. .

Another strategy to discourage plagiarism is diversifying focus. Teachers who concentrate only on the finished product make it easy for a student to hand in a piece written by a parent or taken from the Internet. Engage students in the various stages of the writing process. Require students to submit their prewriting, drafts, revisions, and peer response sheets throughout the process of developing a piece of writing. Rather than give one grade for a final piece, include all of the components of the writing process as part of the final grade. Keep in mind that learning occurs while students are engaged in a process, so why not give credit where that learning occurs? Both Kay and Patti require students to hand in all of their work that led up to the final piece with the final piece stapled on top. Not many parents will be willing to fabricate all parts of the writing process and not many students will want to manufacture those components to accompany a piece lifted from the Internet. This approach to creating original pieces actually makes utilizing the writing process easier for students than trying to plagiarize.

Provide class time for students to engage in the writing process. Devoting class time to every stage of the writing process may not be practical for each assignment, but at intervals this engagement is beneficial on many levels. This practice allows teachers to become familiar with students' subject matter and to intervene throughout the writing process. Teachers can effectively monitor students' progress, keep procrastinators on task, and make plagiarizing much more difficult. .

Patti*'s favorite plagiarism anecdote: Seniors were working diligently to complete state-mandated writing portfolios. Each student was required to include a literary writing such as a short story, poem, or play. A student asked me to look at two poems she had written independently and provide feedback to help her choose one for her portfolio. I glanced at the first one, "My luv is like a red, red rose." Poor girl had the bad luck to choose the one poem every single English teacher in the country would recognize! When she returned for my reaction, I opened a literature book to Robert*

Burns' poem, and showed her the remarkable coincidence. Judging from the nature and quality of the writing in the poem she ultimately included in her finished portfolio, I suspect it was truly her own work, which is what was needed in the first place.

VIII ~ Managing Special Communications

MANAGING PARENT COMMUNICATION

Parent communication is essential for good school relations. Lately, parents are being empowered by school systems and various parent organizations to take control of their children's education. They are provided with guidelines about how to conference with teachers and how to voice concerns and assure they are met. With these guidelines, many parents are becoming adept at wresting control of parent/teacher encounters; some parents may even try to intimidate a teacher, occasionally going overboard in efforts to make their desires known. Today's parents can be aggressive about the demands they make of teachers and the lengths to which they are willing to go to get them met. Moreover, teachers can no longer count on automatic parental support when conflicts arise with students. Some parents even question the teacher's professional knowledge and authority. Teachers, especially those new to today's classrooms, must be prepared to deal with these challenges in a professional manner.

The most effective way for teachers to avert conflicts is to adopt strategies that will build alliances with parents before any problems arise. Once students realize their parents and teachers are "on the same wavelength" and have the same expectations, teachers' jobs become easier and more productive. Keep in mind that students often exercise the adolescent tendency to complain about teachers within earshot of their parents. Of course, they only include details that reflect the students' interpretations. When a difficulty, problem or conflict arises and a teacher communicates with a parent who has heard only the students' perspective about a teacher and his class, interaction can begin on a strained note. The parent's reaction may be anything from defensive to irate. Parents will be much more likely to approach teachers with an open mind, if teachers have used communication to develop alliances with parents *before* there is difficulty.

Phone calls, mailings, individual conferences, and large meetings, such as an open house, offer constructive opportunities for communication between parents and teachers. Each of these methods has guidelines that allow for maximizing optimum communication between parents and teachers.

Phone Calls

Although the most direct method of contacting parents, phone calls have become increasingly difficult for teachers to use effectively. Most parents work, and may become angry if disturbed at work by a teacher call. In addition, students can intercept messages left on home voice mail. Teachers must be aware of the potential for caller ID and consider the desirability of parents and students having access to their home and/or cell phone numbers. If teachers use "Private Caller" to guard their phone numbers, calls may not be answered. When making calls from a school telephone, accessing an outside line during a planning period could be a problem.

With all the reasons to avoid phone calls, the truth is that they work. Personal communication through voice contact provides the personality and warmth absent in form letters and e-mails. But beware a parent who wishes to bend your ear about personal problems. Talk about a student's problems can easily segue into family difficulties and a distraught parent using the teacher as a confidant. Be polite, but make phone calls brief and to the point.

Increasingly, technological advances can help teachers make voice contact with parents without some of the disadvantages associated with traditional phone communication. One such innovation is "Google Voice." Accessed through the Google website, Google Voice allows anyone to create a "Google" phone number that could be used exclusively for parent contacts. Google phone numbers are associated with the *person* rather than with a particular phone device or location and can be used with mobile phones, desk phones or work phones. Google Voice provides numerous options such as custom voicemail greetings, the option to send some callers straight to voicemail, and others. Perhaps our favorite feature is voicemail transcription: voicemail messages can be automatically transcribed to text and sent to you via email. We're confident that the pace of technological advances will continue to provide improved resources that will help teachers be even more effective and maximize the use of their valuable time.

Most teacher calls to parents are prompted by negative concerns such as low grades or behavior problems. Why not try another type of call, which will truly amaze parents? Try the occasional call when students have made progress, been successful with a project or done something worthy of special recognition. Teachers will be delighted with parents' reactions to this positive communication.

*One of **Kay's** fondest anecdotes: In one week four of her students' letters to the editor were published in the local newspaper. She called parents to tell them how proud she was that students' writing had found an authentic audience. Parents relayed their pride and together they congratulated the roles they played in student success.*

Mailings

Sending a **letter to parents early in the school year in which you introduce yourself and your classroom** creates an effective first impression and is a valuable investment of your time. In addition to introducing yourself, your curriculum, important class expectations and policies, outline the ways in which you'll be communicating with parents. A parent who feels well informed is much less likely to become an irate parent. If they can anticipate specific communication at regular intervals, many parents will find that satisfactory. A model Parent Class Information Sheet and a model Parent Communication Letter can be found in the Appendix for this book.

It is also valuable to consider a mailing to parents when students are held responsible for a major class requirement. An informational letter to parents at the origin of the project alerts them to expectations, grading criteria, and pertinent deadline dates. For example, Patti and Kay both send such a letter to the parents of seniors that outlines the writing portfolio graduation requirement. Keeping parents informed and involved from the very beginning of the year helps absolve a teacher if a student is not successful in his class. Furthermore, such interaction provides parents with ways to help their seniors achieve success. This type of communication not only enlists parents as partners but also makes it difficult for them or their child to shift blame to the teacher if the child does not perform.

Consider composing a **notification of success letter**, which includes a number of positive learning behaviors that can be checked. Periodically mail this letter to parents of deserving students, perhaps a few each week so you won't become bogged down. Imagine the reaction when parents receive an envelope with a school return address and open it to find an affirmation! The letter provides something tangible the parent and student can see, feel and save. A parent who has received positive messages from a teacher will be much more likely to become a partner if and when a difficulty arises with her child.

Learning their child has failed a class when it is too late to rectify the situation justifiably angers parents. The last thing you or an administrator wants to hear from a parent is, "Why wasn't I notified about this? I didn't know anything until it was too late." That sentiment puts the teacher in a defensive position and makes it more difficult for an administrator to support that teacher when confronted with an irate parent. It is the teacher's job and in his best interest to **notify parents of their child's potential for failure while there is still time to make a difference.** Yet teachers can't spend hours making phone calls from home to people who might have caller ID. Assigning accountability for the student's performance squarely where it belongs - on the student and his parents - can be strategically accomplished.

*After trying various strategies, **Patti** arrived at a method that doesn't cause her mounds of paperwork or hours of phone calls. Halfway through each grading period she sends notification letters to parents of students with D's and F's. Sounds like a lot of paperwork; but managed effectively, it's not. She created a **template** so she only has to fill in a minimum of information. **Information cards** that students fill out on the first day of class make it easy for an aide to address the necessary envelopes. Some schools may even provide address labels for teachers.*

*Patti's final step is to **document** the communication by making two copies of each letter before mailing - one for her own files and one for the counselor or academic administrator. Providing a copy to the counselor/administrator notifies her of the student's status and provides her with evidence if it becomes necessary to support the teacher in a grade dispute.*

*Zip the letters through the school postage meter, and they're off. In some cases, there may be the possibility of **faxing** printed communication to parents at work or at home.*

Numerous advantages result from this notification procedure:

- *Parents are notified while there is still time to make a difference.*
- *The teacher has documentation of her initiative in notifying parents.*
- *The counselor/administrator has been notified.*
- *Responsibility for the student's performance is shifted to the student and parent(s).*

A model of Patti's notification letter template can be found in the Appendix for this book.

There is, of course, an obvious downside of communicating with parents through mailings. Students can intercept school mailings before parents ever see them or even know they arrived. As teachers, we can cover a lot of bases; but it's impossible to avoid every pitfall. That's why **documentation** is so very vital. Documentation provides concrete evidence that you, as a teacher, have fulfilled your responsibilities; and in many instances even exceeded typical efforts to which parents are accustomed. In a parent conference, when you provide a copy of a mailing to that parent that he has never seen, generally his irritation is directed where it should be – at the child who intercepted the mailing. In addition to your own documentation, it's definitely advantageous to notify the administrator who might be involved in arbitrating any dispute. If administrators are aware that you systematically notify parents, they generally are very willing to support you, if a challenge should occur.

E-mail

E-mail communications to and from parents are yet another, newer form of access. Although it can be quick and efficient, e-mail communications should not be initiated with parents until teachers consider the multiple ramifications that become a possibility with the use of e-mail for this purpose.

The instantaneous nature of e-mail makes it quite easy for a student or parent to impulsively send an e-mail rather than make a phone call and leave a message. When phone contact is the norm, the teacher retains some control over how it is handled. He can determine when to return the phone call, prioritize the phone return with his other important tasks, and limit the duration of the phone call. These limits, or at least their expectation, are dropped when e-mail communication becomes the norm. If one or more parents expect instant and constant communication from him, a teacher could find himself on the wrong side of a parent's ire merely because there aren't enough hours in the day to plan, teach, grade, and continually read and respond to e-mail messages. Refer to the section of this book titled "Managing Technology" for specific recommendations regarding the use of e-mail for parent communication.

Open House

Open house can be helpful in initiating alliances with parents. The first impression a teacher creates with parents is just as important as the one she creates with students at the beginning of the school year. Don't let this opportunity fall to happenstance. Contemplate the desired impression and plan encounters so that it will occur. We want our first impression with parents to communicate that we care about their children, that we are respectful and fair, that we know what we are doing, and that we are all about the business of learning. To communicate these messages, we each prepare informational handouts that tell parents what they usually want to know about a teacher and her class. Some administrators ask teachers to distribute a syllabus at open house; but many parents, especially of younger students, aren't looking for that kind of information. More often, they want to "check out" the teacher to be assured that their child is in good hands. Of course, have a syllabus available for those parents who request such detail; but an informational handout that reflects parents' immediate concerns will serve everyone better. *Refer to the specific suggestions in the section that follows.*

In most districts, open house is not a time for individual conferences; so don't succumb to parents' attempts to conduct one. Many open house meetings offer parents an opportunity to sign up for individual conferences at a future date or to make arrangements for a conference at a specific time on a day set aside for parent teacher conferences. If your school does not formally offer these opportunities, you can recommend them to parents who wish more detailed conversation about their child. Consider providing a sign-up sheet for this purpose.

Parent Information Sheet

A teacher's customized **parent information sheet** (as mentioned above) can be given to parents not only at open house, but also at conferences; mailed as a follow-up to phone conferences; or included as an insert in any parent mailings. For parents who do not attend open house, this parent information sheet, when received in a mailing, communicates a lot about the teacher, her class, her expectations, and their responsibility for their child's success.

Patti's Parent Information Sheet has evolved as she has taken note of questions asked by parents year after year. She's also considered information indicated at conferences of which parents want or need to be apprised. In creating your own information sheet for parents, you might want to consider including some of the kinds of data **Patti** provides:

- An overview of course content
- A rationale for and explanation of learning tools such as learning logs, writer's notebooks, lab book, portfolio, etc. that students are expected to keep and which carry significant weight on their grades

- Information about the learning performance component of students' grades

  *When presenting this item on the information sheet, **Patti** assigns **accountability** with this statement: "This learning performance grade reflects the degree to which a student assumes his/her responsibility as a learner. The grade is directly proportionate to the quality and quantity of learning activity demonstrated by the student while in this class." Consider the message that is sent to parents with this single statement.*

- Necessary materials such as texts and supplies
- Special program components such as college credit, magnet requirements, extended school field trips, out-of-town activities, etc.
- An explanation of any grading procedures specific to that class

  ***Patti** explains the grade review sheet that is sent home for a parent signature each grading period. She points out the dates to look for it and suggests parents put these on their calendars. She uses this opportunity to gently assign accountability to parents for monitoring their child's grade. Patti reinforces this parental accountability with a statement on their information sheet about the planner each student receives upon registration: "In order to monitor your student's progress, require him/her to keep a daily record of assignments, quizzes, tests, and upcoming deadlines in this planner. Examine it regularly."*

- Make-up and extra credit policies
- Grade-impacting deadlines
- Progress report and report card dates
- Expectations regarding conduct grades
- Suggestions for how parents can support their child's learning in the class

You can see a model of Patti's Parent Information Sheet in the Appendix for this book.

> ***Kay** has offered parents brochures produced outside the school by organizations such as NCTE, PTA and the State Department of Education, which provide tips for parents such as <u>How to Help</u>*

Your Child Become a Better Writer, Your Child Can be Published in the PTA Newsletter, Answers About the State Assessment Writing Portfolio. These additional forms of communication distributed by the teacher are evidence of pedagogical soundness. They also point out parents' role in students' success as well as demonstrate a genuine interest in including parents in their children's academic pursuits and responsibilities. Such brochures can be distributed at open house, on conference days or by mail any time during the school year.

Consider developing your own brochures that could be used each year with minor updating; or as a department, create pamphlets which can be tailored to the expectations of the individual school or teachers in your department.

Conferences

Perhaps the tougher communication may be face-to-face meetings with individual parents. These include district-wide conference days often two to four times a year, ones scheduled by teachers and parents or the school counseling office, or the occasional unscheduled "drop-in" by a parent who is unaware of the teacher's schedule or the school's rules for parent/ teacher conferences. All of these occasions demand that teachers take the lead and show true professionalism. Several factors influence the nature and direction of the parent-teacher conference:

- Which party initiated the conference?
- Is the conference a first communication between parents and teacher or a follow-up to earlier contact?
- When is the conference being held and what instigated it? For example, does it take place following a disciplinary referral or before or after grades are issued?
- Is the conference between parents and teacher or is a school counselor or administrator in attendance?
- Will the student be present at the conference?

The answers to these questions can affect the way a conference progresses and the outcomes achieved for all participants. All conferences will be different; there is no one good way to suggest how a conference should progress. A few general guidelines for the teacher, however, may be helpful:

- **Ask a counselor or administrator to participate in individual conferences**. This suggestion is especially pertinent if the teacher anticipates a difficult parent or touchy issue. A conference of this potentially volatile sort should be held in a counselor or administrator's office. The additional school representative can provide support and corroboration for the teacher and serve as a witness or mediator in the unlikely event things don't go well.
- **Be friendly**. Welcome the parent and begin the conference immediately. Take charge of the conference and be aware of both its direction and timing.
- **Use a set-up, which will put both parents and the teacher at ease**. Have both parties sit side by side at a table. If student desks are comfortable, arrange them facing each other. At no time should the teacher hold the conference at her desk. Do not set up a situation where any party feels intimidated.
- **Have appropriate materials at hand** such as teacher notes on student progress, participation checklists, tests, papers, or other indicators of a student's performance - documentation that substantiates the teacher's position. Showing parents a grade book is not a good approach to dealing with the numbers since parents could notice other students' grades and draw comparisons. If necessary, copy only that part of the grade book, which shows the grades for the particular student who is the subject of the conference.
- **End the conference on a positive note**. Suggest teacher or parent interventions, which will guide the student's future progress in a positive direction. For example, "If you (the parent) will monitor Mary's homework and try to make certain she gets it done each evening, I (the teacher) will closely observe her progress on a daily basis and make every effort to keep her on task in the classroom. Between the two of us, we may well get Mary back on the road to good grades and an improved attitude." End a conference by saying something positive such as "Thanks for coming in. I hope we both see some improvement soon." If a parent persists in chatting after the teacher has closed the conference, remind him that you have other conferences on your schedule, a class to teach, or students waiting.
- If a set-up conference time becomes inconvenient or impossible to meet, be sure to reschedule.

> ***Patti*** *begins most face-to-face conferences by thanking the parent(s) for taking time to come to the school. Then she compliments the parent(s) by emphasizing that their child has a much greater chance of success due to their active interest and support of the learning process. She also says something positive about the student. These initial strategies help calm any parent anxiety or defensiveness.*
>
> *Throughout the conference Patti focuses on the* <u>*student's*</u> *performance and/or behavior with concrete examples for support. She* ***anticipates*** *what might come up in the conference and takes* ***documentation*** *with her. Consequently, she's prepared in the event that it becomes necessary to demonstrate the opportunities the student has had in her class, student behaviors that have contributed to a situation or other factors that may arise in the course of the meeting. She often will take a copy of her class information sheet, written directions for the learning log or other standard materials that all students receive in her classes to establish with parents that students have ample information to help them fully understand what they need to do to be successful in her class.*
>
> *She also clarifies what the student and the parent(s) can do to increase the student's potential for success. In her parent conferences Patti subtly, yet specifically, shifts responsibility for the student's performance from herself to the student and his parent(s). She points out to parents that if she (the teacher) and the parents work together as a team, the student will benefit. She concludes the conference by once again thanking the parents for their time and interest.*
>
> *Generally, by following this model Patti is able to build alliances with parents that increase students' prospects for success as well as negate efforts the student may have made to play the teacher and parent against one another.*

Plan ahead for a conference by preparing a **conference report** for the parents. Although conference reports require preparation time and must be filled out prior to scheduled conferences, **Kay** has found them to be the best tool she has for successful parent teacher conferences. Begin the conference by sharing copies with all parties. This report indicates to parents the teacher's concern for their child's well-being and also serves as evidence of the teacher's professionalism. Some of the features that could be part of the conference report include:

- observations of student work habits
- description of academic progress or lack of it
- test scores
- class grade at conference time
- recommendations for improvement

After the conference teachers should keep a copy of the report on file. Although many parents may come prepared to take notes, they will be grateful to have a record of what transpired.

This form or a similar one can be filled out before a conference, used during an unexpected parent conference, or completed by the teacher during or immediately following the conference. In this instance, offer to mail a copy to parents. Always be sure to save copies of any documentation provided to parents. A sample conference report form appears in the Appendix of this book.

All of the above suggestions apply to most face-to-face parent/teacher meetings. The specific kind of conference suggests additional considerations.

Parent/Teacher Conference Days: If the notion of parent/teacher conferences on a district-wide conference day is intimidating (which may especially be the case for the beginning teacher) suggest to school administrators they might offer a large group setting, such as the cafeteria or the media center. In that setting teachers may conduct conferences, yet eliminate the isolation they may wish to avoid when holding conferences alone in their rooms. If handling conferences in an individual classroom, set chairs outside the room for parents who are waiting for their scheduled conference time. They will appreciate the gesture. In addition, this subtle action will discourage one set of parents eavesdropping on another parent's conference. This simple act will convey to parents that you value the confidentiality of your communication about their child.

Unscheduled or "Drop-in" Conferences: Some parents don't stop to realize how busy a teacher's day can be. They suppose they can stop by, the teacher can drop what he is doing and talk to them immediately. This attitude would not be tolerated in a doctor's or lawyer's office, and we don't think it should be allowed in schools. If parents appear at the door unannounced, politely ask them to check in the school office to set up a time convenient for the two of you to meet. Advise them that you can't speak with them unless they have an appointment. Even if they come by on your planning period, remind them that you have work scheduled and will be glad to meet with them at a more appropriate time. Teachers are professionals, and should be treated in a professional manner. Sometimes we must help parents and the general public recognize this status.

Parent/teacher conferences can be one of the most stressful aspects of the teacher's job. But that stress can be decreased or diminished entirely by carefully preparing ahead, providing accurate documentation for parents, and staying in charge of both the conference's direction and duration. With planning, preparation, and practice, conferencing with parents can become a skill that teachers master and even enjoy.

Despite the variety of methods for communicating with parents, we offer one suggestion that applies in all cases. Consider keeping a **Parent Communication Log**. It could be as simple as a spiral notebook or as sophisticated as a binder customized for this purpose. Every time you instigate or experience a parent communication, faithfully record it in your Parent Communication Log. Minimum information would include date of contact, name of parent(s), nature of contact (e-mail, phone call, note to parent, etc.), brief notes about the content of the communication, and outcome(s). You might even include printed copies of exchanged e-mails and/or letters to parents. If you don't want to keep printed copies of e-mail in your Parent Communication Log, be sure to store all e-mail communication in a folder on your computer so you can print any of them if the need should arise. If you send letters home to parents, be sure to keep a photocopy of each letter or at the very least the letter template for future reference. Such documentation will prove invaluable in the event you are called upon to demonstrate your efforts to keep parents informed. An added benefit is that once you've recorded a parent contact, you no longer need to keep it in your memory bank in order to recall the interaction if called upon to do so.

We know. We know. Our recommendations require typing, copying, addressing, writing reports, etc. There's just not time. Remember to employ management strategies such as form letters, templates, plain paper copiers, address cards completed on the first day, and aides to address envelopes. Effective communication can work, but only if teachers are organized, have a plan and system, and manage their time efficiently. Yet another reason to plan rather than hope things fall into place.

MANAGING BOOK AND FILM CHALLENGES

Many teachers delight in enriching their curriculum with books and films. The added richness these resources provide for students can be a major factor in their enthusiasm for and knowledge about the subjects they learn.

Often teachers are able to help choose the materials they teach and can create plans to implement them. Yet, district, state, and soon perhaps national mandates dictate great chunks of the curriculum. **Teachers, therefore, must carefully plan and evaluate any additional materials they will use with students.** Poor choices, failure to seek approval, as well as parental and other kinds of challenges can propel a teacher onto the front pages of the local newspaper and onto the evening news.

A recent incident in our own district resulted in a teacher experiencing unwanted headlines. She had offered several books with mature themes, among numerous others, in a high school classroom library. She had followed district procedure by sending home letters requiring parental permission for students to read from the class library, including explicit permission for students to read any of the controversial titles. Nevertheless, a community group felt that a particular book was objectionable to them and demanded the book be removed from the classroom library.

The challenge, to be expected, was picked up by the local media and front pages spoke of the controversy surrounding the teacher and the reading choices she offered. The issue went to the school board. The fact that she had followed district procedure as well as valiant efforts on the part of students resulted in favor of retaining all titles in the classroom library. The books remained, but the coverage and the way the controversy played out in the community assured that lasting damage was done, even though the conflict was resolved. The attention was a nightmare for the teacher, the school, and the district. In the end, only the students were truly victorious.

In today's climate of parental and community challenges to classroom materials, even books firmly entrenched in curriculum guides are not exempt from challenges. **Teachers must be certain they can make strong cases for everything they teach.** Consulting with district resource personnel, especially if you're new to the curriculum, is a must and essential if you wish to deviate from the prescribed course of instruction.

Also **be prepared to supply alternative assignments for students whose parent(s) wish their child to be exempted from certain assignments.** Students may also object on their own grounds to do a particular assignment. Be sure alternative assignments fulfill the same curricular needs as the original assignment and do not put the student(s) at an undue disadvantage.

Patti *once had a parent who did not want her daughter to read "All Quiet on the Western Front" (which was part of the standard curriculum) due to "violence" in the book. Patti offered several alternatives, and the parent chose for her daughter to read "The Red Badge of Courage" instead. In Patti's opinion, the alternative choice was just as, if not more, violent than the book being read by the rest of the class. She always suspected the parent had not read either book and had unexpressed issues with "All Quiet." Nevertheless, she was relieved to have found an alternative acceptable to the parent that explored at least some of the same themes as the book her full class was reading. Fortunately, she had taught "Red Badge" previously and had a complete unit with materials, so she didn't find herself having to create parallel lesson plans.*

Essential guidelines should be followed when choosing to use an additional book or film, which is not included in the prescribed curriculum. Thinking and planning ahead for possible controversy and challenge is good insurance.

- **Be sure to read the book or see the film with an eye to potential controversial elements before using it with students.** This advice may seem obvious, but often teachers may be unaware of the possible consequences a book or film might present. Taking the word of a colleague that "It's O.K. Your kids will love it;" or a student who offers to bring in a film about which "everyone" concurs is "appropriate for this class;" or even relying on your memory of a past reading or viewing can be a classic mistake on the part of the new, inexperienced, or naïve teacher.
- **Weigh the pros and cons associated with the book/film**. If you choose to use it, the pros should outweigh the cons.
- **Check banned book lists and utilize lists of challenged books, controversial films and their ratings before making choices**. Enlist the help of bookstores, the National Council of Teachers of English and/or the Internet Movie Database. Be sure that you're willing to "take the heat" that could arise when using a potentially controversial book or film.
- **Anticipate the concerns and issues that parents and others may present when challenging a book or film.** Be ready to defend your choice with a strong, well-researched and carefully considered case.

- **Send letters to parents seeking permission for their students to read a book or see a film, which is controversial, has been challenged or, in the case of film, is rated R.** Share a copy with an instructional coordinator or administrator in your building. Keep signed permission forms on file until year's end.
- **In your letter, make a case for the book's or film's relevance to your unit or curriculum.** Mention barriers such as language, violence, sex, religion, race, and other issues, which might concern parents in your community. Assure them of your professionalism in dealing with these materials and issues with their children. *A sample letter is offered in the Appendix for this book.*
- **Offer optional assignments for students, if parents challenge a book "just for their child."** Take care that this student is not singled out or mocked by other students for pursuing an optional assignment. Be sure the optional assignment does not put the student(s) at a disadvantage in any way, particularly when it comes to grading.
- **Don't hesitate to ask colleagues to share assignments that you could offer as alternatives.** As a department, develop some assignments for emergency use, which particularly address those books, or films, which are a part of the prescribed curriculum but may be challenged.
- **Seek out the many resources that exist for dealing with teaching controversial and challenged materials.** Ask your professional librarian to order them.
- **Check with your department head, an instructional coordinator, a district resource person, an administrator, or a trusted veteran colleague** if you're in doubt about proceeding with the inclusion of a book or film.
- **Seek guidance on book choices and challenges from national organizations** such as the National Council of Teachers of English or the American Library Association. NCTE supplies rationales for teaching frequently challenged books. Other organizations and publishers offer information and books about literary and film challenges, banned books, and related issues of censorship.
- **Devise a unit on censorship and discuss its implications with students**. Sponsor a Banned Books Week, perhaps coordinating it with a national effort usually spotlighted in October. Direct students to local independent bookstores that

may mount window or store displays or web sites, which might hold discussions about censorship and present other offerings online.

Some useful websites to start your search for support for controversial materials and censorship include:

- www.ncte.org/action/anti-censorship/rationales
- http://www.edselect.com/challenged_books.htm
- http://readwritethink.org

Dealing with issues around challenged books and films can become a teacher's nightmare. The one thing you don't want to experience is a *surprise* attack. However, if a teacher is aware and prepared to face the challenge, dealing with censorship issues and challenges can be empowering.

RELATIONSHIPS WITH NON-INSTRUCTIONAL STAFF

Teachers and administrators are not the only staff that inhabit a school. Non-instructional staff comprise a crucial component for a school's smooth and efficient functioning. Clerks, custodians, cafeteria workers, and maintenance personnel can make a teacher's life much easier and more pleasant. Keep in mind that these support staff usually do not earn anything near what teachers do, yet their jobs are demanding in a way that most teachers would find abhorrent. They must shuffle lots of paper, continually answer phones, screen people entering the building, push brooms, clear up after student "diners," constantly handle thermostat complaints, and yes, deal with impatient teachers. It is definitely in teachers' best interests to become their friends.

Fostering a positive working relationship with **clerks** can make non-instructional tasks and interruptions more bearable. For instance, a sympathetic clerk can shield teachers from interruptions by walk-ins – parents, publisher's sales reps, insurance sales people, etc. A clerk can facilitate detailed paperwork such as that required for ordering. A bookkeeper can make handling money collected from students as simple or as complicated as her relationship with a teacher warrants. A counseling clerk can offer to type letters of recommendation composed by teachers . . . or not. You get the picture.

Also keep in mind that clerks most often are stationed in close proximity to administrators. Often they share a closer working partnership with administrators than do teachers, if for no other reason than daily association. In that context, they often have an administrator's ear. To be blunt, if a teacher makes one of them mad enough, she could color an administrator's perception of that teacher. On the other had, if clerks have a good working relationship with a teacher, administrators will know. Both Kay and Patti enjoy excellent working relationships with the clerks in their school. This is not by chance.

Kay would put a good relationship with the **bookkeeper** at the top of her list when dealing with non-instructional personnel. During the school year, few teachers will get by without collecting money for some purpose. Whether for book fees, class fees, money for field trips, book orders, tax-exempt documents – money collection and its documentation comprise one of the many functions a teacher must perform. Unfortunately, collecting often becomes tricky. A bookkeeper values teachers who keep good receipt records and turn in their monies on time and in a well-organized manner. A teacher who fails to be diligent about book keeping matters can be a bookkeeper's worst nightmare. Just as teachers must be evaluated, the bookkeeper is audited several times during the school year.

Kay*'s bookkeeper always appreciates attention to detail and promptness with paper work. Once when Kay misplaced several multiple receipt forms, her bookkeeper intoned, "I'm not worried, you'll find them because you're careful with bookkeeping matters." Kay values that reputation. When she needs assistance with money, coordinating funds for out-of-town field trips, or securing permission for making long distance calls, her bookkeeper in turn makes her job easier.*

We can't stress enough that doing your job well so that other workers can do theirs more easily makes a teacher popular among non-instructional staff.

As a department chair, ***Patti*** *is conscientious about ordering paperwork, sometimes spending hours collecting all of the required information – multiple bids, item numbers, shipping and handling charges, etc. Consequently, the* ***ordering and receiving clerk*** *takes care of minor errors here or there and frequently brags on Patti's order forms. Another department chair did not so willingly adhere to the myriad ordering details required by central office. She reached the point that she was afraid to turn her orders in to the clerk who had lambasted her numerous times. She turned to Patti for help even developing the habit of showing her orders to Patti for double-checking before turning them into the clerk.*

In our district the ***principal's secretary*** wields considerable power. In some cases even the principal can be a bit intimidated. Keys, payroll, insurance, state reports, professional leave, sick days and substitutes all come under her control. The best way to gain the good graces of this key staff person is to scrupulously complete and hand in on time any paperwork she assigns. We've seen less organized teachers leave her office almost in tears after being reprimanded for not handing in something on time – again. We've listened to colleagues rant in resentment because paperwork that is totally unrelated to instruction seems elevated to importance higher than instruction. That state of affairs is unlikely to change. Our advice: get used to it and get organized. In the long run, your days will be better for it.

The principal's secretary in our school handles our requests for professional leave, substitutes and funding for attending meetings such as the NCTE Convention. Not a straightforward procedure in itself, it can become further complicated depending on the district climate toward professional leave. Our friend, the principal's secretary, has gone out of her way to assure that we will receive every possible consideration throughout this sometimes arduous process. She also knows that even though our participation may entail multiple days away from our classes, she can feel confident that we will leave quality lesson plans and ample instruction for our substitutes and makes sure those in power know that too. She has gone to bat for us as well as helped us secure substitutes when the district was less than cooperative. We make sure she knows how much we appreciate her and her efforts on our behalf and never return from professional leave without bringing her a small gift.

The **attendance clerk** is another ally a teacher wants on her side. Although teachers can resent the attention paid to daily attendance procedures, it's in their best interest to take it seriously and perform it conscientiously. Often funds are allotted based on average daily attendance. Moreover, daily absentee lists are usually prepared from teachers' morning attendance. A single error could result in six or seven teachers turning a student in for cutting who was actually absent but not marked correctly. Since an administrator has to deal with those multiple reports, it will become clear who repeatedly errs in attendance recording. Since clearing up the error creates unnecessary work for the administrator, do you think he or she will overlook it at evaluation time?

Patti *has trained herself to keep meticulous attendance records. In addition to maintaining her good relationship with the office staff, this attention to detail has served her well. If a student she has turned in for cutting claims to the administrator that he was there but she marked him* *absent by mistake, the administrator usually just laughs. If a student seeks an extension claiming to have been absent when an assignment was due, all Patti has to do is check her detailed attendance book. In fact, when a homeroom teacher has marked one of Patti's students absent from school and a parent challenges this reported absence a day or even a week later, it's not uncommon for the attendance clerk to rely on Patti's attendance records to verify the student's attendance at school that day.*

We can't say enough about the value of positive relationships with **custodial** and **maintenance** personnel. Patti remembers her father - a career teacher, counselor, and teacher educator – saying, "The first friend to make in a new school is the custodian." She took this advice to heart every time she changed schools, and was never disappointed. Nurturing positive relationships with custodians can result in "beyond the call of duty" favors: watering plants over school holidays, helping rearrange furniture, spotting unused or ready-to-discard furniture just to mention a few.

When teachers engage in special events, assistance from the custodial staff can be invaluable. That is the case with the Shakespeare and Poetry Festivals we conducted for many years. Display tables, chairs, microphones, and portable stage were all handled with few glitches because of the relationship we had with the custodial staff. They even took the initiative to guard our set-up the night before the festivals when night school met in our space.

We are lucky to have the best **maintenance person** in our school district. Not only is he excellent at his job, but there also doesn't seem to be anything he isn't willing to tackle.

We lost count a long time ago of the number of times he has adjusted our thermostats – without grumbling. Even though a well-tuned thermostat and a maintenance man willing to keep it humming to your specifications may seem a minor thing, temperature and atmosphere in a classroom have a great deal to do with keeping both teachers and students comfortable, happy and working effectively. No one can be at peak performance when she is uncomfortable. One's classroom is one's domain; its comfort level, just like its space and furniture, is an important concern.

***Kay** likes a cool room and our maintenance man is only too willing to accommodate. She tells her students, who refer to her as "the ice queen," that, "This room is mine. I'm here six and one-half hours a day. If you're cold, bring a sweater or blanket. I'll even reserve a place for you to store them." Kay depends on our maintenance man to keep her happy with constant adjustments to her thermostat.*

Once ***Patti*** *acquired a large, metal, double-door cabinet. There were shelves on the right side of the cabinet, but the left side was open for hanging a coat. Our maintenance man didn't blink an eye when Patti asked if he would install shelves on that side. Another time she obtained an oversized metal bookshelf. Placing it in the back of the room behind student desks, she was concerned that it could tilt and possibly fall on students. Not to worry. Our maintenance man found a way to secure the shelf to the cement block wall. Need a new pencil sharpener or clock? At least for us, we never have to wait long.*

Don't overlook the importance of **cafeteria workers**. Keep in mind that every day they must deal with impatient students in the cafeteria line who want their food "now" and who don't appreciate the challenge of preparing nutritious, yet appealing, meals on a budget for picky adolescents.

Our cafeteria makes especially good cookies. Because of relationships we have built, it is no problem to secure trays of cookies for events. ***Patti*** *always appreciates the effort made by the cafeteria manager when it is her turn to host the district debate meet.*

In the 1980's Patti's principal decided to relieve her from a class to assign her as the first woman to join "the boys" as a cafeteria monitor. Although the assignment relieved her from responding to one set of writing assignments, its non-instructional nature didn't suit Patti's interests, and she was glad when it lasted only one year. The brightest spot of that duty was her acquaintance with the "cafeteria ladies." They reminded Patti of her grandmother, who had once been a "cafeteria lady" herself. They looked after her. Whenever the cafeteria prepared oven baked chicken breasts, without saying a word about it, the "cafeteria ladies" gave Patti a foil wrapped chicken breast to take home in addition to the one on her plate lunch.

Many of our recommendations for developing relationships with students also apply in developing relationships with non-instructional staff. Treat them with respect. Value them and the work they do and appreciate the stresses under which they must perform this work. Be courteous, polite and considerate. Beyond these fundamental considerations, small gestures go a long way toward cementing positive working relationships. A birthday card, holiday card, periodic note of appreciation, small gift on secretary's day, or token of appreciation for a "beyond the call of duty" gesture are all kindnesses that are appreciated far more than their monetary worth.

IX ~ When the Routine Changes

NEW STUDENTS

A teacher has oriented her class regarding expectations and rules. She has taught them to use her classroom procedures. She and her class have bonded. Then a new student appears at her door. The whole dynamic of the class changes when a new person enters the mix. It's not necessarily a negative change, but it *is* different. To avoid upsetting a carefully built environment when new students enter an established classroom, it is essential that they receive orientation and training. Yet a teacher can't quit teaching and take a class period to orient and train this one student. What is a teacher to do?

If a teacher is lucky, it's only one new student at a time. One year Patti returned from Labor Day break to ten new students. Another year, she returned after the winter holiday to discover that twelve students with schedule changes had been assigned to her classes. It's at times like these that a teacher will especially appreciate having an opening routine (such as learning logs) in place so his class is constructively engaged while the teacher deals with new faces that have appeared at his door - especially when there has been no advanced notice.

In the ideal world, teachers would be informed of impending new students; but schools don't operate in an ideal world. Surely it must be possible to provide prior notification of new students in order for teachers to prepare for them; yet, that hasn't always been the case in our experience. Consequently, we have devised strategies to make this situation as minimally disruptive and efficient as possible.

Patti's Procedure

After experiences like those mentioned above, Patti decided to **anticipate** what apparently seems to be inevitable. She keeps several prepared folders with necessary orientation materials handy for just such occasions. Each folder includes:

- Prototype and blank card for the information card all new students complete
- List of Classroom Rules
- Class Information Sheet outlining procedures

- Learning Log directions
- Sample Learning Log grade sheet
- Personal Grade Record sheet for recording all graded work, quizzes and tests
- Sample Grade Review Sheet used to average grades at end of grading periods
- Directions for independent reading
- Reading Record Sheet for recording independent reading

This folder then becomes the new student's classroom folder where he begins to accumulate graded work along with his classmates. The items are particular to Patti's classroom operation and management procedures. In preparing such folders, each teacher would include information and materials specific to his classroom management plan.

After greeting the new student(s) and introducing herself, she directs him to thoughtfully read the information in the folder assuring him that she holds students accountable for following the rules and procedures. This routine, along with the folder of materials, communicates immediately that hers is a serious classroom. With the class working on learning log entries and the new student(s) reading orientation materials, Patti has created time for the paperwork involved with entering a new student(s) into her records. After giving the student(s) time to read the material, Patti seats him near a student who "knows the ropes." She introduces the two and asks the veteran to show the new classmate the "ropes" and to help him get off to a good start. Patti encourages the new student(s) to ask questions of the veteran until he gets familiar with classroom procedure and wishes him luck.

Kay's Procedure

Kay's procedure for introducing new students to her classroom is similar to Patti's. She has the new student fill out the class information card and hands him a packet of orientation materials, the same ones handed out at the beginning of the school year. She then asks the student to review the class log for the five previous days before he entered the class. She seats him close to a "buddy," a reliable student who will answer essential questions during the next few days. She introduces the student to the class, usually saying, "This is _______________. Make him/her feel welcome to our class and school" (if the student is a transfer to the school). As students file out of class, Kay makes sure she adds a reassuring "welcome, we're glad you're here" to the new student. She also asks that he make time after school to briefly conference with her about new procedures and to ask any questions he might have about the orientation materials or other concerns. If the student cannot fit an after school conference into his schedule, Kay tries to accommodate him at a time convenient for both of them.

The addition of new students has the potential to disrupt the established dynamics of a classroom. When teachers have instituted policies and routines to which they consistently adhere, existing students are subtly reassured that the environment with which they are comfortable will remain intact. Furthermore, when teachers have a plan and procedure for orienting and integrating new students into their classes, those new students can become acclimated quickly.

SUBSTITUTES

A day when the teacher is absent from the classroom is a day when outsiders observe whether the teacher employs excellent, adequate, or poor management skills. Of course, that theory will not *always* hold true. We know children and adolescents, and we know the mantras:

- Students will "try anything" with a substitute.
- Students may wreak havoc with the seating chart.
- Students may be extremely talkative.
- Some students may devise clever and inappropriate tricks to flummox both the substitute and their classmates.
- They may even tell the substitute that the regular teacher allows them to . . . . .

The scenario, as we remember it from our own student days, has played out for decades when the regular teacher is absent.

The absent teacher, by **planning, orienting** and using effective management techniques, can assure that an absent day is a pleasant one, or at least a bearable one, for the substitute teacher. Moreover, a teacher can assure that a day with a substitute is still a learning day for students. **Anticipating** and **planning** are the keys to ensure substitute success. Of course, a teacher might not always be able to plan an absence. She may be ill early in the morning, or have a family emergency at the last minute. But with technology in place in most schools and classrooms, handling a substitute situation is much easier than it has ever been in the past.

Let's first consider a planned scenario – the teacher is taking personal leave to attend a professional conference. She plans ahead to make certain that when she is absent, her lessons will be at a place where students can proceed on their own with less direction than normal. In essence students can, if they have been effectively oriented and have practiced the process, be self-directed learners.

*For example, one day when **Patti** was absent, **Kay** promised she would check on her substitute to see that things were running smoothly. They always make these check-up visits to each other's rooms when one or the other is away. Patti's classes mostly consisted of students our system labels "at-risk." To many, the phrase roughly translates as "hard-to-manage, difficult to teach." As Kay entered the classroom about ten minutes after class had started, most students were in their seats working. Some were at a workstation where Patti kept class materials. She had trained students to retrieve these items as needed, and they were doing exactly as she would have expected.*

The substitute stood at the front of the classroom answering questions. She told Kay she was amazed at the students' behavior. They knew what to do, and they were doing it. The substitute's presence in the classroom assured that housekeeping chores were completed and the work started and finished at the proper times. She was there to assist the students in completing the work Patti had left for them. Patti, as a careful manager, has planned, oriented, and effectively managed her students from the first day of class. When she is absent, her hard work pays off.

An **unplanned absence** is more difficult to manage, but it can be accomplished. The first challenge is sending substitute plans to school. If the teacher is on-line at home, she can e-mail plans to school or possibly fax them in. Otherwise the usual methods prevail: ask a colleague to deliver plans, phone a friend and dictate plans, or make an early trip to school.

Anticipating the possibility of an unplanned absence, it's helpful for teachers to keep a copy of their text at home for reference. Increasingly, publishers provide electronic versions of their textbooks: CD or online versions or even both. If this is the case with your text, be sure you're aware of how to access these resources. Even if the only time you make use of them is for reference when you have an unexpected absence, you'll be glad you were able to take advantage of this resource.

Regardless of whether an absence is planned or not, the absent teacher's attention to several factors can ensure that her students' and a substitute's day runs smoothly:

- At the beginning of the year, we inform students that we expect cooperation with and politeness toward substitutes or others occupying our classrooms in our absences.

- In notes for the substitute, we outline *specifically* what we want our students to accomplish and what we want the substitute to do.
- We ensure that our plans are clear and understandable. When possible, we word process our sub plans. When substitutes can't decipher or understand handwritten directions or lesson plans, no one accomplishes much. We keep in mind that a substitute will not be familiar with the context of our classrooms, so we provide all information the sub will need to understand and implement our plans efficiently.
- We leave all **materials** essential to the smooth management of our classroom (class rosters, seating charts, special instructions, etc.) where the sub can easily find them – in a specific desk drawer or visible on top of our desks. In some schools, substitute plans and materials are left in the school secretary's office.
- We leave our written **classroom rules** for the substitute and any printed classroom procedures that students are expected to follow.
- We *do not* leave our official roll book, grade book and lesson plan book accessible for substitutes. It is too easy for these to disappear in our absence. Instead, we prepare separate **attendance rosters** and **lesson plans** for the sub to use. We then transfer data to the official book(s) ourselves upon our return. As changes occur because students are added to or removed from our classes, we make sure to update our sub rosters. In schools where attendance is taken electronically, this may not be an issue.
- We provide an accurate **seating chart** and specifically tell the sub in our written directions that students are expected to sit according to that chart. We point out that because we have provided the seating chart, subs can identify students by name who present problems. We tell our students that we expect them to abide by the seating chart whenever we have a substitute.
- We leave copies of books and other materials students will be using so the sub can assist students with class work.
- We do *not* leave our **teacher's edition**(s) out and accessible. It would be easy for students to help themselves to our teacher's edition leaving us without this useful reference and perhaps giving students an unfair advantage with lessons that emanate

from the text. Instead, we leave photocopies of pages from the teacher's edition to which the sub can refer.

- We ask the substitutes to note details of the day's accomplishments. We urge them to comment on any problems, such as uncooperative or difficult students, so that we can deal with them when we return. We also ask them to identify students who were particularly helpful or those who stood out as exceptionally cooperative, so that we can positively reinforce their behavior. We attach paper to our directions to ease compliance.
- When we know in advance we will be having a sub, we apprise students of the lesson plans we are leaving for their class. Then if the sub is confused, incompetent, or likes the sound of his own voice, students can still proceed with the lesson.
- We identify a couple of students in each class that can answer questions and be helpful to the sub. We ask these students in advance if they are willing to serve in that capacity. Such recognition assures students of our regard for them.
- We review our expectations for behavior and performance with our classes prior to each anticipated absence.

We each keep an easily accessible **folder** in our files with the accumulated substitute materials suggested above. If we need to prepare for an anticipated absence, the materials are close at hand. We each know where the other keeps her substitute folder; so if either of us has an unanticipated absence, the one at school can locate the folder for the substitute.

To promote future good behavior when we have a substitute, we make sure to **follow up** when returning from an absence. Some of the things we do to follow up include:

- Check the sub's records to see if anyone has cut class. If they have, turn that information into the office, even if it is after the fact. This usually has to occur only once for potential cutters to realize that a sub in our classrooms is not a free pass to skip out. The additional message to students is that we are serious about our expectations when we have a sub.
- Address and apply consequences for inappropriate behavior reported by a sub. Since we have left a seating chart, the sub should be able to leave us specific names of problem students so that we need only apply consequences to the offenders.

- Reward, even if only with verbal praise, classes and students who met our expectations.
- Review with each class what occurred instructionally with the sub. We don't assume our lesson plans were followed. We confirm assignments made, completed, and collected so that there will be no "wiggle room" for a student to blame a sub when his work is not handed in on time.
- Find time to go through each class's papers handed in to a sub to see if any might be missing. A common student ruse when a paper does not find its way to the teacher is to assure the teacher she turned it in to the sub. We address any missing papers with the student immediately. Both Kay and Patti instruct students as a matter of policy never to hand in make-up or late work to a sub, reminding them how easy it is for "out-of-pocket" papers to become displaced.
- Review our expectations for students regarding substitutes after each absence.

> ***Patti*** *likes to reward classes that perform particularly well for a substitute with "coupons" awarding bonus points. She makes it clear before the absence that these "coupons" will be awarded only if* <u>*the entire class*</u> *receives a good report from the sub. As a reinforcement measure, these "coupons" (See appendix.) specifically spell out behaviors that earn the reward. She uses a template that requires her to add only a minimum of information to each student's coupon. Sometimes Patti gives students the coupons before an anticipated absence and lets them write their names on them. She then collects the coupons and assures her class they will be returned with bonus points affixed if she receives an appropriate report from the substitute.*

For everyone's best interests, however, **emergency lesson plans** are good insurance. At the beginning of the year, foresighted teachers will design lessons useful for any time during the year under most circumstances. These lessons should be at least loosely aligned to the curriculum for each of the teacher's classes; otherwise, they become busy work with little value. For ideas to consider for use in developing emergency lesson plans, refer to the "Sample Prompts for Writing Activities" in the Appendix.

*In her English class, for example, **Kay's** emergency lesson plans provide for writing a personal narrative – prewriting and drafting steps could span several days, if necessary. She might also include several mini-lessons in standard compositional problems most students battle, or a "special" vocabulary study that will interest students. Kay changes these mini-lessons or updates them if they get used. Kay also includes several reading selections with appropriate assignments – perfect lessons for unforeseen occasions when she cannot prepare plans specific to the immediate course of study.*

Prior planning takes time; but in the long run, plan-ahead efforts like these pay off. The keys to smooth, productive days for the absent teacher, the substitute, and students necessitate planning, prior training, and effective management. A note from the sub – "I had a most pleasant day. – Thanks for everything you did to make it so. Please call for me again." – is the absent teacher's assurance that her planning has been worthwhile.

ASSEMBLIES/SPEAKERS/SPECIAL PROGRAMS

Like many events that take place in schools, assemblies, speakers, and special programs can be both stimulating and intrusive. A well-planned assembly offers students a welcome break from classroom routine. An event with little purpose and structure or one which teachers forget or overlook intrudes upon classroom routine and can be a disaster, which affects planning, management, and a smooth day. Such situations are stressful for teachers and students alike.

Teachers usually have little control over school-planned events such as pep rallies, yearbook pictures, motivational speakers, and class meetings. If teachers have input into planning the school calendar, they can help direct the nature and outcome of these events. Mostly, however, these events are planned and implemented by administrators, counselors, and club sponsors.

The most obvious strategy for keeping events of this sort from wrecking the day and wasting instructional time is planning. Most schools provide monthly calendars of upcoming events; teachers are reminded of these events on weekly and daily bulletins as well. Nothing is worse, however, than arriving at school with the day planned out and discovering a forgotten assembly.

*To alleviate this possibility, **Kay** notes assemblies, meetings, or other events in her lesson plan book. She staples the calendar for each month or* *week in the plan book close to the planning pages it impacts. She finds that a calendar placed here is easy to use and less likely to be lost, considering the vast amount of paper she handles every week. This way, as Kay makes weekly lesson plans, she is aware of events and able to plan around them.*

When notification of an assembly, speaker, or other event that will preempt a class session is announced, ***Patti*** *immediately writes it in her plan book for the week, day, and class period(s) it will impact along with pertinent details. By doing so, it is highly unlikely she will overlook the event when lesson planning.*

Teachers must be realistic about days when planned events interrupt routines and schedules. Students sometimes expect a "free day" when classroom routine changes. Don't avoid instruction on those days, but rather plan instructional activities that accommodate students' heightened energy levels. Teachers can plan the nature of instruction during an interrupted day to actually take advantage of student restlessness. Changing routine does not need to set teachers up for stress and frustration if they are organized and plan appropriately for such days. Be realistic – "go with the flow."

An additional management concern with assemblies and other school-planned events is **student behavior**. Savvy teachers set up guidelines early in the school year, apprising students of the expectations and consequences for their behavior during events outside the classroom. Behavior mandates may include procedures for traveling to and returning from locations quickly and in an orderly manner as well as appropriate student behavior during the events. These directives would vary appropriately according to the nature of the event. Obviously, acceptable behaviors for a pep rally would differ from those for a serious motivational speaker. Behavioral guidelines should be an integral part of event planning. Students must know teachers' expectations for their behavior, if they are to follow them and avoid problems that might arise. **Do not assume** that all students know the appropriate behavior for a given event. Guidelines must be reviewed well before events and, in some cases, students will need to be actively taught appropriate behavior. Shouting instructions as students are leaving the room will not result in the desired outcome.

When monitoring special learning events, such as cultural arts programs involving large audiences, teachers must be especially vigilant. A handful of rowdy students can ruin everyone's enjoyment and compromise the program itself. Try the following ideas for monitoring student behavior at large events:

- **Don't assume** that students know appropriate behavior for the nature of the event. For instance, don't assume that students know it's not acceptable to discuss a dramatic performance with a neighbor during the performance. They may not realize the distinction between a live public performance and televised performances in their homes.
- Actively teach appropriate, expected behavior to your students.
- Think through the event beforehand. Consider what temptations and/or problems might arise and discuss them with students.
- Avoid viewing events as "extra planning periods" in which to accomplish other work. Working with students outside of your classroom is an expected part of your many duties.
- Accompany students to the event, sit with them during the event, and return with them to the classroom.
- Participate actively in monitoring and correcting students in your charge.
- Model appropriate audience behavior.

These guidelines provide the key to successful school events and enjoyment for everyone attending. Moreover, learning appropriate behavior for a variety of "public" events is a life lesson that will serve your students well into their adulthood. Later when students attend events outside of school, they will know how to be good audience members thanks to your efforts.

When teachers tie assemblies, speakers, and special events into instruction, more meaningful outcomes are possible. These occasions are less intrusive when instructional connections are found. Do not be naïve, however. Some events offer no possibilities other than "breaks" and entertainment. Careful planning and foreknowledge of events allow teachers to make the most of them.

Some of the most interruptive events have no relation to classroom activity, yet they are unavoidable. The taking of school yearbook pictures is a prime example. School picture days can be hectic. As with all activities outside the classroom, students must know the teacher's expectations if they are to behave properly. For example, teachers should be certain that students understand rules about not interfering with other classes that may be in session while on their way to and from the picture-taking site. For this, as for all kinds of interruptions, teachers must plan ahead. Therefore, make guidelines for behavior a key part of anticipating these events.

Students must also be aware of the expected behaviors *during* the event. The logistics required to make yearbook pictures will leave some students idle before or after their own sittings. Teachers should be on the site to monitor students and deal with any problems that arise from idle time. Sponsors of school picture days and other events are grateful to those colleagues who take the responsibility to see that their students act appropriately.

Counselors or deans frequently visit classes to schedule students or for explaining graduation, student credits, or special programs. These non-instructional days still require teachers to be "on the scene" and in charge to assist these visitors in their classrooms. Teachers must assure that students behave appropriately during these visits

When teachers plan events solely for their own students in the classroom or in special venues, planning problems and intrusions are lessened. For instance, a teacher may schedule a speaker relevant to a particular course of study to speak to her third period class. Teachers must remain in the classroom during these events. Outsiders do not know students, so teachers must support visitors by their presence and participation; besides it's important for teachers to demonstrate good manners. Furthermore, accidents can happen. Controversial speakers may upset parents and/or district leadership. A speaker may make an unanticipated comment that arouses dissatisfaction. It's important for a teacher to be present to monitor the speaker/guest as well as her students. To avoid unforeseen difficulties with teacher-chosen speakers, most school districts have policies regarding outside speakers in individual classrooms. Be sure to follow these guidelines, if they exist. If a teacher has done so but a speaker makes an unfortunate comment, the teacher and the school are in a much better position if adherence to the established guidelines can be demonstrated.

> ***Kay*** *sends letters to parents explaining potentially controversial events or speakers, and their relation to classroom instruction. She offers a rationale that might ease parents' concerns about the speaker or event. In addition, she always informs the principal well ahead of time when she is inviting outside speakers into her classroom. She cautions that employing good judgment and planning is better than being surprised with disciplinary action or media attention.*
>
> *For more details, refer to the section on "Book and Film Challenges" as well as the Appendix for a sample letter.*

When teachers share speakers with other classes, be sure that colleagues know behavior guidelines and prepare their students for the event. Understanding the hosting teacher's expectations for student behavior and ensuring your students participate in an appropriate manner, can make the difference between a stimulating and enjoyable occasion and an embarrassing disaster.

For several years ***Kay, Patti*** *and various like-minded English Department colleagues mounted a Shakespeare Celebration on or near William Shakespeare's birthday for what our schools call "at-risk" students. The celebration included displays and exhibits created by students, a presentation by the local Shakespeare Festival, student performances and birthday cake. After the first few years, teachers had worked out the kinks and developed a successful format and guidelines.*

The heart of the festival was student performance. These were not merely attempts to perform Shakespearean scenes, but included choral readings, skits, reading of original poetry, even Shakespeare raps. Obviously not professional quality, but often clever and presented from the heart, these performances provided our students with recognition and accolades usually reserved for honors and magnet students.

Much of the success derived from our basic guidelines: no student would be required to perform; instead, incentives were offered that enticed some students to choose to perform. Additionally, teachers fashioned classroom activities that stimulated students to create their own performances. Further, management guidelines were built in that would all but assure students would behave appropriately and enjoy the Shakespeare Celebration.

An English/drama teacher, who joined our faculty one year, was invited to participate in the celebration along with her students. This young teacher, who had been teaching in a parochial school, maintained an unrealistic notion of what our students could and should be able to do. Therefore, we tried to orient her and shared our words of wisdom from prior experiences as well as our guidelines in preparation for the occasion. Coincidentally, a reporter from the local newspaper asked to attend our festival that year to write an article about our event. We were delighted that our "at-risk" students would receive public recognition.

When it came time for our new teacher's classes to perform, she had some reluctant thespians. Despite our numerous suggestions of reasonably attainable formats and unintimidating genres, she expected her students to execute a traditional performance of a Julius Caesar scene wearing sheet togas. It seems this teacher was unable to think "outside the box" and, as well, had ignored our suggestions as well as the event guidelines. Two of her students publicly refused to perform, and she just as publicly threatened them with a discipline referral if they did not. The students stormed out of the Celebration uttering that they would prefer to go to the office than to do this "-----." This scene transpired in front of all of our students and a newspaper reporter!

The reporter, kind in his article, focused on the positives of the student performances with only a brief mention of the incident, presenting it in context. Our new teacher didn't last beyond that one year. Her dismal example assured our firmness with newcomers in subsequent years that they were required to adhere to the established guidelines in order for their students to participate.

Assemblies, speakers and special events can add worthwhile dimensions to any school or classroom program. Value for students, teachers and outside participants doesn't just happen; committed and insightful teachers make the difference between a valuable experience for all involved and a disaster. The means for success, as in many other areas of classroom management, are planning, laying out expectations and consequences for students, and following through with specific guidelines for each event.

FIELD TRIPS

"Field trips not only expand children's learning and experience by providing them with hands-on experiences, they also increase children's knowledge and understanding of the world in which they live." *Making the Case for Field Trips: What Research Tells Us and What Site Coordinators Have to Say,* Martha R. Nabors, Linda Carol Edwards and R. Kent Murray, Education, Summer, 2009.

Field trips. Just the thought of planning a field trip is enough to send shivers down the spines of new teachers and teachers who have "kept the kids home" for a long time. Yet, taking students on the road need not be a hassle. **The key to successful field trips is planning and preparation of students.** Planning a field trip, however, requires multiple tasks and cannot be done effectively at the last minute. Long range planning and careful attention to detail are the management essentials here.

First comes the idea, then the tie-in, and finally the contact. **To be truly successful, the experience outside the classroom must have a relevant tie-in to your curriculum** – the closer and the more current the connection, the more effective the outing.

Recently, ***Kay*** *has had several opportunities that were perfectly suited to highlight the concept of connection to the curriculum, plus enrichment. For several years, she had wanted to work a unit on the history of photography into her humanities curriculum. With a stroke of luck, the local art museum provided that opportunity to connect. Before school even started, Kay found out the good news. A traveling exhibit of Ansel Adams' photographs was coming to the museum.*

She planned her photography unit to overlap the show, quickly scheduled the museum visit and began planning assignments around the trip. By the time Kay's students visited Adams' photographs at the museum, they knew enough about the history of photography, ways to analyze photographs, and other aspects of photography as art to make the visit a rich, enjoyable, and worthwhile experience. Long range planning and careful preparation as well as pre- and post- visit assignments provided necessary links to make this excursion a highlight of the year for Kay's humanities students.

Careful design and planning are essential for the teacher who desires a profitable day outside the classroom. Students must know *why* they're going on the trip, *what* they will be expected to learn, and *how* they will use the learning when they return to the classroom.

Without a design and strategies for success, a field trip becomes just what many students want it to be – a day out of class with "free time" and lunch at a fast food restaurant. Without design, the teacher gets a powder keg ready to explode – noisy students, with little direction, who have minimum interest or none at all, in a place where they're unsure about what to do and/or how to act. But these worthless endeavors shouldn't be the norm.

In the early 1980's, ***Patti*** *took a group of "at-risk" students to see a professional production of Whose Life Is It Anyway? She engaged in her usual field trip preparation routine: outlining her expectations and consequences for ignoring them, teaching appropriate theatre etiquette, and informing students about the play. As her students were ushered to their seats, she realized there was something she had failed to anticipate. Many of her male students were wearing hats - not caps, but large, brimmed hats popular at the time. She knew they placed high value on their hats and, even if willing to remove them, would not want to put them under their seats or hold them in their laps. Looking around, Patti noticed a low retaining wall along the side of the auditorium near the section where they were seated. She explained to her young men that hats were not worn during performances because they obscured the view of patrons* *behind them. Before they had a chance to protest, she suggested they line up their hats along the retaining wall where they could see them at all times during the play. They reluctantly decided this was a reasonable alternative and did so.*

The main character in Whose Life Is It Anyway? is an artist paralyzed from the neck down. This challenging role required the actor to conduct his entire performance from a hospital bed, without using his hands or arms. The students were so intrigued by someone who could do so and still be captivating that they completely forgot to keep an eye on their hats. At intermission Patti's student aide, who had observed the boys' shenanigans in class, commented about how attentive to the play those same young men were. Detailed preparation, strategic quick thinking, and the power of the arts provided these students, who had never previously seen a live theatrical performance, with an experience that opened new doors to them that enriched their lives for years afterwards.

To assure field trip success, most museums, zoos, theatres, and other venues have education departments that will work with teachers to plan educational and enjoyable field trips. Be sure to take advantage of their resources. Often the institution you visit has designed procedural guidelines for teachers and students. Be sure to observe them, particularly if you think you might ever want to return with another group of students. Venues with tours as the main focus, such as museums and zoos, often require students to tour in small groups of ten or so with a chaperone. The teacher may choose the tour or sometimes is able to tailor a tour to meet specific curriculum needs. Most field trip venues and their offerings are light years ahead of where they were, even ten years ago.

A few years ago, **Patti** *took a group of one hundred "at-risk" students to a professional production of Having Our Say. She took several steps to ensure that it was an instructionally and behaviorally positive experience for her students. By taking the initiative to see the play prior to the field trip, she could identify specifics for students to look for throughout the performance:*

- *Patti encouraged her students to watch the actresses' elderly shuffles and palsied hands to see if they ever failed to maintain that manner.*
- *She asked her students to observe how much the actresses had to juggle in a particular scene – remembering lines, staying in character, maintaining blocking so each was where the other*

expected her to be at the appropriate time, and believably interspersing line delivery with food preparation.

- *Then she also suggested students consider the characters' similarity to their own grandmothers, great grandmothers, or aunties.*

This preparation provided numerous aspects of the play on which students could focus, therefore enhancing their viewing experience.

Furthermore, Patti shared reviews and articles about the play from local newspapers with students. Behind-the-scenes insights garnered from the theatre subscriber's newsletter further enlightened them. Students read popular magazine articles about the actual Delaney sisters upon whom the play was based. Copies of the book from which the dramatic adaptation was derived were made available in the classroom library. Although a handful of students showed interest in the books before the field trip, many more became interested as a result of the trip to the theatre.

Due to the reputations and prior records of many of Patti's students, other teachers never considered taking them out of the building. After teaching proper theatre etiquette and clearly outlining expectations for their behavior, Patti pointed out to students that teachers from other schools in attendance, theatre staff, and volunteer ushers from the community would make judgments about them and their school based on their behavior. She asked them to consider whether they wanted to confirm stereotypes others had assigned to them or if they preferred to demonstrate the inaccuracy of those perceptions. Since her group was heavily comprised of male students, Patti made sure to include some male faculty chaperones. While observing students board buses, one male faculty member looked at Patti with wonderment and asked, "Are you sure you really want to do this?"

Patti's students were wonderful! Once the play began, they were intrigued with the performance as well as the story of the Delaney sisters. They looked for the things to which Patti had alerted them and were duly impressed. When students in the balcony shot spit wads down on them, Patti's students exercised self-control commenting to her at intermission, "Can you believe they're so immature?" It was clear this was a positive experience for her students; but Patti's impression was confirmed when Greg, one of her most "behaviorally challenged" students, declared, "That play was jammin'!" Patti invested considerable time and exerted substantial effort into planning and executing this field trip. It was this attention to detail that ensured its success. Greg's enthusiastic endorsement made it all worthwhile.

Each field trip you take will have its own sets of expectations: those that the organization provides, those you provide for your students, and those you prepare for the adult chaperones. A list of important items to remember follows:

- **Have enough chaperones for the number of students you take**. Some venues will specify this number. Be sure to clearly outline their responsibilities to the chaperones, particularly those that are not school staff.
- **Have a way to identify the students by their names.** Students can make nametags or use the "Hello, My Name Is" tags. Your school office may have some; ask the secretary. This ID will ease the chaperones' job, and help docents or guides personalize their connections with your students.
- **Be sure students understand your academic and behavioral expectations for them.** Remind them they represent many parties beyond themselves in this public arena – all young people, their school, their teachers, and their parents. When they act appropriately, everyone notices; when they are incorrigible, no one forgets.
- **Make a checklist before the trip in order to cover all your bases.** A few examples:
    - Did you remember to call the restaurant several days ahead to tell them you'll be turning sixty students and six adults loose in their establishment at 12:30?
    - Did you turn in all permission slips to the office?
    - Did you inform the cafeteria manager to expect sixty fewer lunch customers than normal?
    - Did you let other teachers know some of their students would be on the field trip?

Administrators at some schools require checklists that must be approved before a field trip can take place. Using a checklist helps keep all parties happy and makes your job a little easier. In the absence of a school checklist, you can make your own template to use and refine each time you take a field trip, rather than continually relying on your memory. You might share your template with the administration for general use. Refer to the Appendix for a sample checklist.

Be advised that your field trip may not always be popular with some of your colleagues. Many teachers are concerned about the proliferation of field trips, which cut into their teaching time with students. Kay and Patti give fellow teachers ample notice of their trips, so they can plan accordingly for activities such as scheduling tests and projects. No matter how carefully we plan and give notification, however, there will be those colleagues who disparagingly dub us "field trip kings or queens." Why not present your written curriculum rationale for your field trip to those naysayers to assure them your field trip has instructional significance and isn't just a frivolous outing? That may not quiet all of the complaints, but it will establish your credibility with colleagues who are broader minded. It goes without saying; there will be fewer complaints about field trips when teachers have made the effort to clearly integrate the field trip experience into their curriculum. When the instructional value of an outing is apparent and teachers have taken pains to minimize the inconvenience to their colleagues, it's harder to be critical.

For solace in this matter, ***Kay*** *always returns to the venerable article in the November-December 1998 issue of Teacher magazine. John Falk, founder and director of the Institute for Learning Innovation in Annapolis, Maryland, said, [he] "once asked groups of college students as well as elementary school children to think back to a museum field trip they had taken previously. He found that 95 percent, regardless of age, could recall exactly what they saw, what they did, and whom they were with. And more than 70 percent of the details the students remembered had to do with the content of the program or the exhibits." Those statistics support the benefit of field trips and experiences outside of the world of the classroom and textbooks. Kay has kept this magazine and when colleagues complain about field trips, she hands them the article, "What a Trip," and urges them to read it. Those words make obvious the benefits of out-of-class experiences.*

Faculties can take steps to minimize school disruption caused by numerous field trips. Kay and Patti teach at a school where numerous teachers take frequent field trips. Although historically there had been some effort to avoid conflicts, it had never been very systematic. While a member of the school management committee, Patti designed an addendum to the standard parent field trip permission form that required teachers to also give approval for students to miss their classes. This amended form, which alerted teachers to the impending event, quickly became a standard part of the school approval procedure. Eventually, teachers proposed a policy, which the administration endorsed, that field trips during the last week of each grading period were prohibited. When a staff collaborates, students can experience benefits derived from experiences beyond school walls without unduly intruding upon the rest of their classes.

Our best evidence, however, which makes us keep on planning and taking field trips, comes from our students. We hear them excitedly talking about what they've seen, heard, and experienced. Their quality of follow-up work usually reinforces the value of the trip and the time it took to plan and execute it. A letter **Kay** received recently from a graduate said it all. She thanked Kay for introducing her through field trips to many of the experiences that "as an adult have enriched my life and keep me happy." What more could a teacher ask of a field trip?!

MANAGEMENT AND SCHOOL SAFETY

Everyone is concerned about school safety these days. We can no longer take anything for granted. It's not the same world that it was even ten years ago, and we have all been affected. Without a doubt, there are serious implications for all teachers. Effective classroom management is one of the most valuable tools a teacher can employ to ensure safety in her classroom.

The atmosphere a teacher creates and maintains in her classroom determines if it is easy or difficult for violence to occur. A teacher who is an effective manager is much more likely to provide a consistently safe environment for learning. A classroom where:

- students are focused on learning deters violence.
- the teacher is *actively attentive* to *all* aspects of her classroom is more likely to sustain stability.
- students are consistently engaged in learning activity limits the opportunities or impetus for violence.
- the teacher respects all students as learners and fosters that same respect among the students discourages the attitudes and situations that lead to outbursts.
- the teacher is continually alert to the activities, attitudes, and behaviors of all students is less likely to erupt.
- the teacher is present from the time students enter the room until they depart will be less likely to have problems.
- all students are confident they will be treated fairly and in the same manner as all other students discourages volatility.
- students are mentally challenged and stimulated will focus on thoughtful and constructive ideas rather than disruptive negativism.
- all students genuinely feel they can be successful if they are willing to put forth the effort fosters positive attitudes.

The teacher sets the tone and ultimately determines the classroom atmosphere.

Imagine a classroom where the students wander in at will because they are used to the teacher standing in the hall chatting with her colleagues even after the bell has rung to begin class. When she does enter, students are loitering in small groups around the room engaged in private conversations. Imagined or real insults hurled in the hallway have found their way into this classroom and the body language of some students suggests they are on their guard as a result. The teacher raises her voice in order to be heard and commands the students to take a seat and get out their books. Several students do not have their books. When the teacher admonishes them, a student (under his breath) comments, "She never chews out so-in-so." The teacher instructs students to read pages 25-35. Those without a book ask to go to their lockers to get them. The teacher replies with a sigh, "Oh, all right." They saunter out. Those who have books do not feel compelled to jump into their reading since a number of class members just left the classroom. A student moves to the teacher's desk to ask a question about an assignment and the teacher becomes engrossed with that student. Another student takes advantage of the teacher's inattentiveness to hurl an insult to a student a few rows away who shoots a paperwad in return. Students begin to straggle back with books in tow. As various ones enter, they comment, gesture, or sneer at someone still in the room. While the teacher is collecting her notes and trying to get organized, a student wanders over to the pencil sharpener, sticks his head out the door and makes a comment to a passerby in the hallway. And so it goes . . . .

Now imagine another classroom where students move into the room and their assigned seats promptly because they know it is expected, and they know there will be consequences if they are not in their seats ready to learn when the bell rings. The teacher is at the door greeting them with positive comments as they enter. As they sit down, students get out their learning logs and begin copying the prompt that is projected on the screen because they have learned this is the way most class periods begin. When the bell rings, most students are already contemplating the thoughts they will record in response to the prompt. While they are responding in their learning logs, the teacher quickly and silently takes roll using seating assignments to determine absentees. After ten minutes or so, the teacher asks for volunteers to share their thoughts or ideas related to the day's prompt. The teacher and the rest of the class take each response seriously because such a tone has been established and reinforced since the beginning of the year. Next the teacher asks students to get out their books. All but one or two students have their books because they know there are consequences for not bringing them to class. After making a short reading assignment, the teacher gives alternate directions to those students without books. When a student requests to go to his locker to get his book the teacher politely but definitely reminds him that, "We do not do that in this class, but be sure to record the reading pages in your planner so that you can do the reading later when you have your book." A student raises her hand and asks the teacher if she will look at a revision of a writing assignment and the teacher replies that she will be glad to conference with this student once the class is working independently on the day's assignment. After completing the reading assignment, a student quietly moves to the shelf where the class notebook is kept and takes it to his seat to check on make-up work for the day before. Can you predict how the rest of the period will go in this classroom?

- Which scenario provides numerous opportunities for eruptions?
- Which scenario focuses students on their learning thus distracting them from "baggage" they may have brought with them upon entering the classroom?
- Which scenario presents a situation where students have been taught learning practices in which they engage independently?
- How can those practices discourage nonacademic, undesirable disruptions?
- Which scenario fosters mutual respect?
- Why is one scenario less likely to generate or allow safety-threatening situations or violence to occur?
- In which classroom would you feel that your own son or daughter was safer?

In these challenging times when schools and classrooms are often featured in negative or frightening ways in the media, individuals readying themselves for the teaching profession are bound to be anxious. No doubt exists, however, that safe schools are vital if public education, as we know it, is to continue. Many suggestions are proffered about how to have a safer school. Will school uniforms make schools and students safer? Our answer is, "Not by themselves." Will metal detectors and hall monitors curtail violent behavior in the schools? Our answer is, "Not totally." Will new, tougher rules and zero-tolerance policies change the atmosphere of our schools and make them safer? Our answer is, "Possibly, but not without other fundamental changes in society."

So what are teachers to do to ensure a safe school? **Teachers must do everything possible to make individual classrooms safe havens for learning.** If classroom teachers engage students in productive learning, schools themselves will be safer. Many strategies are available to make classrooms safer and more learning-centered. No strategy, however, is foolproof. Safe classrooms have the following characteristics:

- The teacher is always present in the room.
- Students are continuously involved in learning with little or no "free time."
- The teacher is circulating in the classroom, monitoring and assisting students with their learning.
- Students know the class rules and the penalties for breaking them.
- The teacher quells student disruptions immediately as they occur.
- Students not responding to teacher intervention are removed from the classroom.

The remarkable truth about these characteristics is that they almost always are observable if teachers are teaching and monitoring learning, and students are working and learning in the classroom on a daily basis. Think of the contrasting classroom scenarios described earlier in this section. When the teacher has established a classroom atmosphere and learning routine, fewer problems occur and therefore fewer opportunities for unsafe classroom conditions arise. Exceptions to this rosy scenario, we know, might occur - especially during the first few years of a teacher's experience. Just as any new skill for teachers or students must be tried and practiced, the guidelines for a safe classroom are no exception. But for safety's sake, mastery and successful implementation must occur swiftly.

By necessity, situations will arise once in a while that challenge the "never" qualifier in the above characteristics. Take the first one – a teacher should never be out of her classroom when students are present. If she is forced to leave, someone should know of her absence and be monitoring her students – a teacher across the hall or next-door is a likely choice; a hall monitor or school administrator could be summoned; a teacher on planning period might fill in for a few moments. However, running to the workroom to make copies, going to the restroom except in an emergency, leaving to get a soft drink, or chatting with teachers in the hall do not rank highly as reasons to exit a classroom full of students. Yes, there are exceptions from time to time. But if everyone abides by the mandate that instruction should begin when class begins, and end when class is over, teachers should have practically no reason to be away from their classrooms when students are present except in a rare emergency. **Safe**

classrooms require a framework where teaching and learning are constant.

Circulating and monitoring students as they work is an integral part of teaching time. Sit in on group work, listen to discussions, offer suggestions, praise good ideas, steer bad ideas in new directions – all of these maneuvers keep a teacher involved and help her to get in touch with her students' learning styles. As teachers expect students to stay on task, so should teachers expect the same of themselves. Don't just assign work; be a part of that work. Keeping in touch on a daily basis with what happens among students in a classroom will help maintain that classroom as a safe haven for learning.

> *Students often ask for "free time" or a "free day". Occasionally,* ***Kay*** *gives students a task which may appear to be free time such as shelving books, putting up bulletin boards, or producing signs for a class occasion, "Trust me. It's all a ruse; students just don't notice they're learning as they work."*

Our final recommendation for a safe and effectively administered classroom is simple. **Handle any discipline problems yourself, when feasible**. Do not debate with an unruly student in front of a class. Step outside the door if the discipline can be delivered quickly. Ask the student to stay after class is over. For example, one problem **Kay** successfully and quickly handled herself happened one year when she taught two, hot-headed, young mothers:

During class, they persisted in making audible, crude remarks to each other to the delight of the entire class. I asked both of them to step outside; I left the door partially open to monitor the class. I quietly and calmly chided these young mothers: "I imagine your children would really be embarrassed if they heard their mothers talking this way in public. I think you should apologize to each other, and quietly walk back into that classroom with your heads held high. Your classmates and I will respect that gesture." These two mothers embraced, said they were sorry, and did exactly as I had suggested. I was amazed and relieved and so was my class.

Kay's discipline in that situation took few words. But often much greater intervention may be required. If need for discipline is immediate, ask another teacher to watch the class while you deal with the offender, or call a security guard or an administrator to come and escort the student from the classroom. Many disciplinary situations exist which call for individual means of approach. Teachers can locate whole books and seminars that deal with disciplinary issues too massive to cover in this book. Just remember to use your best professional judgment. Do not let yourself be forced into dealing with a problem in an unprofessional manner. Always reflect about how you handled each situation and how you might effectively improve your approach. By doing so, you'll be better prepared for upcoming incidents that require your intervention and more able to stifle them before they can escalate.

As almost every teacher knows, student behavior can deteriorate quickly under certain circumstances. When the teacher stays engaged in teaching and keeps the class on task, continual focus on learning is the likely outcome. When a teacher has established and worked from the first day of school to consistently maintain constructive learning behavior in the classroom, the likely emergence of difficulties is diminished.

Safe classrooms and safe schools are a challenge for all of us who work with young people in today's school environments. We will need new strategies, courage, and patience to deal with these challenges during the 21st century.

COPING WITH CRISIS

A decade or so ago, we may not have thought it essential to include a section on "crisis" in a book about classroom management. However, recent events that have impacted students, teachers and classrooms have made crisis management a teacher concern and a very real responsibility.

Students and teachers have always been confronted with crises that touch them individually. Students may lose a parent, sibling, other relative or close friend to illness, accident or natural causes and teachers will be called upon to contend with these emotional experiences in their classrooms. Although personal crises are always sensitive to handle, a roadmap of experience exists to guide teachers.

More challenging are events that impact greater numbers of students, perhaps an entire school. For example, fire, robbery, accidents, or the death of a student or teacher may cast a pall over an entire student body and staff. Often the whole school will pull together to deal with such events. Widespread crises such as floods, hurricanes, tornadoes, and even large-scale illnesses such as flu epidemics touch entire communities, yet require specific, personalized responses from school staff. Under such circumstances, support services are usually available to guide and assist school staff in addressing student needs.

Unfortunately, nothing prepared us for numerous instances of school violence, which shook our belief in the notion that schools are safe havens. Teachers and administrators have been called upon to muster inner resources in the absence of prescribed strategies for dealing with the unthinkable. Sadly, school violence has not remained limited to isolated incidents, but has come to seem almost epidemic. Fortunately, most teachers do not have to deal with school violence firsthand; but they do have to cope with the impact on their students whenever such events have occurred elsewhere. Students, parents, and the community have become increasingly vigilant in efforts to anticipate and prevent occurrences of school violence. This vigilance has impacted school atmosphere and has added a new dimension to school and classroom operation.

Significant national crises, especially those that occur during the school day, pose a major challenge to school personnel. Events such as the Challenger and Columbia explosions, the bombing of the Oklahoma City federal building, and the September 11 terrorist attacks on the World Trade Towers and the Pentagon have heightened awareness of our nation's vulnerability. Due to the ubiquitous use of cell phones, the Internet and television news broadcasts, teachers often find themselves as the first line of defense and support when these catastrophes unexpectedly occur. None of us can be adequately prepared to deal with the intensity of such events, yet teachers must respond immediately when faced with crises during the school day. Under these circumstances, teachers may be the initial sounding boards for students as well as their source of comfort. Consequently, it is crucial that teachers anticipate how to handle such episodes before they are faced with making quick decisions without time for contemplation.

We do not presume to prescribe appropriate teacher response to student reaction when crises surface. We aren't psychologists or grief counselors who are professionally trained to deal with these kinds of issues. However, since teachers may be the first adults students encounter when an event occurs, they must be prepared to deal with students' reactions.

Consider this scenario:

It's nine a.m. on September 11, 2001. You are teaching. Students begin to learn about the attack on the World Trade Towers from cell phone calls, text messages, and word of mouth.

- Do you turn on the television for students to witness the unfolding historic event?

- What about parents who may object to their child observing the horror over and over again on television?
- What about students who might become distraught from the frightening spectacle?

Teachers are confronted with challenging dilemmas in the face of unexpected crisis. Make no mistake. How to approach such situations is a very, very difficult call. Certainly, teachers should not wait for a tragic event to occur before contemplating how they might handle it. We suggest teachers weigh the following considerations prior to actually facing tragedy or crisis:

- How your emotional display may affect students.
- How modeling appropriate response and reactions guides students.
- How classroom structure and routine could offer a sense of comfort and security for students.
- How parental preferences might influence treatment of events in the classroom.
- How viewing continual television coverage could emotionally impact students.
- How continual news coverage could easily become a substitute for meaningful lesson planning.
- How much time, if any, to spend talking with students about the event.
- How allowing students a brief forum to discuss the event could be handled.
- How such a forum could overwhelm the classroom unless the teacher establishes parameters.
- How to allow students to engage in uninfluenced exploration and decision-making as a crisis evolves.
- How much time should be spent focused on the event before moving on.

Keep in mind that every incident is different; therefore, the teacher must assess the tone of her class and parental preferences in making decisions about how to handle individual crises. It is probably a good idea to err on the side of self-restraint until you are confident in your approach to the crisis. Seeking recommendations from crisis management professionals can provide a guide for teacher decision-making. It is wise to follow administrative instructions during any kind of drill or crisis and to make students aware that you are serious about their compliance. Remain objective and allow students the dignity of making their own decisions once the initial shock of a crisis has waned.

Real world events can offer rich opportunities for curriculum connections. Although teachers could integrate related issues into their lesson planning at the moment of the crisis, they should consider the wisdom of waiting until the initial heat of a crisis has passed. Certainly, once the emotional impact of such an event has dissipated, teachers could consider the value of incorporating related issues and analysis into their course of study. This approach could help prepare students if and when they are faced with similar unexpected crises in the future.

It appears that crisis is likely to continue to affect our students and us; therefore, it is wise for teachers to keep abreast of continuing developments in our world. Since students look to us for knowledge and explanations, it is the duty of teachers to keep up-to-date and well informed about current events. Obviously, teachers cannot be experts on all topics; nevertheless, the ability to explain significant events and major issues in a way that students can understand provides opportunities to take full advantage of teachable moments. Although teachers can reasonably be expected to have only general knowledge of many events and issues, they would be well advised to be prepared to recommend reputable websites, reliable newspapers and news magazines for students who seek more detailed information. Many online services for newspapers and magazines offer educational support, which may be enhanced during times of major crisis. For example, primary news services such as CNN, NBC, ABC, NPR, *Time, Newsweek, The New York Times, The Wall Street Journal,* and *USA Today* all offer online resources with educational components.

There are no easy answers to the questions confronting teachers in terms of crises that impact our schools. Although there are guidelines, no hard and fast rules for addressing crisis situations can assure classroom teachers that they will effectively handle the next unexpected crisis that arises. Crises seem to have become a phenomenon of the late twentieth and early twenty-first centuries; thus teachers, no matter how wary, must develop coping strategies.

Therefore, the committed and enlightened teacher will find time to:

- create opportunities to discuss crisis management methods with colleagues
- develop crisis plans with school or system personnel
- assist in devising a school crisis policy
- explore resources such as The National Association of School Psychologists

- take advantage of staff development to learn ongoing crisis coping strategies

Crises don't seem to be disappearing anytime in the near future, no matter how devoutly we wish they would. As teachers and caretakers of our nation's children, our best defense is to anticipate the unknown and prepare for what awaits our students, our classrooms and our schools.

Appendix

RULES FOR SUCCESS

1. Be in your seat and prepared to begin to learn **promptly** at the beginning of class. Make all preparations such as sharpening your pencil, getting out materials, etc. before the tone sounds. If you are not *in your assigned seat* when the tone begins to sound, you will be counted as unexcused tardy.
2. If you are tardy to class without a legitimate pass, you will be given an unexcused tardy. You will not be excused to go get a pass once you have reported to class.
3. You are required to supply and have the following in class **every day**: your own paper, pen or #2 pencil, necessary book(s), assignment(s), and/or supplies. Be responsible for your own property and do not rely on others to provide materials for you.
4. Bring all necessary materials, supplies and tools with you to class **every day**. You will not be excused during class to go to your locker or anywhere else in the building for materials.
5. Do not talk when the teacher or another student is talking. Do not talk when the loud speaker is on. Raise your hand and wait quietly when you wish to be recognized by the teacher.

PROCEDURES

1. Head **all** papers with your **full name, date of origin, and class period** in the top right corner. Put an **identifying title** on the top line of **all** papers.
2. When you have been absent, present your **absentee slip** to your teacher at the *beginning* of class.
3. When you have been absent, check your **make-up assignments** in the class notebook/log. Give the teacher a note with your name and a list of anything you need for make-up work. Complete and hand in your make-up work within the designated time limit.

TIPS FOR ORAL PRESENTATIONS

NOTE TO TEACHERS: Guidelines for preparing students to meet learning objectives, such as these student tips for giving oral presentations, can be used to guide students to meet those learning goals. Learning aids help students to be successful and hold them accountable for all facets of their learning. Such aids are also useful for creating assessment rubrics that students can review prior to engaging in their preparatory activities. KET

1. Be organized. Know what you want to accomplish and have a plan for doing so. In group presentations plan who will do what.
2. Be familiar enough with your material so you don't have to read from notes. You should have and make use of notes; however, don't be so dependent on them that it seems you're reading rather than presenting.
3. Plan your opening. Introduce the topic and give an overview so the audience knows what to expect. Don't' start with "I'm going to do ______________." or "Our group has pages 15-20." Instead, do it. Begin with information related to the presentation's focus, purpose, or thesis. One way to accomplish this is to begin with a generalization e.g. "Egypt's system of religion had similarities to Mesopotamia, but there were different approaches to their spiritual nature."
4. Make sure the audience is aware of your focus from the outset. If you use a handout, it may take care of this need; but it never hurts to reinforce your purpose, focus, or thesis. Don't encourage your audience to interrupt with questions; save these until the end of the presentation.
5. Put unfamiliar terms or key phrases on the board before you begin or project them in a PowerPoint slide, particularly if they're important to the content.
6. Be familiar with difficult pronunciations. Look up pronunciations in the dictionary, text or glossary or ask the teacher for guidance. Mark your notes so you'll remember the pronunciation and practice saying the new expressions in advance so you will be able to use them fluently during your presentation.
7. Make eye contact with your audience, not just with the teacher. If you're familiar with your material, this contact is not so hard because you're not afraid you'll lose your place in your notes.

8. In group presentations, know your speaking order and be prepared to make oral transitions between speakers. e.g. "Darlene has described the physical gods and goddesses, but just what did these mythological figures symbolize to the people? John will elaborate." Phrasing of this sort will provide smooth transitions between speakers and help the audience follow your train of thought.
9. Act like you're enthusiastic about your material, even if sometimes you're not. You can't expect your audience to be interested, if you're not.
10. Use visual aids effectively. Make sure everyone can see them; use a pointer, if you are comfortable with one. Incorporate your visuals into your presentation rather than just letting them hang/stand there. Refer to your visuals to make points or to illustrate something you're explaining.
11. Know your material well enough so you can answer questions, if there are any, from the class or the teacher. Save a few minutes at the end for questions or any necessary clarification.
12. Relax. We're all friends and your job here is to transfer and explain information in a pleasant, well-organized and efficient manner to help us all better understand your topic.

THINKING SKILLS

We feel it is essential that teachers help students develop their thinking skills. Planning lessons and learning activities around thinking skills such as those in the sample list below can make classroom instruction meaningful far beyond memorization, recall, and identification and therefore more relevant in the larger world. Engaging students' thinking skills on a regular basis maintains the instructional **rigor** important for preparing them for life beyond the classroom. Teachers should not assume that students know how to perform the various thinking processes, but rather should teach students how to effectively perform the thought practices they ask students to demonstrate.

Analyze	Break into parts and examine each part separately.
Apply	Use previously learned information in different situations or in problem solving.
Argue	Take a position on an issue, put forth reasons to support the position, support those reasons with evidence and reasoning.
Classify	Place entities in groups on the basis of common attributes.
Compare	Examine similarities between or among entities. Can mean to examine similarities *and* differences with emphasis on similarities.
Conclude	Come to a reasoned judgment about the unknown using evidence and reasoning based upon the known. (Draw conclusions)
Contrast	Examine differences
Critique; Criticize	Examine the good and bad points of a situation or idea
Define	Give a clear, concise meaning for a term or concept. Usually consists of identifying the class to which a term or concept belongs and how it differs from other things in that class.
Demonstrate	Show how a concept or thing can be used.
Describe	Recount or relate something in a sequence or story form. Provide a good word picture of a concept.
Diagram	Organize in a pictorial way – a flow chart, map or some other graphic device. Should include appropriate labeling of both the whole figure and each of its parts.
Discuss	Examine in a complete and detailed way, usually by connecting ideas to examples.
Distinguish	Emphasize differences in descriptive form.
Elaborate	Add details, explanations, examples, or other relevant information from prior knowledge.
Enumerate	Write in list or outline form a set of related facts, ideas, objects, or issues.

Evaluate	Make a value judgment, a statement of negative and/or positive worth. Back up the judgment with evidence (facts, figures, instances, etc.)
Explain	Make clear, analyze and clarify. Although similar to "discuss," explaining implies more emphasis on cause-effect relationships or step-by-step sequences.
Formulate	Create something new. Similar processes are: compose, design, construct, and develop.
Generate	Produce new information, meaning, or ideas.
Illustrate	Show by means of a picture, word picture, diagram or some other graphic aid. May also be used to call forth specific examples or instances, which "illustrate" a law, rule, principle or concept.
Infer	Go beyond available information to identify what may reasonably be true.
Interpret	Explain, translate or show a specific application (how it works) of a given fact or principle. Should go beyond previously cited examples or instances.
Justify	Tell why a position or point of view is good, right or proper. Should be mostly positive and stress the advantages of a position over its disadvantages.
List	Provide a formal numbering or sequencing of data.
Order	Sequence entities according to a given criterion.
Outline	Organize a set of facts or ideas in terms of main points and sub points.
Predict	Anticipate an outcome based on the use of existing knowledge.
Prove	Provide confirmation or verification. Establish something with certainty by evaluating and citing evidence or by logical reasoning.
Relate	Show how two or more things are connected because of similar reasons for being, similar results, or similar characteristics.
Review	Reexamine or summarize the key characteristics or major points of an overall body of facts, concepts, principles, or ideas.
State	Present a brief, concise statement of a position, fact or point of view.
Summarize	Present the main points of an issue in condensed, shortened form. Details, examples, illustrations are not given.
Trace	Present in step-by-step sequence a series of facts which are somehow related either in terms of time, order of importance, or cause and effect.
Verify	Confirm the accuracy, truth, or quality of an observation, hypothesis, claim, or product.

References:
"Basic English Revisited: A Student Handbook", 5th Edition, written and compiled by Patrick Sebranek and Verne Meyer
http://www.adprima.com
http://www.umanitoba.ca/virtuallearningcommons/files
http://www.temple.edu/rcc/TestTakingStrategies/commonactionverbsessaytests.htm

SUGGESTIONS FOR STUDENTS: MAKE EFFECTIVE USE OF YOUR TEXTBOOK

NOTE TO TEACHERS: Preparing students to make effective use of classroom tools nourishes learning and enhances opportunities for student success. Making suggestions for using texts, tools and equipment is a valuable investment of teacher instructional time and another indicator of effective management techniques. These suggestions may vary according to the textbook used in a particular course. KET

- Use the section headings and sub-headings as keys to the major ideas in each chapter. This method is particularly effective if you outline your notes.
- Pay close attention to photographs, illustrations, charts, diagrams and their captions. They provide important details.
- Read all footnotes, which will help clarify special concepts, add extra information or define unknown terms.
- Use the glossary at the back of the text to assist with the meaning of specialized terms.
- Read and try to answer all parts of sections such as *Comments and Questions* or *Ideas for Learning* in the text. Material from some of these sections may occasionally be assigned for class work or homework; but even if they aren't, reading them and quizzing yourself will offer insight into the text material.
- Look over time lines or other aids at the text's beginning and coordinate this information with your reading assignments.
- Use the *Table of Contents* and the *Index* to help locate information.
- Take careful reading notes during your first reading to keep from having to reread. Use "sticky notes" to mark important areas or items you need to remember, especially if you are not allowed to write in your text. Review your notes for discussions or quizzes before coming to class.
- Keep materials and information (including notes) well organized and always bring them to class with you.

NOTE TO TEACHERS: This evaluation form is designed for collaborative use by teacher (T) and student (S) to evaluate a student's bulletin board. Point values for each bulletin board component are indicated. Average the student and teacher points to determine a maximum of 50 points on the evaluated components. The teacher then determines a maximum of 100 points based on the quality and timeliness of the assignment's completion. The total number of points a student can receive is 150. KET

BULLETIN BOARD EVALUATION

Does this bulletin board follow the unit being taught in class? **(5)** ____ S ____ T

The theme of this bulletin board is ______________________

____

____ **(10)** ____ S ____ T

SKETCH of BOARD

What are the media and materials used in this board? **(5)** ____ S ____ T

____

Provide a simple sketch of your bulletin board in the space provided above. **(15)** ____ S ____ T

On the back of this page:

List **one** print resource used in your research in **standard reference format**. **(5)** ____ S ____ T

List **two** additional resources (website, CD-Rom, DVD) used in your research in **standard reference format**. **(10)** ____ S ____ T

What did you learn by creating this bulletin board?

Teacher Total: ________

Student Total: ________

Average student and teacher points = ______ **(50)**

Completed by teacher:
Overall quality & timeliness
of completed board: ____________ **(100)**

Completed by teacher:
Final score ________ **(150)**

PROJECT PLANNING REPORT

Note to Teachers: A planning report such as this can be used for individual students or groups to keep the teacher apprised of their project activity. It further helps focus students on their task. PAS

Describe what your finished project will look like:

When is it due?

Outline the steps you plan to follow to develop your project:

1.

2.

3.

4.

5.

6.

7.

8.

9.

10.

Use the back if you need more space.

Outline your timeline for implementing the steps in your project:

1.

2.

3.

4.

PROJECT LOG

NOTE TO TEACHERS: One way to keep students focused on their task while working on individual or group projects, is to require each student to keep a Project Log. This group log can be easily modified for use by students working on individual projects. PAS

GROUP #: ________________

PROJECT: ______________________________________

Every time that you work on your project (both individually and with your group), log specifically what you did using the format below.

DATE	DESCRIBE WHAT YOU DID	TELL WHAT YOU ACCOMPLISHED	TIME SPENT

BRIEFLY DESCRIBE YOUR MAJOR CONTRIBUTION(S) TO YOUR GROUP'S PROJECT:

SIGNATURE OF YOUR GROUP MEMEBERS VALIDATE THE ACCURACY OF THIS LOG:

1. ____________________ 3. ________________ 5. ______________

2. ____________________ 4. ________________ 6. ______________

PROJECT UPDATE

NOTE TO TEACHERS: Requiring students to submit periodic Project Updates can help them organize their tasks as well as remind them to plan ahead in order to complete their projects by the established deadline. Such updates help teachers monitor the progress and work habits of students in time to intervene and provide assistance, if necessary.

Describe what you have accomplished so far:

What do you have left to work on?

With what are you having difficulty?

Describe your plan for addressing this difficulty:

What are the very last few things that you must do in order to put the finishing touches on your project?

Outline your timeline for completing your project and handing it in on time:

GROUP RULES

NOTE TO TEACHERS: The first time our students work with partners or in a group, we teach our group rules. It is helpful to keep a poster stating these rules visibly displayed in the classroom. It's also worthwhile to review group rules when making any group assignment. Finally, we incorporate adherence to group rules as a grading component for assignments or activities that are completed collaboratively.

1. Move quickly and efficiently into your group.
2. Talk only to those in your group.
3. Stay on topic and on task.
4. Everyone should participate.
5. No one should dominate.
6. All paperwork from your group should contain your group number and the names of participating group members.
7. Move desks back to their original positions before leaving class.

INDIVIDUAL SELF-EVALUATION
GROUP ACTIVITY

DIRECTIONS: Constructive group behaviors are listed below. For each group behavior, **circle** "YES" or "NO" indicating whether or not you demonstrated that behavior.

For each "YES," write a specific **example** of how you demonstrated that behavior. For each "NO," **explain** why you did not demonstrate that behavior.

1.	CONTRIBUTED IDEAS AND OPINIONS	YES NO
2.	ASKED FOR OTHERS' IDEAS AND OPINIONS	YES NO
3.	ASKED FOR HELP WHEN NEEDED	YES NO
4.	HELPED THE GROUP STAY ON TASK	YES NO
5.	HELPED THE GROUP FOLLOW GROUP RULES	YES NO
6.	HELPED RELIEVE GROUP TENSION	YES NO
7.	USED GROUP MEMEBERS' NAMES AT LEAST ONCE EACH	YES NO
8.	DIDN'T INTERRUPT	YES NO

DIRECTIONS: Now respond to the following items.

9. I'm proud of the way our group ______________________________

____

10. Tell specifically what you contributed to your group's project/assignment: ______________________________

____

GROUP SELF-EVALUATION by INDIVIDUAL GROUP MEMBERS

DIRECTIONS: Each group member should complete this self-evaluation individually. Respond to each item as specifically as possible.

Tell what your group accomplished:
Tell *your* contributions to the group: **What was your *greatest* contribution to your group?**
Did your group listen to one another's ideas? Explain.
Did one or two people dominate the group? **If so, describe how they did so:**
Describe how your group made decisions:
Describe how your group divided responsibilities:
Explain how your group updated members who may have been absent:
Describe what you have learned about working in groups from this experience:
What will you do next time you work with a group to help it function even more effectively?

TEACHER NOTE: Self-evaluations of this nature not only guide students to assess their group for a specific activity but also help them reflect on group processes. As such, this self-evaluation tool helps students learn about effective group functioning and how it is achieved.

GROUP SELF-EVALUATION

DIRECTIONS: Work together as a group to **very specifically** describe the contributions each member made to your group's project.

NAME:
NAME:
NAME:
NAME:
NAME:
NAME:

TEACHER NOTE: This can be used along with the Group Self-Evaluation Confirmation that follows.

CONFIRMATION
GROUP SELF-EVALUATION

DIRECTIONS: Read what each of your group members wrote on your group's self-evaluation. Then tell if you agree or not. If there is anything that you do not agree with, explain on this sheet and sign your comment. Any comments you make are confidential and will be seen only by you and the teacher.

CHECK ONE:

☐ **I agree** with what my group wrote in our group's self-evaluation.

☐ **I do not agree** with everything written in our group's self-evaluation.

What do you disagree with?

Explain why:

Signature:

Make any other comments about your group's process that you think I need to know about:

Signature:

TEACHER NOTE: This confirmation sheet is used in conjunction with the Group Self-Evaluation sheet also included in this Appendix.

COLLABORATION RUBRIC

4 - Thorough Understanding

- Consistently and actively works toward group goals.
- Is sensitive to the feelings and learning needs of all group members.
- Willingly accepts and fulfills individual role within the group.
- Consistently and actively contributes knowledge, opinions, and skills.
- Values the knowledge, opinion and skills of all group members and encourages their contribution.
- Helps group identify necessary changes and encourages group action for change.

3 - Good Understanding

- Works toward group goals without prompting.
- Accepts and fulfills individual role within the group.
- Contributes knowledge, opinions, and skills without prompting.
- Shows sensitivity to the feelings of others.
- Willingly participates in needed changes.

2 - Satisfactory Understanding

- Works toward group goals with occasional prompting.
- Contributes to the group with occasional prompting.
- Shows sensitivity to the feelings of others.
- Participates in needed changes, with occasional prompting.

1 - Needs Improvement

- Works toward group goals only when prompted.
- Contributes to the group only when prompted.
- Needs occasional reminders to be sensitive to the feelings of others.
- Participates in needed changes when prompted and encouraged.

INDEPENDENT READING GUIDELINES

NOTE TO TEACHERS: I developed these guidelines for use with classes populated with students who generally don't read or don't think they like to read. These guidelines establish the structure for students' independent reading. This procedure has worked very successfully and has resulted in students who have never read a complete book, doing so and enjoying it. I'm convinced that a major key in this success is student choice. Students choose the books they read from the very extensive collection in my classroom. If a book they have chosen turns out not to appeal to them, they may keep trying others until they find a book that "grabs" them. Over time, I have learned what titles particularly appeal to different types of students and will offer my suggestions. Also, students complete recommendation cards that we keep on file to which other students can refer when choosing a book.

This independent reading procedure has also proven to be a valuable management tool. Instead of becoming idle if they complete their daily work, students get their books and read. They really do! Not only does this keep them constructively engaged, but it also limits the number of extra credit activities that I need to keep ready for such contingencies. PAS

1. Choose the book that you will read from the choices in the classroom library.
2. If after reading <u>25 pages</u> you do not like your book, you may exchange it for another one.
3. All reading of this particular book will be done *in class* during designated reading sessions or when you have completed and handed in all class work. The books may not leave the classroom. If you would like to check out a copy of your book from a library or buy one from a bookstore in order to read outside of class, you are invited to do so.
4. Points will be given for each designated reading session. These will accumulate and be recorded as a *test grade*. In order to receive your points for each designated reading session, you must engage in *actual* reading for the *full length of the reading session*. No points will be given for reading done outside of the classroom.
5. If you have an excused absence, you may *make up designated* reading sessions by reading for *thirty minutes* in room 228 during fifth or sixth period or after school. You may also do make-up reading once *all* of your daily class work has been completed and handed in.

6. Fill in your reading record sheet *completely* and *accurately* at the end of each reading session in order to receive full points for that session.
7. If you finish your book, complete a recommendation card for other students who might consider reading that book. Then begin another book from the choices provided in the classroom.
8. BONUS READING: Any time you complete *all* of your daily class work (including your Learning Log entry), you may get your book and reading record sheet and read for bonus points. When you do this, record your reading on your reading record sheet and return it to your teacher by the end of the class period in order to receive bonus points.

READING RECORD #______

BOOK____

AUTHOR_____________________________________

DATE	STARTING PAGE	STOPPING PAGE	STARTING TIME	STOPPING TIME	NO. MIN. READ	POINTS (Teacher Completes)

THOUGHTS ABOUT LEARNING LOGS

Since writing is a progressive skill that develops with practice over time, it makes instructional sense to give students an abundance of writing practice. Learning logs, as I use them in my classroom, provide regular, consistent, focused writing and thinking practice. In addition, learning log entries can build time into each class period for the teacher to take roll, sign permission forms, regroup, tie up loose ends from the previous class, or deal with individual student needs. There are multiple variations for how such a tool could be implemented in your classroom. PAS

Format and Procedure

The physical format of the learning log is simple: a binder, notebook, folder, or spiral that is used exclusively for the learning log in which students can regularly copy each prompt and write their responses. It works this way:

1. I prepare for display (on the chalkboard, overhead transparency, PowerPoint slide) the next day's prompts before leaving school each day. (This requires **consistency** and **accountability** on my part.). Each class has a designated section of board or a screen where students know their daily prompt can be found.
2. The majority of the time, I begin class with learning log writing; although from time to time, this activity is more appropriate at another point in the day's lesson.
3. When they enter class or at the appropriate time in instruction, students copy the prompt, write their responses, then count and record the number of words they have written. Ten to twenty minutes is devoted to learning log entries, depending on the complexity of the prompt and its role in the day's lesson. If students aren't finished when it is time to move on to another activity, they finish outside of class.
4. Often I plan learning log writing so that students can determine individually how much time to spend on their responses before moving on to a previously described activity. Other times I solicit volunteers to share a response or part of one with the class or we spend a few minutes discussing their ideas that the day's prompt has generated.

It is not difficult for students to earn a high grade on the Learning Log. Therefore, it is essential for them to be held accountable for following the directions and procedures.

Word Counts

Each grading period, prompts are assigned a designated minimum "word count" that each student must write in order to receive full credit for that entry. I start the minimum word count at something students can easily attain such as 50, 75 or 100 minimum words, depending on the class. Each grading period I increase the word count perhaps by 25 or 50 words, again depending on the group of students. I want the word count to be something that all students can accomplish with some students able to exceed the word count when a topic particularly motivates them. By gradually increasing the word minimum that students must write, they are nudged to develop their writing fluency. I'm careful to build suggestions for elaboration into prompts as the year progresses. I have never had a problem with a student who absolutely could not achieve the word minimums. In a class of non-academic students, the word count minimum might progress in this manner:

50 word minimum – First grading period
75 word minimum – Second grading period
100 word minimum – Third grading period
125 word minimum – Fourth grading period
150 word minimum – Fifth grading period
175 word minimum – Sixth grading period

Bonus Points

I award bonus points when an entry demonstrates exceptional effort in response to a day's prompt; most often this is reflected in an entry that goes *significantly* beyond the word minimum. Initially, I may consider 25 words above the minimum worth 1 bonus point and 50 points above worth 2 points. I may increase that to 50 points for 1 bonus point, 75 for 2, etc. as the year progresses. This must be monitored so that the bonus remains attainable for students who apply themselves but not so easy to achieve that a majority of entries receive bonus points thus skewing the grades. Students can receive over 100% on their Learning Logs, but too much over 100% would cause issues with overall grade averaging. Bonus points are only given when a student exceeds the word minimum *with meaningful thoughts in direct response to the day's prompt.*

Grading

I "grade" the learning logs once each grading period. Students can turn down the corner of up to five entries to which they'd like for me to respond. They know I will respond to their thoughts and ideas and not evaluate their writing. I scan each Learning Log with the Learning Log Grade Sheet in hand to assure that students are responding appropriately to the prompts and following directions. Then I go back, read and respond to the designated entries.

I tally the points on the Learning Log Grade Sheet and convert the total to a percentage. I'm not concerned if some students end up with over 100%., The learning log grade is an indication of learning activity and 100%+ is an acknowledgement of quality effort. The learning log grade provides an alternate form of assessment over which students have a great deal of control. For a student who doesn't test well, this grade is an opportunity to maintain a respectable average while developing his writing and critical thinking fluency. A high learning log grade indicates that a student is exerting appropriate, even exceptional, learning effort which is an important component of success and mastery measurement.

LEARNING LOG GRADE SHEET

Each entry is worth ___5__ points. In order to receive all of the points, an entry must be complete and according to the specifications, must meaningfully address the prompt, and must include the date, title, prompt and word count.

DATE	NO.	SPECIFICATIONS	PTS. RECEIVED
		Name & period **distinctly** on outside front cover	2 1 0
		Previous Log Grade Sheet (Second Six Weeks)	2 1 0
12-1	51	No., complete prompt, 175 words, word count	5 4 3 2 1 0
12-2	52	No., complete prompt, 175 words, word count	5 4 3 2 1 0
12-7	53	No., complete prompt, 175 words, word count	5 4 3 2 1 0
12-9	54	No., complete prompt, 175 words, word count	5 4 3 2 1 0
12-11	55	No., complete prompt, 175 words, word count	5 4 3 2 1 0
12-14	56	No., complete prompt, 175 words, word count	5 4 3 2 1 0
12-15	57	No., complete prompt, 175 words, word count	5 4 3 2 1 0
12-16	58	No., complete prompt, 175 words, word count	5 4 3 2 1 0
1-4	59	No., complete prompt, 175 words, word count	5 4 3 2 1 0
1-5	60	No., complete prompt, 175 words, word count	5 4 3 2 1 0
1-7	61	No., complete prompt, 175 words, word count	5 4 3 2 1 0
1-11	62	No., complete prompt, 175 words, word count	5 4 3 2 1 0

1-12	63	No., complete prompt, 175 words, word count	5 4 3 2 1 0
1-13	64	No., complete prompt, 175 words, word count	5 4 3 2 1 0
1-14	65	No., complete prompt, 175 words, word count	5 4 3 2 1 0
1-15	66	No., complete prompt, 175 words, word count	5 4 3 2 1 0
1-20	67	No., complete prompt, 175 words, word count	5 4 3 2 1 0
1-21	68	No., complete prompt, 175 words, word count	5 4 3 2 1 0
1-22	69	No., complete prompt, 175 words, word count	5 4 3 2 1 0
1-25	70	No., complete prompt, 175 words, word count	5 4 3 2 1 0
		TOTAL NUMBER OF POINTS POSSIBLE	**104**
		YOUR GRADE (Total number of points received)	

SAMPLE PROMPTS FOR WRITING ACTIVITIES

NOTE TO TEACHERS: These sample prompts illustrate the instructional array that can be achieved with writing prompts. Such prompts can be used with learning logs or similar informal writing practice as well as for fully developed writing activities. Once teachers become accustomed to designing effective writing prompts, they will be pleased with the instructional diversity provided by this learning format. Notice the ease with which thinking skills can be incorporated into writing prompts plus how such prompts can engage students in the world beyond the classroom. The astute teacher will find inspiration for stimulating writing prompts everywhere - newspapers, magazines, current events, etc.

ART

What makes something "artistic"? **List** features that determine artistic quality. Then **explore** the nature of art. Finally draft a **definition** of art.

BUSINESS

Select a product that interests you. Then describe that product in a way that will entice a buyer to part with their hard-earned money.

CIVICS/GOVERNMENT

"Good people do not need laws to tell them to act responsibly, while bad people will find a way around the laws." - Plato

Explain how you **interpret** Plato's philosophy. Does his philosophy have relevance in our 21st century society? If so, **describe** how by **citing** and **explaining** with **examples.** If not, **explain** why not, using **reasons** supported with **evidence.**

Explain the concept behind the collection of taxes. **List** at least six services/benefits that are made possible because of tax dollars. **Suggest** what alternative method(s) of funding could be employed to provide each of these services/benefits. **Explore** whether or not there is a need to improve our taxation system. **Defend** your position with **reasons** and **evidence.**

ECONOMICS

What determines value? For example, why is a generic tee shirt valued less than one with a designer logo? Is this genuine or contrived value? What makes gold more valuable than a gold-painted brick with a designer label? Generate a list of criteria that determine value. Then apply your criteria to something you value.

HEALTH

Most U.S. adults should eat less than a teaspoon of salt each day, but only 1 in 18 meets that goal. Salt increases the risk of high blood pressure, which is a major cause of heart disease and stroke. Research indicates that most dietary salt comes from processed and restaurant foods. Construct a **persuasive argument** that you could present to a restaurant owner that would motivate him/her to reduce the amount of salt in his/her menu items.

MATH

Choose a math concept. **Describe** a real world application of that concept. Then **explain** how that math concept functions in that real world application. .

MUSIC

Music surrounds us in our daily lives. **Explore** reasons why music is so pervasive. Then consider what effects, both positive and negative, music has on various individuals or groups. Finally, **identify** qualities of music that make it an effective form of therapy for people who are suffering.

PHYSICAL EDUCATION

Much is being said these days about childhood health and fitness. Explore why physical fitness is important. Then consider who is responsible for the physical fitness of society's youth – parents? schools? government? someone else? Take a position on this question and **defend that position** with **evidence** and **reasoning.**

SCIENCE

In 2007 a baby wooly mammoth preserved for 42,000 years was discovered in Siberia almost perfectly intact. Named Lyuba, she has been extensively studied and is now touring the world for museum displays. First, **explain** why discoveries of this sort are valuable. **Support** your explanation with **reasons** and **examples**. Then explore **reasons** why people come to see them on display. **Cite** at least two **reasons** and **discuss** whether or not such displays are important. **Support** your position.

Select a chemistry concept. **Describe** how you could demonstrate this concept for youngsters, say fifth graders, in a way that is fun and interesting. Then **tell** how you would explain the concept behind your demonstration in language the youngsters could understand.

SOCIAL STUDIES

Is it important to preserve historical artifacts? **Explain** why or why not. What particular kinds of historical artifacts are more important to preserve than other kinds? **Support** your position with concrete reasons.

Explore concepts behind this quote from William Shakespeare's play, *The Tempest:* "What's past is prologue". First of all, **explain** what you think Shakespeare meant. Then **state** if you agree or disagree. **Support** your position by citing **examples** that support or refute Shakespeare's position. Finally, **relate** the quote to your study of history in this class.

TECHNOLOGY

The Internet has been hailed as the greatest means of interpersonal communication that has ever existed. **Cite** new issues that have arisen due to the communication capabilities provided by the Internet. **Choose** two of those issues, **present** the pertinent facts surrounding each, and **explore** the implications each issue presents.

Although the advent of the Internet has provided unparalleled communication opportunities, it has also created serious questions about freedom of speech. Consider whether freedom of expression should be protected by law in all circumstances, or if new laws are needed to protect citizens from the consequences of unrestricted use of the Internet. Take a position and **defend that position** with **evidence** and **reasoning.**

THEMES & ISSUES

Explore the issue of **role models**. What is a role model? Explain how a role model is different from a hero or someone you admire. List qualities that you think a role model should have. Then describe how to pick a role model. Finally, discuss the value of having role models.

Is **genius** a special, rare quality or does everyone have it in some area and to some degree? Draft a brief article that could be submitted to your school newspaper in which you provide an extended definition of genius. Cite specific people who fit the criteria of your definition and support your classification with specific examples.

What is the **American Dream**? Do you think it is realistic or unrealistic for a person today to aspire to rise from rags to riches through honesty and hard work? Explain why you think someone can or cannot using concrete reasons and examples for illustration.

"**Power** should always be distrusted, in whatever hands it is placed." Sir William Jones

State whether you agree or disagree with this quote. Then support your position using examples from history, current events, personal experiences, literature, and/or film. Be specific.

STATE ASSESSMENT PREPARATION

A state assessment test tip: "Explain, support and justify your answers to open-ended questions." **Describe** specifically what this direction means. Use **examples** to illustrate your description. Then tell how you will put this tip to work while you're taking the state assessment test.

Describe everything that you can do while you're taking the state assessment test *before* you actually start writing a response to a specific open-response prompt that will make your finished response receive high points. **Explain** how each step will contribute to the effectiveness of your finished response.

SELF-EVALUATION/REFLECTION

To analyze, examine the individual parts of something then explain how each part relates to the others and to the whole. **Analyze** your academic performance in this class this grading period. Then **draw conclusions** that will influence your efforts for the rest of the semester.

Describe your goals and resolutions for this semester. Then **outline** your plan for accomplishing your goals and sticking to your resolutions.

VIEWING VIDEO

Describe your response to ____________(character) and ____________(incident). Do you think that's the way the director wanted you to respond? **Explain** why or why not. Then **explain** how you could tell that was/was not the desired response.

Describe one scene from the film we viewed in class that you would choose to see again if you could only see one scene again. **Explain** why that is the scene you'd choose. Then **demonstrate** how you could incorporate your description into a review of the film.

WRITING PROCESS

Prewriting

Think about the subject of the writing piece you're contemplating for your portfolio. Consider the audience for this piece. Why would they want to read about this subject? What would they get out of reading your finished piece (information, motivation, inspiration, suggestions, etc.) on this subject? **Explain. Describe** what you will do in developing this piece to maximize its usefulness/meaningfulness for your target audience.

Planning

Describe how you are going to hook a reader's interest in the first paragraph of your portfolio piece. What are some of the details you will use? **Explain** why a reader will want to continue after reading your first paragraph.

Drafting

Explore **drafting**: What is it? What do you do when you draft a piece? What can you discover from drafting? What decisions might you make while drafting?

Describe how you have **organized** the ideas in your draft. Explain what effect this organization will have on a reader. Then describe the organizational revisions that would make this draft an even better, more effective finished piece.

Revision

Contemplate the **revision** of your draft. What major changes will you make? Why? What minor changes will you make? Why? Describe specifically how you plan to go about revising your draft. Explain how this will strengthen your finished piece.

Some people think that a first draft is fine as it is and doesn't need to be revised. Examine the value of **revision** by comparing and contrasting the nature of revised and unrevised writing.

Editing

Describe **editing**. Tell at least five things that should be done when you're editing. Number them 1-5 within your paragraph.

Writing Reflection

Explore your experience in developing this piece for your writing portfolio. What do you like best about the finished piece? Was your way of writing different from the way you usually write? If so, describe how it was different. What challenges did this writing present? How did you address them? What will you do differently in your next piece of writing? Why?

Personal Writing

Draft a brief **memoir** of a childhood experience that made an impression on you. This may not necessarily have been a major life experience, but rather a small, quiet moment from your youth. Express the meaning of this experience to help a reader understand its significance.

According to Henry David Thoreau, "If one advances confidently in the direction of his dreams, and endeavors to live the life he has imagined, he will meet with success." Draft a **personal essay** using this quote as your central idea. Use incidents from your life to define and explain what success means to you in supporting the central idea.

Expository Writing

Increasingly schools are shifting to mandatory uniforms. Is this a good or bad idea? **Defend your position** in the draft of a speech that you might give before your school board. Be sure to support your position with solid **reasons** and **evidence**.

Draft a letter that you could send to the superintendent designed to persuade him/her that Friday the 13th should be a day off from school. Use **evidence** and **reasoning** in order to **present an argument** so strong that he/she can't possibly disagree with you.

Portfolio Development

Choose a learning log entry to develop into a piece for your writing portfolio. **Explain** your reasons for choosing this entry for further development. Furthermore, **explain** why it will develop into an effective portfolio piece.

LITERATURE

Literary Analysis & Interpretation

Beneatha and Asagai discuss the difference between "idealists" and "realists" in *A Raisin in the Sun*. Which characters in the play are idealists and which are realists? **Explain** by citing illustrations from the play. Which are you? **Explain.**

What does the play *A Raisin in the Sun* say about the importance of self-respect? How does the play make this point? Do you agree or disagree with the play's message about self-respect? **Explain** why.

Reader Response

What would you like to ask one of the characters in the book that you are reading? How would he/she respond? Write a brief **dialogue** between yourself and this character from your book.

Describe what has probably happened to the chief characters ten years after the end of the story we read in class. Then use **evidence** from the story and concrete **reasons** to **explain** why you think that has happened.

Literary Elements

Describe the **initial incident** in the book that you are reading. What did the author do to make you want to keep reading? Describe something in your own or someone else's (real or fictional) experience of which the initial incident in your book reminded you.

What opinion does the author express throughout this book/story? **Describe** *how* the author expresses this opinion throughout the book giving concrete **examples** from the text. Do you agree or disagree with this opinion? **Explain** why.

LEARNING PERFORMANCE GRADES
Notes for Teachers

Patti uses of what she calls the "Learning Performance Grade" which provides a multitude of instructional, behavioral, and classroom benefits.

- Encourages students to regularly assume positive learning behaviors.
- Teaches students to behave and perform like seasoned learners on a regular basis.
- Reinforces learning practices that Patti wants all students to regularly demonstrate.
- Rewards students for their constructive learning efforts.
- Gives students a high degree of control over an aspect of their final grade.
- Accommodates multiple learning styles and varied student strengths.
- Provides diversity in the form of assessment.
- Introduces an alternate measure of effort and achievement.
- Measures a variety of skills, traits and behaviors.
- Offsets low quiz or test scores.
- Contributes to student opportunities for success.

Many schools and districts include "class participation" as a required component of students' grades. "Participation" implies that activities such as oral presentations or class discussion are required. I call my grade a " learning performance" grade because it measures and reinforces practices that I want all students to regularly employ. I identify it as "learning" performance because it focuses on learning behavior distinguished from conduct.

Orientation & Rationale

In orienting students at the beginning of the school year, I point out that the Learning Performance Grade will be averaged with other grade components and can help offset possible low quiz or test scores. Characteristically, some of my students may struggle with traditional grading; e.g., they may not perform well on tests, are often reluctant to engage in class discussion, etc. When such students consistently operate like active learners, their Learning Performance Grade will reward them accordingly.

Procedure

- I give students the Learning Performance Grade Sheet (See Appendix.) at the beginning of each grading period and ask them to fill in their names, class periods, etc. This not only reminds students about the grade but also saves me time in grade reporting.
- Using the multipurpose grid that is provided in the Appendix, I fill in student names for each class as well as the class dates along the top. This is kept on a clipboard that I can quickly reference or even carry around the classroom.
- Every student begins each class period with five points. During class, I only make entries on the grid when a student loses points (designated with a minus sign) or earns bonus (designated with a plus sign.) Between classes, I quickly fill in the actual numbers based on the number of minus signs, plus signs, or nothing at all (indicating five points.) Most students receive five points. I can do a quick conversion of minus and plus signs to points.
- I've disciplined myself to keep up with this documentation because it's such a valuable management tool. Periodically there is a day that I just can't manage to deal with the documentation along with everything else going on in the classroom. Although I don't announce to students that I'm skipping a day, once they've become accustomed to this procedure, a skipped day here or there doesn't matter.
- At the end of each grading period, I tally the points and convert the total to a percentage based on the number of days when points could have been earned. Due to the bonus awards, some students may end up with over 100%. That doesn't concern me. Such a score is an indication of their constructive learning activity and the high grade is a reward for quality effort. Furthermore, if a student doesn't test well, this is an opportunity for him to maintain a respectable grade that reflects his daily effort and performance. Numerous students come to appreciate the opportunity to demonstrate their learning with an alternative measure. As such, the Learning Performance Grade functions as a valuable tool to assess student effort and progress as well as a useful tool for classroom management.

This procedure, that has evolved over several years, isn't for everyone. It requires focus on detail and consistent attention. Although it has worked effectively for my classroom for several years, other teachers may have alternative strategies that work better for them. Most of what we've arrived at as our personal classroom procedures originated with at least the grain of an idea from a colleague. We encourage all teachers to engage in collegial discussion and share strategies.

LEARNING PERFORMANCE GRADE

_______________________________**NAME**

____________**DATE**

__________________**PER.**

In order to receive the maximum daily Learning Performance points, you must be in class and on time.

Appropriate learning behavior and learning activity on a **daily** basis as well as student effort are reflected in this grade. This includes:

- Listening
- Paying attention
- Following directions
- Attentiveness
- Focusing on class activity and learning
- Responding appropriately when called upon
- Bringing necessary materials and assignments to class
- Participating according to instructions in oral, listening and viewing activities
- Using class time for **maximum learning activity**

Putting your head down on your desk results in an automatic "0" for that day.

______________________**GRADE**

NOTE TO TEACHERS: When the Learning Performance Grade is introduced to students, we spend time clarifying what is appropriate and what is inappropriate learning behavior. I explain to students that "Responding appropriately when called upon" doesn't necessarily mean always having the correct answer. More often, it means " knowing where the class is located in a text, being engaged in the lesson or topic, providing a thoughtful response, etc." Some students might be intimidated about learning, if they feel the expectation is to always provide a correct response to a question. PAS

SEMESTER SUCCESS

NOTE TO TEACHERS: It is worthwhile for students to reflect on the factors that contribute to their grade in a class; but if left to do so independently, most students will never take the time. Requiring them to reflect on the factors that influenced a grade and set goals for the next grading period helps them plan for their success. Furthermore, requiring parents to share in this process is not only of value to the student, but also points out parents' shared responsibility for student success. PAS

DIRECTIONS: Respond in complete sentences.

List the specific things that students must do to be successful in this class:
1.

2.

3.

4.

5.

6.

Describe what success is for you in this class:
7.

Tell in detail how your **attendance** affected your success in this class this semester:
8.

Tell in detail how your **behavior** affected your success in this class this semester:
9.

Tell in detail how your **attitude** affected your success in this class this semester:
10.

What factors had the greatest impact (positively and/or negatively) on your grade in this class this semester?
11.

What practices and/or behaviors are you going to continue next semester? Explain why.
12.

What practices and/or behaviors are you going to change next semester? Explain why.
13.

What **grade** do you want to make in this class next semester?
14.

What **conduct grade** do you want to make in this class next semester?
15.

What is your **attendance** going to be like in this class next semester?
16.

List specifically what you are going to do to be successful in this class next semester:

17.

18.

19.

20.

POINTS FOR THIS ASSIGNMENT WILL NOT BE RECORDED UNTIL IT IS RETURNED WITH A PARENT/LEGAL GUARDIAN SIGNATURE.

____
PARENT/LEGAL GUARDIAN SIGNATURE

DAILY LOG

NOTE TO TEACHERS: A daily log, which students keep to help each other with the responsibility for making up work when returning from absences, reinforces the need for careful organization and following classroom procedures. KET

Date: ______________________________**Day:** ____________________________

Logger: ____

What We Did (discussion, group work, video, quiz/test, presentations, etc.)

What We Used (Textbook, Handout, Notes, etc.)

What Was Turned In Today (essay, project, class notes, etc.)

What Is Due/Homework – Other Assignments (include page number(s) and due date.)

Other Things That Happened (Assembly, class visitors, counselors, pictures, etc.)

Logger's Comments or Suggestions

LOGGER'S SCHEDULE

Class: ______________________________ **Period:** __________________

DATE	LOGGER'S NAME	COMPLETE
Aug. 31-Sept. 4		
Sept. 8-11		
Sept. 14-18		
Sept. 21-24		
Sept. 28-Oct. 2		
Oct. 5-9		
Oct. 12-15		
Oct. 19-23		
Oct. 26-30		
Nov. 2-6		
Nov. 9-13		
Nov. 16-25		
Nov. 30-Dec. 4		
Deb. 7-11		
Dec. 14-18		
Jan. 4-8		
Jan. 11-15		
Jan. 19-22		
Jan. 25-29		
Feb. 1-5		
Feb. 8-12		
Feb. 15-19		
Feb. 23-26		
March 1-5		
March 8-12		
March 15-19		

NOTE TO TEACHERS: Adjust the dates on individual log sheets to correspond to a given school year. KET

MEMO: Make-up work from excused (WITH NOTE) absence
FROM: MS. TWARYONAS – ENGLISH/HUMANITIES

NOTE TO TEACHERS: Memos to students, such as this one about make-up work, send a clear message about understanding a teacher's expectations and students' accountability, both of which contribute to student success. KET

1. You will have as many days as you were absent **plus one** to make up work. For example, if you were absent on Tuesday you will have until 2:20 p.m. on Thursday to get your make-up work turned in or your assessment, quiz, etc., made up. I will be available to make up work after school except on Tuesdays or other days when I might have meetings. Please check with me before you make plans to stay after school. Remember, you were absent; therefore, it is YOUR RESPONSIBILITY to get your work made up according to the guidelines.
2. You may make up work during the school day *only* if you are an aide for a teacher or work in the office. Do not tell me you're not doing something in a class and can get out to make up your work. I will have a note available for you to get permission from the person for whom you're an aide. You may make up only written work during the day; any work, such as a quiz which was given orally, must be made up after school. Please make the necessary arrangements to do this. Most work can be made up in 10-15 minutes. Major assessments may take longer.
3. These guidelines will help us to make up missed work quickly before it becomes burdensome for either of us. There may be exceptions to this policy if your absences extend over a long period of time. Please be sure you have a note if you are absent and a note if you have an early dismissal and miss work, particularly an assessment or quiz. Being on the early dismissal list does not tell me any reason for your absence.

______________________________ who is an aide for me during the ______________ period has permission to come to Room 216 (4th period) to make up English or Humanities work missed because of an excused absence.

Thanks, Kay E. Twaryonas
Date ________________________________

Teacher Signature _________________________________

You may get one of these notes from me if you are coming in to make up work during the school day.

PARENT INFORMATION SHEET
Junior English
P. Slagle, Teacher

COURSE CONTENT

Literature will focus on American authors. The approach to literature will be response-based and will include reading comprehension as well as vocabulary and language study. **Writing** will be process-oriented providing practice in writing for a variety of audiences and purposes and in a variety of forms. Emphasis will be on the STATE ASSESSMENT TEST skills and the STATE-MANDATED writing portfolio assessment criteria. Other areas of emphasis will include **study skills, collaboration, critical thinking,** and **critical viewing skills**.

LEARNING LOG

This writing log provides regular practice using skills that are assessed on the STATE ASSESSMENT TEST and in the STATE-MANDATED writing portfolio that is required for graduation. **Class time is provided for this practice**, and students are expected to use this class time to practice on-demand writing like that expected on the STATE ASSESSMENT TEST. This log is graded once every grading period and reflects a student's commitment to developing his/her thinking and writing skills.

LEARNING PERFORMANCE GRADE

In this class students are expected to be responsible learners, and they are held accountable for **constructive learning behavior.** The Learning Performance grade reflects the degree to which a student assumes his/her responsibilities as a learner. The grade is directly proportionate to the quality and quantity of learning activity on the part of the student while in class. Behavior that is necessary for optimum learning to occur includes: listening thoughtfully; paying attention; following directions; participating according to instructions in oral, listening, and viewing activities; bringing necessary materials to class; using designated class time for maximum learning activity. Accountability, focus and concentration on learning as well as the quality of effort by the student are reflected in this grade.

EXTRA CREDIT

Extra credit will *only* be available to students when *all* required class work has been completed and handed in. Extra credit will be made available to students at various times throughout the grading period; consequently, it will *not* be an option at the end of a grading period. Students should take advantage of offered extra credit opportunities during the grading period, if they feel they may need grade enhancement.

GRADE REVIEW SHEET

Each student is required to average his/her grade prior to each progress report/report card. This Grade Review Sheet provides a detailed picture of the factors that determine each student's grade. **It will be sent home for a parent/legal guardian signature each six weeks.**

PROGRESS REPORT AND REPORT CARD DATES: Oct. 8, Nov., 19, Jan.16, March 2, April 21, June 12

PLANNER

Each student has received a school planner. In order to monitor your student's progress, require him/her to keep a daily record of assignments, quizzes, tests, upcoming deadlines, etc. in this planner. Examine this planner regularly.

CONDUCT GRADE

Conduct grades will be lowered for **un**excused tardies and **un**excused absences; Tardy Hall; cuts; sleeping during class; not following class rules and procedures; disruptive behavior; and/or not following directions.

WHAT YOU CAN DO TO SUPPORT YOUR CHILD'S SUCCESS:

1. Make sure that he/she attends class daily.
2. Require him/her to keep a daily record of class activity as well as a grade record in his/her planner and review it regularly.
3. Remind him/her that you will be expecting to sign his/her Grade Review Sheet each six weeks. Ask him/her to explain the grade information to you.
4. Put progress report dates on your calendar and expect him/her to show you the progress report on those dates.
5. When your child's absence from class is unavoidable, make sure that he/she assumes his/her responsibility to do make-up assignments, quizzes, and tests within the prescribed time limit.

PRE-PROGRESS REPORT PARENT NOTICE

Name of School
Street Address
City, State, Zip Code
Phone Number
Fax Number

Date ________________
Course ________________
Period ________________
Homeroom ____________

Dear Parent,
This letter is sent concerning your child's progress.

________________________ is showing difficulty in the area(s) checked below:

__________Tardies to Class
__________Irregular/poor class attendance
__________Required work late and/or incomplete
__________Low quiz/test grades
__________Missing assignments. The final deadline is ____________.
__________Failure to consistently pay attention
__________Directions frequently not followed
__________Class time not used effectively
__________Not consistently prepared with materials and supplies
__________Deadlines not consistently met
__________Unsatisfactory behavior and/or attitude

Learning Log is due on ____
Comments:
____
____
____

Please require your child to record all assignments, quizzes, tests, upcoming deadlines, and grades in his/her school planner. Examine this on a regular basis in order to monitor his/her progress.

A **Grade Review Sheet** will be sent home for your review and signature during the week of ____________________________________.

If you would like for your child to carry a weekly progress report, contact his/her counselor, ______________________________, at XXX-XXXX.

Thank you for your support and cooperation.

Yours truly,
Teacher Signature

STUDENT COMMENDATION

TO THE PARENT(S)/GUARDIAN(S) OF ____________________

DATE ______________________

I would like to take this opportunity to recognize your student for his/her outstanding effort in my sophomore English class.

This recognition acknowledges particularly exceptional effort in the area(s) indicated.

____________**ATTENDANCE**
Attends school regularly. Consistently punctual to class.

____________**ATTITUDE**
Displays consistently positive attitude. Employs tact and courtesy. Shows enthusiasm.

____________**COOPERATION**
Works well with teacher and other students. Performs productively in partner and group activities. Cooperates effectively in partner and group activities.

____________**EFFORT**
Exerts quality effort on a regular basis. Comes prepared with materials, supplies, and assignments. Consistently follows directions.

____________**IMPROVEMENT**
Has made a concentrated and visible effort to improve.

____________**INITIATIVE**
Shows readiness to assume responsibility. Shows willingness to work beyond minimum requirements.

____________**PERFORMANCE**
Demonstrates outstanding work quality and accuracy. Provides outstanding work production.

I value the efforts of students in my classes. High grades are not the only measure of success. Students who demonstrate the above qualities have a high degree of probability for success not only in the classroom, but also in the world beyond the school. Thank you for *your* efforts in supporting your student's success.

Teacher Signature

NOTE TO TEACHERS: This form or another can be filled out before a conference, during a conference or after a conference. KET

CONFERENCE REPORT

DATE: ____________________

PRESENT AT CONFERENCE:

Teacher: ____________________

Parent(s): ____________________

Student: ____________________

Administrator/Counselor: ____________________

CONCERNS:

____

____

____

____

____

RECOMMENDATIONS:

The student will ____________________

____

____

The parent(s) will ____________________

____

____

The teacher will ____________________

____

____

SAMPLE LETTER FOR PARENTS
RE: CONTROVERSIAL MATERIALS IN THE CLASSROOM

NOTE TO TEACHERS: Sending a letter or note to parents about controversial materials being considered for classroom use can offset problems which might later surface as challenges to the material and the teacher's judgment in choosing it for students. An effort such as this sample letter can help make parents feel involved in the classroom and its work. You might include with the letter any addenda about the film/book, such as reviews or articles, especially any which come from respected educational sources.

Underlined content in the sample letter is specific to the particular lesson and would appropriately be customized for each use of the letter. Teachers would fill in necessary information to complete the blanks. KET

Dear Parent(s),

As your student's teacher, I am writing to obtain your permission for your son/daughter to see a film/read a book which I have chosen to use in connection with our recent study of *literature inspired by the war experience.* This film/book, ____, contains *harsh language and wartime violence*; but those factors are present in the context of *war and the many challenges it presents for soldiers and others involved in its undertaking*. As a professional educator, I feel these actors are overwhelmed by *fine direction and stunning performances*, as well as the close connection which this film/book makes to our classroom study of *war literature*. I will work with students to discuss this film/book, including its merits, shortcomings, *language and violence*, in connection with our study of *themes of war explored through literature.*

I hope that you will trust my professional and personal judgment in bringing this film into our classroom to expand and enrich our reading and study of *the war theme*. If you prefer that your son/daughter not participate in this viewing, I will provide them with a replacement activity of similar value. Please sign this letter and have your son/ daughter return it to me at school no later than ____________________ (day) ____________________________(date). I will keep these signed permissions on file until the end of the school year.

If you have any questions about this assignment or the permission form, please call me at ______________________________(school phone number). Thanks for your attention to this matter.

Sincerely,

____ (signed by teacher)

- -

I hereby give my son/daughter ____________________________ (student's name) permission to view __________________________________ (teacher fills in title of film/book) in the classroom of _______________________________________ (teacher fills in name.)

Parent Signature ____

Date signed ____

SUBSTITUTE PREPARATION PERSONAL CHECKLIST

NOTE TO TEACHERS: I created this personal checklist to use for anticipated absences. It saves time and assures that I don't overlook significant preparation activity. This model is specific to my classroom as well as my procedures and routines. I've added personal notes for teachers that elaborate on my checklist items. Teachers will want to customize their own checklist. PAS

________ **Update class lists for sub folder.** (I never leave my attendance/grade book for a substitute. Instead I leave photocopied class lists and grade rosters for a sub to use.)

________ **Copy current seating chart for sub folder.** (My seating charts are fluid. Consequently they may not be the same for each sub instance. It's important to update them or their value to a sub is critically limited.)

________ **Call sub center. Notify principal's secretary.** (This may seem obvious, but in the heat of teaching, grading and preparing for a sub, it actually can be overlooked.)

________ **Put grading keys for assignments in key folder.** (If you expect subs to grade class work, they must have the essential tools to do so.)

________ **Add assignments to grade book.** (Typically, I add assignments to my grade book as they are made. Therefore, it is helpful to add the ones students are to complete while with a sub. I record them in pencil just in case things don't go according to the plan I leave.)

________ **Add quizzes to grade book.** (Typically, I head the column for recording assignments, quizzes, and tests as they are assigned. Consequently, I add them as part of my sub preparation.)

________ **Make hard copies of learning log prompts.** (These are needed for daily updates of the class notebooks. Additionally, if a sub will be there for more than one day, he/she will need complete prompts to put on the board, project on the overhead, etc. Students will need them for reference in the class notebook.)

________ **Put assignments and learning log prompts in class notebooks.** (Typically, I update the class notebooks daily either on my planning period or at the end of the day. It's better for students, if I anticipate what they will need to refer to while I'm away and make it available to them. If things don't go according to my sub lesson plan, I revise the class notebooks upon my return.)

________ **Count dictionaries.** (These are available to students at all times. When I'm there, I do a regular visual scan to make sure they're not "walking" off. When I have a sub, it's important that the dictionaries do not disappear.)

________ **Lock up or return AV equipment.** (Leaving AV equipment out and accessible when I'm not there to monitor it is not a good idea.)

________ **Photocopy pages in teacher's editions.** (I never leave my teacher's editions for subs. It's too easy for them to disappear in my absence.)

________ **Put away materials on lectern and teacher's desk.** (Materials that I want to have when I return should not remain accessible when there is a sub.)

________ **Put away hall pass.** (Students could abuse the pass or even take it when there is a sub. I leave a temporary hall pass in my sub folder.)

________ **Put upcoming quiz dates and deadlines on board.** (Even though I'm not there, students will look to the designated spot for upcoming deadlines.)

________ **Make lesson plans and learning log prompts for day of return.** (Not only do I have to prepare lesson plans for the days I'm away, but I also need to be prepared for the first day back.)

GENERAL INFORMATION
SUBSTITUTES FOR P. SLAGLE

PLEASE READ AND ADHERE TO THIS INFORMATION WHEN YOU ARE SUBBING FOR ME. THANK YOU.

1. I have provided a **seating chart** to help make your job easier. Students sit according to these seating assignments when I'm here, and they know I expect them to sit according to this seating chart whenever I have a substitute.

2. The seating chart makes it possible for you to leave **specific names** of students who are disruptive, cause you problems, and/or do not do their work. Please do so.

3. Also leave me the **specific names** of students who leave the classroom during the period and the reason they left the classroom.

4. Please leave all **student work** sorted by period and labeled. Indicate if the assignments are complete or incomplete.

5. **Numbered assignment sheets** should be collected before the end of each period, put in numerical order and checked to see if any were not turned in.

6. If **paperback books, dictionaries,** or any other classroom supplies or materials were used by students during the course any period, be sure those items are returned to where the student got them from before the end of the period. They should not be left on, under or around student desks.

7. Students should not have access to my desk or anything in or on it.

8. I expect anyone who subs for me to follow the lesson plans that I leave. Thank you for doing so.

9. I have three student aides: Give Name (1st period)
Give Name (2nd period)
Give Name (6th period; my planning period)

Name and Name sit at the large table, and Name sits at the small table adjacent to my desk. They are well-versed in our classroom procedures and are available to assist you.

SUBSTITUTE LESSON PLAN FORM

NOTE TO TEACHERS: The teacher is in charge of the classroom and the students at all times, even when absent. A clear outline of plans and suggestions for a substitute is an important management tool. You can adapt this template for specifics related to your school; e.g., specific information regarding block schedule on the day of the absence, directions for taking homeroom attendance electronically, etc. KET

LESSON PLANS

Teacher ________________________ **Room #** _____**Date**____________

Below is an outline of my classes and notes to assist you with management.

Homeroom: ____
will take HR folder to the office.

(Name of student/student aide)

Materials for your use including a **seating chart** and copies of pages from **teacher's editions** are located:

____

____

Students should not **have access to these teacher materials:**

____

____

1st Period Class:______________ **Helpful student(s)** ________________

2nd Period Class: _____________ **Helpful student(s)** ________________

3rd Period Class: _____________ **Helpful student(s)**________________

4th Period Class: ____________ Helpful student(s) _______________

5th Period Class: ____________ Helpful student(s)_______________

6th Period Class:_____________ Helpful student(s) _______________

7th Period Class: ____________ Helpful student(s) _______________

Additional notes that will assist the substitute:

____

____

____

____

____

____

If you need any assistance, please see _______________ **in room #** ___
(Name of teacher)
_______________ **in room #** ___
(Name of teacher)

I hope you have a good day. Please **leave a note** on an attached sheet, to let me know how my classes worked and behaved and how your day went on the attached sheet. Thanks.

____(Teacher's Name)

*****COUPON*****

____NAME

____SUB DATE(S)

YOU ARE AWARDED THIS COUPON FOR COOPERATIVE AND APPROPRIATE BEHAVIOR WHEN HAVING A SUBSTITUTE. THIS INCLUDED BEING ON TIME TO CLASS, STAYING IN THE CLASSROOM THE ENTIRE PERIOD, NOT REQUIRING A CONDUCT NOTE OR NEGATIVE REPORT FROM THE SUBSTITUTE. GOOD JOB! I APPRECIATE YOUR EFFORT AND COOPERATION. (Fill in whatever you would like to reward students for.)

You may use this coupon for:

- ☐ Five bonus assignment points
- ☐ Five bonus learning performance points
- ☐ Five bonus Learning Log points

Check one and return to Ms. Slagle. You must turn in this coupon no later than

_____________________________ in order to redeem it.

Congratulations!
Keep up the good work!

Ms. Slagle

FIELD TRIP CHECKLIST

NOTE TO TEACHERS: Although this is not a completely comprehensive list of field trip responsibilities, it provides an idea of the numerous arrangements necessary for a successful field trip. We suggest preparing your own checklist to use for each field trip. As you discover, often from experience, items that were overlooked, revise your personal checklist for future use.

VENUE

- ✓ Contact the venue: find out availability, requirements, deadlines, etc.
- ✓ Secure a date with the venue that is approved on the school's master calendar.
- ✓ Reserve tickets, date, etc. with the venue.
- ✓ If no reservation is required, still notify the venue to alert them of your intentions
- ✓ Purchase tickets by the venue's deadline. Determine accepted form of payment.
- ✓ Clarify the venue's cancellation policy.
- ✓ Determine the venue's handicap accessibility arrangements.
- ✓ Determine requirements/rules of the venue and any special directions.
- ✓ Determine what entrance to use, arrival directions, and bus parking.
- ✓ Notify the venue a day or two before the field trip to confirm and review details.

TRANSPORTATION

- ✓ Contact and reserve transportation source.
- ✓ Determine payment deadline. Determine accepted form of payment.
- ✓ Clarify the transportation source's cancellation policy.
- ✓ Determine the transportation sources parameters; e.g., the bus must return students to school in time to make its regular afternoon run.
- ✓ Notify transportation of pick-up and return time. Apprise them of any intermediate stops; e.g., at a restaurant for lunch.
- ✓ Contact the transportation source a day or two prior to the field trip to confirm.

PERMISSIONS

- ✓ Secure school administration approval for your field trip.
- ✓ Observe all school/district field trip policies and procedures.
- ✓ Prepare permission approval forms for parents & distribute to students with directions and deadline.
- ✓ Prepare permission approval forms for teachers whose classes will be missed & distribute to students with directions and deadline.
- ✓ Elicit information about any medical conditions (students and chaperones) that might unexpectedly emerge during the field trip. Inform all chaperones of this medical potential.

FEES

- ✓ Determine cost to students: admission, tickets, etc. plus transportation
- ✓ Determine source of funding.
- ✓ Determine funding for students in the free and reduced lunch category.
- ✓ Determine deadline for student payments.
- ✓ Collect money from students. Provide payment verification (receipt) for each student. Have students sign a sheet when they pay for a record of payment confirmation.
- ✓ Regularly turn in money to bookkeeper according to school policy and procedures.

CHAPERONES

- ✓ Determine number of chaperons based on the venue's as well as school's or district's guidelines. Be sure to have enough chaperones to secure your students' safety and appropriate behavior.
- ✓ Determine how many teachers, administrators and parents to recruit as chaperones.
- ✓ Determine what kind of clearance is required for non-staff chaperones and make arrangements to secure that clearance. Keep it on file at the school
- ✓ Recruit your chaperones.
- ✓ Prepare your chaperones with:
    - background materials about the venue
    - academic rationale and background for the students' experience

  - brief itinerary of activities
  - list of duties & expectations
  - your needs and expectations for them
- ✓ Be sure that chaperones understand their first responsibility is to monitor students.
  - For example, if your students are attending a play, chaperones ' primary responsibility is to monitor students, rather than focusing on the play.
  - Assign chaperones among students. For example, chaperones will often want to sit together at a play or concert. This does not facilitate effective management of students during the event.
  - Apprise chaperones of guidelines such as not leaving students unattended, not smoking, etc. This is especially important for non-staff chaperones.
- ✓ Assign specific students to each chaperone.

FOOD

- ✓ Communicate clear directions to students regarding food; e.g., whether or not snacks be allowed on the bus, in the venue, etc.
- ✓ If lunch occurs during the field trip, communicate clear directions to students; e.g., bring a sack lunch, money for a restaurant, where you will be going to lunch, etc.
- ✓ If going to a restaurant or food court, notify the establishment in advance so they can be prepared for an influx of customers at a designated time.

NOTIFICATIONS

- ✓ Provide detailed information for parents, not just a permission form.
- ✓ Notify the school cafeteria if a significant number of students will not be eating lunch at school on your field trip day.
- ✓ Provide a list of all participating students with departure and return time for all teachers whose students will miss their class for the field trip as well as all administrators and clerks.

YOUR ARRANGEMENTS

- ✓ Make coverage arrangements for any of your classes not going on the field trip or your students that will not be on the field trip.

- ✓ Leave a note on the door to your classroom indicating when you will be gone and when you will return.

BEHAVIOR PREPARATION

- ✓ Teach appropriate behavior specific to the venue; e.g., theatre etiquette, museum etiquette, zoo behavior, etc.
- ✓ Clearly and thoroughly communicate your behavioral guidelines well in advance of the field trip and review at least twice prior to the trip.
- ✓ Instruct students about appropriate dress, if a dress code applies.
- ✓ Clearly spell out consequences for behavioral guidelines that are not followed.
- ✓ Clearly outline prohibitions: separating from the group; talking, using a cell phone, texting, etc. during a live performance; throwing anything into animal cages or habitat, etc.
- ✓ Create a contingency plan for students to follow in case they get separated from the group. Clearly communicate this plan to all students and chaperones going on the field trip.

ACADEMIC PREPARATION

- ✓ Clearly communicate the academic rationale for the field trip to students, their parents, and chaperones.
- ✓ Prepare your students with background information that will allow them to maximize the field trip learning experience.
- ✓ Engage students in pre-field trip lessons, activities and research.
- ✓ Explain post field trip activities, projects, reports, etc. prior to the field trip so students are sure to look for information that will be valuable for their post field trip lessons.

PAPERWORK

- ✓ Assure that you have a signed permission form for each student who goes on the field trip. Alphabetize and file signed permission forms.
- ✓ Prepare a complete alphabetized list of all students participating in the field trip and distribute it to all faculty, administration, clerks (e.g. attendance clerk), and chaperones.
- ✓ Create name tags for students and chaperones.

DAY OF THE FIELD TRIP

- ✓ Make sure that you and every chaperone has a complete list of all students participating on the field trip.
- ✓ Check students off the list one at a time each time they get on and off the transportation or enter or leave the venue.
- ✓ Give clear, concise, and repeated directions regarding when and where to report, when to return to the transportation, restroom arrangements, etc.
- ✓ Provide a brief itinerary of activities to administration, chaperones, and students.
- ✓ Provide and exchange cell phone numbers with the school administration, all chaperones and bus driver(s).

MULTI-PURPOSE GRID

MULTIPURPOSE GRID – You'll be surprised at the multiple uses you will find for a simple grid of this kind.

CPSIA information can be obtained
at www.ICGtesting.com
Printed in the USA
BVOW10s0045301117
501340BV00003B/36/P

9 781457 503962